READINGS
IN
NATURAL
RESOURCE
ECONOMICS

Edited by

John E. Reynolds
Food and Resource Economics Department
University of Florida

J. Martin Redfern
Agricultural Economics Department
University of Arkansas

Robert N. Shulstad
Agricultural Economics Department
University of Arkansas

MSS Information Corporation
655 Madison Avenue, New York, N.Y. 10021

This is a custom-made book of readings prepared for the courses taught by the editors, as well as for related courses and for college and university libraries. For information about our program, please write to:

MSS INFORMATION CORPORATION
655 Madison Avenue
New York, New York 10021

MSS wishes to express its appreciation to the authors of the articles in this collection for their cooperation in making their work available in this format.

Library of Congress Cataloging in Publication Data

Reynolds, John Everett, comp. .
    Readings in natural resource economics.

    1. Natural resources — Addresses, essays, lectures
I. Shulstad, Robert N., joint comp. II. Redfern,
J. Martin, joint comp. III. Title.
HC55.R5   333.7'08   74-13248
ISBN 0-8422-5202-9
ISBN 0-8422-0449-0 (pbk.)

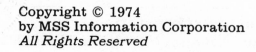

CONTENTS

PART IV. Benefit-Cost Analysis

PREFACE

This collection of readings was put together in response to the expressed need of members of the Southern Land Economics Research Committee. There is a substantial volume of readings in the broad area of natural resource economics. These readings have been published in scattered sources that are not always easily accessible to the researcher, teacher or student. This volume pulls together selected articles that can be used as a reference book and a basis for teaching advanced undergraduate courses in natural resource economics.

The editors have served as a subcommittee of the Southern Land Economics Research Committee in developing this collection of readings. The Southern Land Economics Research Committee and the Interregional Resource Economics Research Committee offered valuable suggestions and comments concerning the selection of articles for this volume. However, it has not been possible to publish all the articles that merited reproduction.

We thank the authors of the articles included for readily granting permission for their use. We would also like to thank the Farm Foundation for their support of this project through the Southern Land Economics Research Committee.

July, 1974

John E. Reynolds
J. Martin Redfern
Robert N. Shulstad

Introduction

Natural resource economics is that subset of economic theory concerned with the economic use of the natural resources of the universe and with the physical, biological, economic and institutional factors that affect, condition, and control how these resources are used. It deals with land, water, minerals, air, marine products, forest products and the environment in general, and includes the study of the ownership, utilization, development, management and conservation of these resources.

The uniqueness of natural resource economics is derived from the emphasis placed on externalities and the importance of their evaluation in public policy determination.

This text is not a comprehensive treatment of natural resource economics. The readers will quickly spot several areas that are ommited, such as the economics of mineral extraction, environmental economics, and the estimation of the demand for recreation. The papers collected in this volume were chosen to expose the student to the mainstream of natural resource economics and enable the student to learn and apply the basic logic and techniques it encompasses to the various resource areas. Some readers might applaud the selection of these articles that are relatively non-mathematical in presentation -- others may desire more quantitative offerings. For this latter group, the references at the end of each included article often provide a more mathematically rigorous treatment.

Part I, The Market System, Externalities, and Alternative Corrective Action, presents the theoretical "guts" of natural resource economics. It examines the development of natural resource economics, the failure of the market in evaluating true social values, the importance of evaluating externalities and possible solutions to market failure. The Reynolds article demonstrates the application of the traditional Lagrangian optimization model for the allocation of water among alternative uses and users. Castle and Stoevener present an overview of the market, its limitations and its uses, giving three examples of market failure where the logic of resource allocation together with market-provided data are valuable in creating alternatives to the market system. It also can be viewed as a pragmatic approach to benefit-cost analysis and the conditions for public intervention. Castle, in "The Market Mechanism, Externalities, and Land Economics," provides a general review of externality theory including an excellent bibliography in the footnotes. He suggests that it is the emphasis on externalities which makes land and resource economics unique and argues that a primary criteria for judging the success of non-market solutions in resource allocation is how well they cope with externalities. (For readers who wish to pursue externality theory further, the editors recommend Mishan, E. J., "The Postwar Literature on Externalities," Journal of Economic

Literature, 9:1-28, March, 1971.)

The articles by Randall and Davis and Kamien examine possible solutions to externality problems. Randall presents a concentrated examination of the effects of transactions costs (the costs of making and enforcing a decision). He argues that transactions costs are the primary barrier to the use of practical market solutions even in cases of full liability rules. In contrast to Randall's theoretical approach, Davis and Kamien provide a practical exposure to alternative non-market policies for dealing with externalities and argue that there exists no single most superior policy.

Turvey's essay delineates three new ideas not explicitly presented earlier in this text nor in other well known articles on the divergence between private and social costs, i.e. Coase, Bator, or Buchanan and Stubblebine. These are, first, the great difficulty inherent in determining the optimum level of controls; second, Turvey argues the importance of equity considerations, stating that even though benefits exceed costs, a payment should actually be made to those adversely affected by externalities; and third, that the income distribution resulting from any corrective government action must be socially desirable if action is to be taken.

On one level readers may view Part I as showing the theory of optimality and how to obtain optimality. On another level readers may correctly infer that the articles point to the difficulty involved in carrying out policies which are acceptable not only to the political constituency, but also to theoretical natural resource economists.

Common property resources, the subject of Part II, are an extreme example of externality problems and the need for effective public policy in the management of natural resources. This is because their uncontrolled exploitation will result in zero or negative net benefits to society. The articles by H. Scott Gordon and James Crutchfield combine to give an excellent exposure to the problems of managing common property resources. Gordon presents the essential theory, stressing the divergence between the use of the resource resulting from independent individual decisions and the use under controlled private or public ownership. Crutchfield then provides a practical example of this misallocation of resources by examining the Pacific Coast halibut fishery.

Part III contains two articles on resource conservation. This subject area has always been an integral part of resource economics. The first, prepared by a National Academy of Sciences Committee on Soil and Water Conservation, presents an elementary but comprehensive review of basic definitions and principles needed to maximize the returns from investment in conservation programs as well as practical constraints to optimum action. Krutilla's "Conservation Reconsidered" is primarily concerned with the optimal intertemporal utilization of fixed natural resource stocks. Krutilla calls for the conservation of the national stock of amenity producing resources, such as a wild and scenic river, on the basis of their eventual decreased need in production due to technological advancements and their uniqueness in providing utility and scientific information.

The last three selected readings are contained in Part IV, Benefit-Cost Analysis. The article by Prest and Turvey may be described as a comprehensive classic on B-C analysis. Part of this article covers the choice of a discount rate for public projects and several alternatives are discussed. Baumol's article, "On the Social Rate of Discount," examines discount rate issues not covered in Prest and Turvey, such as the role of taxes in determining actual rate of return on private investment and an explicit recognition of external costs and irreversibilities inherent in many public investment projects. Baumol proposes the use of high interest rates in benefit-cost analysis on the grounds of both efficiency and equity and calls for more, but less durable, government investments. Finally, Pavelis has written a practical guide to the appropriate use of the B-C ratio, the information needed for its application and the conditions where it is not applicable.

PART I. THE MARKET SYSTEM, EXTERNALITIES,
AND ALTERNATIVE CORRECTIVE ACTION

ALLOCATING WATER AMONG ALTERNATIVE USES[a]

By John E. Reynolds

Rainfall is not uniformly distributed with respect to time or location. This characteristic has brought about attempts to manage water resources to minimize floods during the wet seasons or store the water for later use during dry seasons, or both. The use of water has been important to the economic development of areas. People in the humid East as well as the arid West are aware that water is either presently or rapidly becoming a scarce resource. As a result water use is often burdened with uncertainties and conflicts between users and potential users. These conflicts are intensifying as the demand for water increases and necessitate the making of decisions to allocate a limited amount of water among alternative users.

Relevant economic criteria for allocating water among alternative uses are examined herein. The approach is to consider first the increasing demands for water and then to examine economic criteria for allocating water and the interrelationships between economic, physical, and institutional considerations in making allocation decisions.

INCREASING DEMAND FOR WATER

Although man has manipulated the supply of water with respect to time and plane, the total supply of water on earth today is about the same as it was thousands of years ago. However, this is not the case with the demand for water. The demand for water has increased because there are more people using it today than ever before. Population in the United States has been increasing about 1.6 % per yr. At this rate the population in conterminous United States will reach 468,000,000 in 2020 (6).

The use of available water supply is expected to increase steadily over

Note.—Discussion open until August 1, 1971. To extend the closing date one month, a written request must be filed with the Executive Director, ASCE. This paper is part of the copyrighted Journal of the Irrigation and Drainage Division, Proceedings of the American Society of Civil Engineers, Vol. 97, No. IR1, March, 1971. Manuscript was submitted for review for possible publication on February 13, 1970.

[a] Presented at the November 5-7, 1970, ASCE Irrigation and Drainage Division Specialty Conference, held at Austin, Tex.

time. Withdrawal uses of water in the United States are expected to reach 1,368 billion gal per day in 2020, five times more than in 1965 (6). Increases in the use of water are not expected to be uniform with respect to types of use or regions of the country. For example, the withdrawal quantities needed for municipal uses are expected to be three times greater in 2020 than in 1965, while withdrawals for steam-electric power are expected to increase more than tenfold during this same period.

The nine western water resource regions accounted for about 64 % of all withdrawals in 1954, but withdrawals in these regions are projected to fall to 40 % of U.S. withdrawals by 2000 (3). In Florida, agricultural use of water is expected to increase about 70 % from 1968 to 1980 (7). For the United States, however, total withdrawals for agriculture are only expected to increase about 23 % from 1965 to 1980 (6). The relative importance of agricultural withdrawals is expected to decline from about 42 % of total withdrawals in 1965 to about 12 % in 2020 (6).

Many factors have contributed to the increased use of water. New household devices such as the automatic washing machine and the dishwasher have contributed to the increases in municipal water uses. Increased industrialization has led to large increases in the industrial uses of water. Expansion in irrigated acreage will account for most of the expected increases in the agricultural uses of water in Florida.

In many areas of the country, such as Southern Florida, there will be strong competition among agricultural, industrial, municipal, and other users of water. Problems of allocating water among alternative uses arise when water becomes scarce and there is competition for it.

ECONOMIC CRITERIA FOR ALLOCATING WATER

The process of matching the quantity of water demanded with existing or potential supplies of water may involve many important decisions affecting the development and use of water resources. Economics provides criteria for determining the allocation among competing uses and users of resources (water and other resources).

To develop these criteria, assume that one of the goals of society is economic efficiency. [Society may have other goals besides economic efficiency, such as, some goal relating to the distribution of goods and services among individuals in the community. Economic well-being is an important component of the total well-being of society and is therefore, closely related to the public welfare (1). It is recognized that economic efficiency may not be the ultimate goal of society, but economic efficiency is probably a means toward achieving a higher goal (e.g., a rising level of living).] Also assume that production functions can be estimated for all outputs. The production function specifies the physical relationship between output and the inputs used to produce that output. The production functions for different outputs and producers can be expressed in general mathematical terminology as

$$Y_{jk} = f(X_{1jk}, \ldots X_{ijk}, \ldots X_{nmp}) \quad \ldots \ldots \ldots \ldots \ldots \ldots \ldots \ldots (1)$$

in which Y_{jk} represents the jth output produced by the kth producer; X_{ijk} represents the ith input used by the kth producer to produce the jth output; and $i = 1, 2, \ldots n$, $j = 1, 2, \ldots m$, and $k = 1, 2, \ldots p$. In other words, Eq. 1

represents the production functions for m outputs produced by p producers using n inputs.

For simplicity, assume that the concern is with perfectly competitive product and factor markets. [It can be assumed that there are perfectly competitive product and factor markets so the price of the output (or input) will not vary with the level of the output (or input). This assumption simplifies the presentation; however, the criteria could be developed without this assumption.] Profit can then be defined as the sum of the gross revenues (output multiplied by the product price) for all producers minus the sum of the production costs of all producers. This can be expressed as

$$\pi = \sum_{k=1}^{p} \sum_{j=1}^{m} \left(P_j Y_{jk} - \sum_{i=1}^{n} P_i X_{ijk} \right) \quad \dots \dots \dots \dots \dots \dots \dots \dots (2)$$

in which π denotes profit; P_j denotes the price of the jth product; and P_i denotes the price of ith input. Profits are maximized at the point where the use of an additional unit of any input increases costs by an amount equal to the increase in revenue. By substituting Eq. 1 into Eq. 2, the profit function is expressed as a function of inputs and prices. The first-order conditions for profit maximization are defined mathematically by setting the partial derivatives of the profit function with respect to each of the inputs equal to zero [For the second-order conditions for profit maximization see Henderson and Quandt (2)]:

$$\frac{\partial \pi}{\partial X_{ijk}} = P_j \frac{\partial Y_{jk}}{\partial X_{ijk}} - P_i = 0 \quad \dots \dots \dots \dots \dots \dots \dots \dots \dots \dots (3)$$

in which $\partial Y_{jk}/\partial X_{ijk}$ is the marginal physical product (MPP) of the ith input used by the kth producer to produce the jth output. Shifting the input price, P_i, to the right side of Eq. 3 yields

$$P_j \frac{\partial Y_{jk}}{\partial X_{ijk}} = P_i \quad \dots \dots \dots \dots \dots \dots \dots \dots \dots \dots \dots \dots \dots \dots \dots \dots (4)$$

The price of the output, P_j, multiplied by the MPP is called the marginal value product (MVP) and indicates the rate at which a firm's revenue would increase if the input were changed a small amount. Therefore, Eq. 4 indicates that for profit-maximization each input should be used to the point where the marginal value product equals the price of the input.

Now apply this criterion to water allocation problems. First, assume the quantity of water that will be used to produce A (citrus) must be determined. Eq. 1, the production function, specifies the estimated relationship between the production of citrus and water (and other inputs). From Eq. 4 it can be seen that the firm will allocate water to citrus until the marginal value product, MVP, equals the price (cost) of water. If he goes beyond this point the MVP will be less than the price (cost) of water, and it would be more profitable for him to reduce the quantity of water applied because it is costing him more than he receives in return. [The principle of diminishing marginal returns indicates that the MPP curve (and the MVP curve) will slope downward and to the right over the rational stage of production.] Conversely, if he stops short of this point, the MVP will be greater than the price (cost) of water and it would be profitable for him to apply more water as the added return would be greater than the added cost. Therefore, if the quantity of water is not restricted, a firm will allocate water to a particular use until the marginal value product equals the price (cost) of water.

The allocation of water also involves the problem of allocating water among alternative uses. Assume one firm produces A (citrus) and B (tomatoes) with the use of water (X_W) and other inputs. If the output of citrus is denoted as Y_A, the output of tomatoes as Y_B, the price of citrus as P_A, the price of tomatoes as P_B, and the price of water as P_W Eq. 4 can be rewritten as

$$P_A \frac{\partial Y_A}{\partial X_W} = P_W \quad \dots\dots\dots\dots\dots\dots\dots\dots\dots\dots\dots\dots\dots\dots\dots\dots \quad (5a)$$

to denote the condition for determining the quantity of water to use on citrus. Similarly, the condition for tomatoes would be

$$P_B \frac{\partial Y_B}{\partial X_W} = P_W \quad \dots\dots\dots\dots\dots\dots\dots\dots\dots\dots\dots\dots\dots\dots\dots\dots \quad (5b)$$

If there is an unlimited supply of water, Eqs. 5 specify the quantity of water that will be allocated to citrus and tomatoes. However, if there is a limited supply of water available and these uses are competing for water, the firm may not be able to apply enough water to equate the MVP and the price of water for each crop. However, the firm will still want to use each unit of water where the net contribution to profits is the greatest. By combining Eqs. 5a and 5b, the following solution can be obtained:

$$P_A \frac{\partial Y_A}{\partial X_W} = P_B \frac{\partial Y_B}{\partial X_W} \quad \dots\dots\dots\dots\dots\dots\dots\dots\dots\dots\dots\dots\dots\dots \quad (6)$$

Eq. 6 indicates that the firm should allocate the given supply of water between A (citrus) and B (tomatoes) so that the MVP from the last unit of water applied to citrus will be equal to the MVP of the last unit of water supplied to tomatoes. If a limited supply of water was allocated in a manner such that the MVP from citrus was greater than the MVP from tomatoes it can be seen that profits could be increased by allocating more water to citrus (where the return is higher) and less to tomatoes. Therefore, it can be concluded that in allocating water among competing uses, it should be allocated in such a manner that the marginal value product is equated for all uses. [The criterion for an optimal allocation of water among competing uses has also been referred to in the literature as "the rate of substitution among products is equal to the product price ratio" (5). By rearranging the terms in Eq. 6 it can be shown that these are equivalent conditions.]

The allocation of water among users is also of interest. There are users associated with each use and therefore the allocation of water to each use suggests the allocation among users. For purposes of illustration, assume that there are two users R and S that produce A (citrus) and B (tomatoes) from the use of water and other inputs. If the water supply is unlimited, Eq. 4 indicates that each producer would allocate water to each product until the MVP equals the price (cost) of water. This can be illustrated in Eqs. 7:

$$P_A \frac{\partial Y_{AR}}{\partial X_{WR}} = P_W \quad \dots\dots\dots\dots\dots\dots\dots\dots\dots\dots\dots\dots\dots\dots\dots\dots \quad (7a)$$

16

$$P_B \frac{\partial Y_{BR}}{\partial X_{WR}} = P_W \quad \dots\dots\dots\dots\dots\dots\dots\dots\dots\dots\dots \quad (7b)$$

$$P_A \frac{\partial Y_{AS}}{\partial X_{WS}} = P_W \quad \dots\dots\dots\dots\dots\dots\dots\dots\dots\dots\dots \quad (7c)$$

$$P_B \frac{\partial Y_{BS}}{\partial X_{WS}} = P_W \quad \dots\dots\dots\dots\dots\dots\dots\dots\dots\dots\dots \quad (7d)$$

in which Y_{AR} = citrus produced by R; Y_{BR} = tomatoes produced by R; X_{WR} = the quantity of water used by R; Y_{AS} = citrus produced by S; Y_{BS} = tomatoes produced by S; and X_{WS} = the quantity of water used by S. By combining Eqs. 7a to 7d the profit maximizing solution can be determined when water is in short supply:

$$P_A \frac{\partial Y_{AR}}{\partial X_{WR}} = P_B \frac{\partial Y_{BR}}{\partial X_{WR}} = P_A \frac{\partial Y_{AS}}{\partial X_{WS}} = P_B \frac{\partial Y_{BS}}{\partial X_{WS}} \quad \dots\dots\dots \quad (8)$$

From Eq. 8 it can be seen that for profit maximization water will be allocated so that the marginal value productivity of water will be equated for all uses and users. Eq. 8 could be generalized to include other inputs, outputs, or producers.

The examples used have considered only one quality of water. However, water of different qualities could be considered by denoting each quality of water as a different input. From the profit maximizing conditions specified in Eq. 4 the quantity of each type of water to allocate to any competing use could be determined.

In this section, it has been assumed that the price mechanism can be used to reflect the wishes of consumers to the users of the resources. In many uses, prices can be used to allocate water. However, for some uses prices can not be used as a choice indicating mechanism. For example, a price system does not reflect esthetic values. But just because the price system does not work for some uses is insufficient reason for abandoning it. Other means must be discovered for determining the relative value of water in these uses. [For a more complete analysis of this point and some alternative allocative indicators see Timmons (5).] Water should be allocated to the use that has the highest marginal value product. This is also true for nonmarket commodities; the marginal value product can not be adequately measured for these commodities.

ECONOMIC, PHYSICAL AND INSTITUTIONAL INTERRELATIONSHIPS

The process of making and implementing water allocation decisions involves physical, economic, and institutional considerations. These three considerations should be integrated into any water allocation decisions or policy.

The physical consideration involves what is physically possible from the use of water resources. It involves the range and limits of physical possibilities in terms of water sources, supplies, and uses (4). The range of physical possibilities is expanded by technological discoveries. An example of the physical possibilities is the production function (Eq. 1) which specifies the physical relationship between inputs and output. The physical response to varying quantities of water is needed in order to estimate the marginal value product of water in alternative uses. The physical limits for the application of water to any use must also be determined. The quantity of water available to allocate must be determined.

Water allocation decisions should also be appraised in terms of what is economically desirable. Economic desirability changes with the prices and costs associated with the different alternatives. From Eq. 4 it can be seen that the marginal value product varies directly with the price of the output. The demand for goods and services reflects consumer tastes and preferences and determines the price of the output. The price (cost) of water is also directly related to the quantity of water that will be allocated to any particular use. The physical possibilities are necessary, but not sufficient information upon which to base water allocation decisions. Economic desirability is dependent upon the physical possibilities and is a necessary ingredient to water allocation decisions. However, both the physical and economic considerations are contingent upon what is institutionally permissable.

Institutions mean group control exerted on individual and group decisions. Water rights and zoning regulations are examples of formal controls over individual and group decisions and define to some extent what is institutionally permissable. Customary practices are informal controls. Institutions may either facilitate or obstruct the allocation of water. They facilitate water allocation when they help put allocation decisions into action. They obstruct water allocation when they prevent allocation goals from being realized. For example, assume that water in Lake Waterhole has not been drawn down below 20 ft because of the political consequences that would result. If the allocation goal was to allocate water to the use with the highest marginal value product and there were higher value uses downstream, the political consequences of a drawdown to 10 ft would be an institution that obstructs the goal of allocating water to its highest value use.

APPLICATION TO RESEARCH

The economic principles outlined herein and their interaction with physical and institutional constraints can be integrated in research on the allocation of water among alternative uses. The Agricultural Economics Department at the University of Florida and the Central and Southern Florida Flood Control District are cooperating in a research project concerning the allocation of water among alternative uses. The purpose of this section of the paper is to relate how economic criteria for water allocation can be integrated with physical and institutional constraints.

To allocate water to the use that has the highest value, it is necessary to know the value of water in alternative uses. Data on the response of different crops to varying amounts of water are not readily available. In the study at the University of Florida it will first be necessary to estimate the value of water in alternative uses. After these values have been estimated, water allocation models can be constructed and the optimum allocation of water among alternative uses can be determined.

One of the objectives of the project is to determine the optimum allocation of water over a number of different time periods as well as the allocation among alternative uses in a given time period. By including a number of different time periods in the analysis, it will be possible to determine the relative importance of water storage. A dynamic linear programming model will be used to determine the optimum allocation of water subject to physical and institutional constraints.

The model will be structured to account for the total amount of water manageable by the Central and Southern Florida Flood Control District for each time period, including rainfall and inflow, and to allocate this supply among alternative water using activities, storage and release. The objective function of the model will be a mathematical expression representing benefits from water use. To the extent possible, the benefits from the use of water for municipal, industrial, and recreational purposes will be developed. When it is impossible to obtain data on the benefits from these nonagricultural uses, restrictions will be used to satisfy the water requirements for the uses and the opportunity cost of satisfying these requirements will be determined.

The existing physical and institutional restrictions will be varied to determine the effect on the optimum allocation of water. This allows the determination of the amount of unrealized benefits that are foregone when existing restrictions are met. For instance, if a specific amount of water is held in a lake for esthetic purposes, it can be determined (by changing the restriction) how much that water would be worth in another use. This will give an indication of the opportunity cost to society for providing that amount of water for esthetic purposes. Different levels of water availability will also be used to determine the effect of water supply on the allocation of water.

CONCLUSIONS

In summary, the demand for water has increased rapidly and projections for the future indicate the demand will continue to expand. This has resulted in the need for making decisions to allocate a limited amount of water among alternative uses. A profit-maximizing firm will allocate water to a particular use until the marginal value product from the use of the water equals the price (cost) of water. If there is a limited quantity of water available and there are many competing uses and users water should be allocated so that the marginal value productivity of water will be equated for all uses and users.

The application of the economic criteria presented herein involves many and difficult problems of estimation. These problems include obtaining estimates of production functions, marginal physical productivities and marginal value productivities of water, costs of obtaining water and the supplies available for allocation. However, the economic criteria presented should indicate the nature of the data needed for allocating water among alternative uses.

ACKNOWLEDGMENTS

This paper is a part of the study "An Optimum Water Allocation Model Based on An Analysis for the Kissimmee River Basin, Florida Water Resources Research Center Project No. B-005-Fla. The project is funded by the Office of Water Resources Research, U.S. Department of Interior and the Central and Southern Florida Flood Control District. The Florida Agricultural Experiment Station has approved this paper for publication as Journal

Series No. 3421. The writer is indebted to W. F. Edwards, J. R. Conner and K. C. Gibbs for their helpful comments and suggestions.

APPENDIX I.—REFERENCES

1. Gardner, B. D., "State Water Planning: Goals and Analytical Approaches," *Utah Agricultural Experiment Station Bulletin 463,* 1966, pp. 2–9.
2. Henderson, J. M., and Quandt, R. E., *Microeconomic Theory: A Mathematical Approach,* McGraw-Hill Book Company, Inc., New York, 1958, p. 54.
3. Senate Select Committee on National Water Resources, "Water Supply and Demand," *Water Resources Activities in the United States,* Committee Print 32, 1960, p. 41.
4. Timmons, J. F., "Problems in Water Use and Control," *Iowa Law Review,* Vol. 41, No. 2, Winter, 1956, pp. 160–180.
5. Timmons, J. F., "Theoretical Considerations of Water Allocation Among Competing Uses and Users," *Journal of Farm Economics,* Vol. 38, No. 2, Dec., 1956, pp. 1244–1258.
6. United States Water Resources Council, *The Nation's Water Resources,* U.S. Government Printing Office, Washington, D. C., 1968, pp. 1–32.
7. University of Florida Institute of Food and Agricultural Sciences, "1969 DARE Report: Florida Agriculture Plans for the 1970's" *Florida Institute of Food and Agricultural Sciences Publication No. 7,* 1969, p. 158.

APPENDIX II.—NOTATION

The following symbols are used in this paper:

MPP = marginal physical product;
MVP = marginal value product;
P_A = price of citrus;
P_B = price of tomatoes;
P_i = price of i th input;
P_j = price of j th product;
P_W = price of water;
X_{ijk} = i th input of the kth producer to produce the j th output;
X_W = quantity of water input;
X_{WR} = quantity of water for user R;
X_{WS} = quantity of water for user S;
Y_A = citrus output;
Y_{AR} = citrus output produced by R;
Y_{AS} = citrus output produced by S;
Y_B = tomato output;
Y_{BR} = tomato output produced by R;
Y_{BS} = tomato output produced by S;
Y_{jk} = j th output produced by kth producer; and
π = profit.

WATER RESOURCES ALLOCATION, EXTRAMARKET VALUES, AND MARKET CRITERIA: A SUGGESTED APPROACH*

EMERY N. CASTLE   HERBERT H. STOEVENER

The market is a man-made institution. Specialization, trade, and exchange are human responses to comparative advantage. To be operative the market must exist within a particular cultural setting and must be protected by well defined laws and/or customs. It has come to symbolize many things to different people. To some it is simply a tool for accomplishing certain functions of an economic system. To others it has great normative significance either of positive or negative nature. To another group it represents a set of values and demands allegiance or enmity which exist independent of the performance of the market as such.

The literature in economics dealing with the market tends to focus on price as the signal for the allocation of resources as well as a means of distributing income. Yet universal satisfaction does not exist with the market either as a resource allocator or as a distributor of income. Galbraith[1] argues that the market is no longer viable for the really large allocation decisions in an industrial society. Nevertheless, much of the public tinkering with market prices and quantities has actually stemmed from dissatisfaction with the distribution of income resulting from market performance.

This dissatisfaction with market performance has resulted in a pragmatic action program in this country. As a group we have modified the market when its results have failed to satisfy. The arguments about its performance both by economists and non-economists are often highly doctrinaire. There is a failure to view the market in an objective fashion—as a means to an end. If this were to be done, one would need to establish criteria against which market results could be judged. Only in this way could objectivity be achieved. Obviously these criteria would need to be formulated independently of market results. A weakness of economics literature is that there is so little developed in the way of objective criteria

*Technical Paper No. 2387, Oregon Agricultural Experiment Station. This paper was presented during a conference entitled "Competition for Water in an Expanding Economy" of the Irrigation and Drainage Division, American Society of Civil Engineers, Sacramento, California, Nov. 1, 1967.

1. J. Galbraith, The New Industrial State (1967).

NATURAL RESOURCES JOURNAL, 1970, Vol. 10, pp. 532-544.

against which the market and alternative institutions might be judged.

The position taken in this paper is that the market is a means to an end. As such, it should be judged in terms of its efficiency in achieving a particular end. We ascribe no particular normative significance to the market as such.

I
MARKET OPERATION

In the case of water resources the market has often been modified or eliminated as a means of performing the economic functions associated with the use of a scarce resource. Nevertheless, the traditional functions of the market can be discussed profitably in this connection.

In the case of resource allocation, it can be shown that the market will result in optimum allocation if certain conditions are present. However, this is not the case with income distribution[2] where there is no *a priori* assurance that optimum distribution will result. As mentioned above, it is probably dissatisfaction with the distribution of income rather than dissatisfaction with resource allocation that has led to much of the modification of market operation. It may seem surprising that in view of this, income distribution is not attacked directly through taxation and subsidies. However, there are at least two reasons which help explain this state of affairs:

1. Historically we may have been more interested in equality or provision of opportunity than in income equality in a static sense.[3] This may have particular relevance to such programs as that of the Bureau of Reclamation where one of the objectives was to provide opportunity in agriculture.

2. Income distribution and "effort" have been closely linked in our value system. Only recently have we been able to accept the idea that income may be a function of the social environment as well as individual effort. Poverty, therefore, becomes a social as well as an individual problem.

If the above is correct, then a possible rationale exists for attempting to affect the environment by modifying market operation with respect to resource allocation as opposed to leaving this allocation to the market and attacking income distribution directly. The latter approach is that advocated by Milton Friedman and others

2. Bator, *The Simple Analytics of Welfare Maximization*, 47, Am. Econ. Rev., 28, 29, 31-34 (1957).

3. For example, *see* Brewster, *The Impact of Technical Advance and Migration on Agricultural Society and Policy*, SLI J. Farm Econ. 1169-1184 (1959).

who generally favor considerable reliance on the market. Proposals such as a negative income tax are some evidence that this approach is gaining in favor.

II
MARKET EVALUATION CRITERIA

Water, in particular, raises additional points that must be considered. Are there unique characteristics of water as an input in production or consumption that will affect the capacity of the market to serve as a resource allocator?

Much has been made of water being essential to life, but many have pointed out that this is also true of other commodities.[4] The relatively minor role of water in the total production and consumption process is more relevant. The decision process in water resource development in this country can be more easily understood if we recognize that historically water has been abundant and cheap, rather than scarce and expensive. We have had considerable public participation in water resource development which can be viewed as an expression of the public's desire to continue a policy of abundance. Subsidizing the cost of water to its most important user, irrigated agriculture, by general public funds and revenues from hydroelectric power generation can be cited as an example.[5] Because water has been made relatively cheap and abundant, the consequences have been:

1. the substitution of water for other inputs in production; and
2. water developed with public funds has served as a substitute for the political action needed for reallocation or efficient water use.

There is evidence that water will become more expensive in the future. Yet there is almost no method of evaluation that automatically results in a comparison of the opportunity cost of failure to stimulate more efficient use of water or to reallocate it, with the cost of developing additional water resources. It is this state of affairs that has led any number of economists to advocate greater market reliance to correct many of the obvious misallocations existing in the water field.[6]

Why do we have this pessimistic attitude with respect to the role of the market in water allocation? Are there technical economic

4. *See* Eckstein, Water Resource Development 192 (1961). For a more recent empirical study see R. Young and W. Martin, *The Economics of Arizona's Water Problem,* Arizona Review, (1967).

5. J. Hirschleifer, DeHaven and Milliman, Water Supply: Economics, Technology and Policy 1 (1960).

6. E. Renshaw, Toward Responsible Government (1957).

reasons why the market will not work as an allocator, or is the answer to be found in the political arena? Bator cites three reasons why the market may fail. These are:

(1) The existence of technological interdependencies. This means that one person's consumption or production will automatically and inevitably affect another's production or consumption because they are physically linked. Water pollution is the classic example. The market may be unable to cope with such a problem because property rights cannot be appropriately defined.

(2) The existence of indivisibilities. In this case decreasing costs prevail in production. It would be impossible to utilize marginal cost pricing (charging beneficiaries for the costs which they incur), a necessary condition for an efficient resource allocation, because such pricing in this case would make impossible the recovery of the full costs of production.

(3) The existence of public goods. This is a special case of indivisibilities which exists when it is not possible to define private ownership rights without significantly reducing the public welfare. An example might be a spot of unique natural beauty when demand has not yet grown to the point where one person's use would result in the reduction of another's utility.[7]

Later in this article, the above technical economic conditions are examined in some detail, with particular reference to water problems. However, we need to mention here the relationship of economic and political power as they influence water development in this country. Quite apart from questions of economic efficiency as defined by the theory of markets is the incidence of economic benefits arising from water development. Associated inputs, ranging from the professional services of engineers and attorneys, to fertilizers and other chemicals, are examples. Water makes the West green both literally and figuratively. There are also economic benefits associated with the output resulting from water development projects. The result has been that water development and economic growth have been associated in many areas of the West.

Coupled with this has been a particular form of democratic government that results in our representatives being highly oriented to a particular geographic area. There is much less party discipline in the United States than in the parliamentary democracies such as Great Britain. The consequence is that the executive branch has lost

---

7. Bator, *The Anatomy of Market Failure*, Q. J. Econ.

effective control over many water development agencies.[8] The agencies quite accurately recognize that Congress determines their fate. Not surprisingly, they become responsive to Congressional desires. Water development then often becomes primarily a method of transferring income, in the form of government expenditures from one region to another, and secondarily—quite often incidentally—a means of correcting a water shortage in any meaningful economic sense. By meaningful, we mean as a shortage would be defined in the context of market economics.

The reasons then for the development of alternatives to the market in the allocation of water resources stem from a number of interrelated sources. These include our value system, some technical water production relationships, and political institutions exogenous to the decision-making process in water resource development. Market alternatives cover a range almost as broad as the causes of their origins. We shall restrict our comments here to a discussion of public investment in water resources and certain kinds of water use regulations. We shall also attempt to focus upon those characteristics of these alternatives which are especially relevant to their evaluation.

Before proceeding with our assignment, a caveat is in order. Logically, we would be concerned with the evaluation of the market in comparison to other allocative mechanisms, noting their respective performances in "welfare maximization." While economists agree that this goal would be Utopian, there is disagreement about the extent to which the characteristics of our world differ from those of the imaginary ideal island. Krutilla has summarized the conditions which must exist to enable us to conclude that an action leads to an increase in welfare:

(1) Gross benefits of the action must exceed all costs associated with it;

(2) costs must be borne by beneficiaries in such a way that the initial income distribution is not disturbed;

(3) the initial income distribution must in some sense be judged as "best"; and

(4) the marginal conditions for an efficient resource allocation and exchange must be fulfilled in all cases except the one which is the subject of the action to be undertaken.[9]

If the economist were strictly doctrinaire, he would probably cease to be an economist. In any event, his knowledge that at least

---

8. Marshall, *Rational Choice in Water Resources Planning,* Economics and Public Policy in Water Resource Development, (Smith and Castle ed. 1964).

9. Krutilla, Welfare Aspects of Benefit-Cost Analysis, 227 (1961).

conditions two through four would be violated, even if the first condition were met, would severely restrict his interest in policy oriented economic research. We take a more pragmatic approach.

First, we would insist on a careful evaluation of the benefits and costs associated with the action to be analyzed. While this may be difficult, opportunities for achieving greater accuracy and reliability exist. We shall return to this point later.

Second, except in some cases to be discussed below, it may be desirable to insist upon greater coincidence of benefits and costs. This would not only come closer to fulfilling the second condition with respect to leaving the income distribution undisturbed, but it would also have significant implications with respect to efficiency. We shall not treat these here in detail. Let it suffice to say that failure to hold beneficiaries responsible for the costs incurred on their behalf leads to an expression of demand for the services provided to them not only by those willing to pay the full opportunity cost of these services, but also by those willing to pay only the lower price at which they are actually supplied.[10] When changing the income distribution is among the objectives of the action under analysis, or when it is impossible for other reasons to insist upon reimbursement of costs, the income distributional effects should be spelled out so that they can be taken into account explicitly.

Third, we subscribe to the idea that in a democratic society the prevailing income distribution is not a totally inappropriate framework within which to analyze changes in resource allocation. If such a society were greatly dissatisfied with its distribution of income it has available numerous direct political means for changing it.

Returning to the subject of public investment in water resource development, we argue for the existence of at least one of the technical conditions enumerated above as a necessary condition for an intervention of this nature. It appears that indivisibilities, giving rise to decreasing costs of production, may be most widespread among these. For example, they are likely to exist in many developments for hydroelectric power, navigation, and irrigation. "Natural monopolies" might arise, if uncontrolled private development would take place in these areas. Controlled private development as it is exercised with public utilities generally is one of the alternatives against which the benefits and costs of public development ought to be evaluated. This is being done in some cases. Certain proposals for the development of the Hells Canyon provide an example.

10. Krutilla, *Is Public Intervention in Water Resources Development Conducive to Economic Efficiency*, 6 Natural Resources J., 60-75 (1966). Stoevener & Brown, *Analytical Issues in Demand Analysis for Outdoor Recreation*, J. Agricultural Econ., (1967).

Public goods externalities, where products or services of a development are consumed collectively, may represent another case for abandoning the market. When public goods exist—as for example in the control of flood damages and water quality improvement—an individual's consumption of the service does not impose any costs upon others. From a social viewpoint, charging him for the service would result in a misallocation of resources. It appears that any project seeking to provide these services and avoid a misallocation in consumption would have to involve a substantial public subsidy. In this case, attempts to place greater emphasis upon market forces would have to alter the nature in which the services are provided. Therefore, such an alternative as compulsory insurance against floods, which is really an alternative to providing flood protection collectively, deserves careful analysis as an approach to the reduction of flood damages. It should be pointed out that compulsory insurance against flood damages and control of floods by structures are not mutually exclusive.

Finally, the existence of technical interdependencies must be considered as a condition for public investment. The nature of these interdependencies was probably the primary reason for the development of quite different kinds of property rights in water than those developed for land. We would argue that the existence of these externalities is probably the most important reason for public intervention in water use, but not necessarily for public investment. The case for public investment is a rather narrow one to which we alluded previously. It relates to the creation of social overhead capital for the development of a depressed area, for example. Here it is important to evaluate investment in water resources as one alternative approach among others using public capital for achieving the developmental objective. The case for the use of non-investment alternatives can be made much stronger.

III

MARKET ALTERNATIVES AND THEIR EVALUATION

The range of alternatives to the market is quite wide. Even in those instances where the market may fail, the logic of resource allocation, which is a part of market price theory, may be of great value in creating and evaluating market alternatives. The reason for this is quite obvious. As water in quantity and quality becomes increasingly scarce, the social cost of providing it will increase. A rational society will evaluate returns relative to costs in deciding the optimum level of use and will consider and choose on the basis of cost from alternative ways of supplying that level of use. The theory of resource allocation resulting from market price theory provides for such a system of logic. A laissez-faire market does not have to be in operation to make use of this powerful body of logic. We illustrate this by a discussion of three topics of considerable public interest: (1) water quality improvement, (2) water diversion, and (3) water-based recreational values.

A. Water Pollution

As will be recalled, the nature of this externality problem stems from the market's failure to reflect to the decision-maker certain costs stemming from waste disposal for which he is responsible. These costs are borne by the downstream water user. Kneese[11] has suggested a regulatory alternative, namely a system of charges or payments. Such a system represents an explicit attempt to correct the failure of the market system to provide appropriate incentives against waste disposal. In the case of a system of charges, polluters would be charged, for example, a fee per unit waste discharged equivalent to the downsteam costs resulting from the discharge of this waste. This would force polluters to consider off-site costs in their production decisions.

The contributions which such a system could make toward the efficient allocation of water resources are considerable. In addition to giving polluters incentives to substitute changes in production processes, recovery of materials, and effluent treatment for waste disposal, the assimilative capacity of the receiving water and downstream water supply treatment costs can be reflected appropriately. Furthermore, locational differences in water pollution costs both within a river basin and among basins, can be taken into account. Thus these differences will serve as an incentive for a potential polluter to locate, say, at a downstream point or in a river basin where few other water uses are affected and pollution costs (charges) are relatively low, assuming that the downstream location does not add more to his production costs than the savings in water quality costs.

Given all these desirable attributes of the system of charges, it might be difficult to understand why this system has not been widely adopted. Only in the Ruhr Basin in Germany is a scheme with these general characteristics in operation on a significant scale. Difficulties from putting such a system into operation arise basically from two sources: the framing of appropriate institutional organizations, and the lack of engineering, biological, and economic information necessary for the determination of the level of charges. It can be readily

11. A. Kneese, The Economics of Regional Water Quality Management (1965).

seen that in a complex river basin where externalities are many, and sometimes reciprocal, the estimation of damage functions is a formidable task. Nevertheless, from the point of view of the framework outlined above, a system of charges or payments holds the greatest promise of becoming a feasible, economically efficient solution to the water pollution problem.

Quality standards in the effluent or the receiving water have been the most widely used method of public intervention in water quality management. Conceptually, the enforcement of water quality standards is consistent with the requirements of the framework outlined above. It is necessary, however, that the quality standard be set in such a way that incremental changes in its level will equate marginal treatment costs with the marginal costs of damages avoided. That this condition is fulfilled in many practical situations is doubtful, because the informational requirements for doing this would be the same as those for the determination of effluent charges. As an ad hoc procedure water quality standards can be defended. However, a policy establishing uniform water quality standards for large areas, or even nationally, as the principal solution to the water pollution problem must be questioned on the grounds of economic efficiency. Such a solution would fail to account for widely different ratios between benefits and costs in different decision-making contexts. The system of charges would be preferable as it would provide for greater flexibility and would require less information than would be needed to design an economically efficient system of standards.

B. Water Diversion; Operations Research and the Public Sector

Robert McNamara has brought considerations of efficiency analysis in the public sector to the attention of the public to an extent unmatched by any other public official. The logic of production economics combined with modern computing equipment has been applied to a wide variety of problems which extend far beyond the Department of Defense. Those who argued for the modest expansion of these techniques in water resources development a decade and a half ago appear to be "pikers" in comparison. It is almost ludicrous that the debate was still raging among water economists as recently as 1960 when benefit-cost analysis was pioneered in the water resources field. The value of the techniques and the use of the computer is without question and it seems somewhat surprising in retrospect that they were questioned to the extent they were.

It is now possible to draw some generalizations from this experience. First, as noted above, the approach is here to stay. Second, these techniques are not a substitute for the decision process but an aid to it. Anyone with visions of the bureaucracy withering away as a result of operations research techniques will be disappointed. Third, and this is a subtle point, this development represents a triumph of the market *in absentia* because the logic of these quantitative techniques is based squarely on firm theory. Furthermore, many of the data used stem rather directly from market operations. The market is being "simulated" by such studies to solve certain "sub-optimum" problems.

In the case of wide-scale water diversion, given the present state of technology, it is obvious that indivisibilities exist. If such transfers are to occur they would do so as a result of public intervention. Yet a rational society will consider alternatives to water transfer. Operations research techniques applied in the context of market price theory is a way of considering these alternatives in a systematic way. The estimation of the empirical relationships to make the following model operational is much needed.

$$M_{11} + M_{12} \gtrless M_{21} + M_{22} + M_{31} \tag{1}$$

Where

M_{11} —marginal value use of water in the area of "deficit" for primary purposes.

M_{12} —marginal value use of water in the area of "deficit" for secondary purposes.

M_{21} —marginal value use of water in the area of "surplus" for primary purposes.

M_{22} —marginal value use of water in the area of "surplus" for secondary purposes.

M_{31} —transfer cost of marginal water use.

When

$$M_{21} + M_{22} + M_{31} < M_{32}, M_{33} \ldots M_{3n} \tag{2}$$

Where

$M_{32} \ldots M_{3n}$ are the costs of all alternative means of supplying water to the marginal water uses in the "deficit" water area. Estimation of equations (1) and (2) would permit society to decide if the sufficient and necessary economic conditions for water transfer existed. To estimate these equations one would need to "simulate" market operations and make use of the data generated by the private sector of the economy. If only a fraction of the cost of debating, planning and fighting for and against this issue were spent estimating the relevant economic magnitudes, society would have some basis of judging its effect on resource allocation. The other side of the same coin would show the amount of regional income transfer that would be involved. It is apparent that it is dollar importation rather than water importation that is the real issue.

C. Market Performance and Intangibles
with Special Attention to Recreation

S. V. Ciriacy-Wantrup has treated the semantics of "intangibles" as related to benefit-cost analysis and water resource development in a logical and definitive way.[12] He makes a strong case for the use of the term "extra-market" rather than "intangible" to describe those benefits that are not routinely valued in the market place. He also argues that attempts to quantify such benefits should be encouraged. He suggests that such quantification need not be confined to estimating dollar benefits; there are numerous physical attributes that may be helpful in decision-making.

The fact that extra-market values exist is evidence of a real or imagined failure of the market. In this connection outdoor recreation is often mentioned as an example. The failure may be real in the sense that the market would bring about socially undesirable results. The failure may be imagined in that actual market performance might be superior to administrative management.

The market would undoubtedly fail to do a satisfactory job of managing some of the great natural wonders of the outdoors. The National Parks are an example. A site such as Crater Lake would become a monopoly and would be highly commercialized if left to the market. Yet the fear that some have of a commercial outdoor recreation industry seems, in some instances at least, to be unfounded. The market does provide these kinds of services in many circumstances. It is difficult to argue against an outdoor recreation market on income distribution grounds. It is easy to demonstrate that at the present much outdoor recreation is enjoyed by those with average or better incomes. Equipment expenditures are testimony to this fact. An additional site charge would not appear to be a major factor in discouraging consumption by those with lower than average incomes for those outdoor recreational experiences that involve large equipment expenditures or high travel costs.[13] Special provision might well be made, of course, for those of low income; the point is that much outdoor recreation that is provided by the public sector is not enjoyed by the low income segment of the population.

One of the more interesting developments pertaining to the eco-

---

12. *Benefit-Cost Analysis and Public Resource Development,* Economics and Public Water Policy in Water Resource Development (Smith and Castle ed. 1964).

13. The above argument is couched in general terms. There is need for more precise formulations if one were to make a detailed statement on outdoor recreation policy. Joe B. Stevens has estimated income elasticities of demand for different kinds of outdoor recreation experiences on Yaquina Bay in Oregon. An outdoor recreational policy may wish to use studies of this kind to identify areas for possible interference and public subsidy. Stevens, *Recreation Benefits and Water Pollution Control,* 2 Water Resources Research, 167-182.

nomics of outdoor recreation is the development of a methodology which permits economic evaluation of this intangible. Such techniques have progressed to the point where outdoor recreation can be evaluated with as much confidence as flood control or navigation. Again, the market is operating *in absentia* through the use of economic theory based on market processes and data generated in the private sector of the economy.

A trend is underway to subject more and more outdoor recreation problems to the rule of the market. As the demand for outdoor recreation increases, more such recreation will be supplied by the private sector of the economy. The public sector will also be forced to use market processes either to allocate a scarce resource or to increase its supply. This trend is not particularly distressing to these writers. One frequently hears it said that dollars simply cannot measure the satisfaction that comes from viewing a beautiful sunset or an unspoiled mountain lake. But at the same time the food and clothing necessary to the maintenance of life itself have been subjected to the rule of the market. Does anyone contend that the consumer's surplus has been eliminated in the market for any commodity? The evidence is not available to substantiate the argument that outdoor recreation is "different." This does not mean that the market should be relied upon entirely; it does mean that greater reliance on the market might well bring about some desirable results.

EVALUATION

It becomes obvious from the foregoing that the important social issues relative to the future of the market as an institution for the allocation of water cannot be simplified to the point where one argues for the complete acceptance or rejection of the market. The really relevant questions are of the following nature:

1. To what extent and what kind of regulation of the market will there be?
2. How will market performance be judged?
3. How is market performance affected by (a) taxation, (b) subsidy, (c) property loans, (d) zoning, (e) price supports, (f) other collective devices affecting economic decisions?

Arguments on purely doctrinaire ground about the market may be interesting but they are hardly worth the attention of the modern economist. To be relevant to the problems of the world he must consider government intervention in terms of specific problems.[14]

14. For an eloquent statement of this point of view see George Stigler's 1964 presidential address to the American Economic Association, *The Economist and the State,* 55 Am. Econ. Rev. (1965). Stigler traces what economists have had to say about government inter-

There are many important tasks the market does exceedingly well; there are many important tasks the market does not do well at all; there are many important tasks where it is not clear whether the market is superior to another kind of organization. The first category is of interest to the economist as he studies the market for an under-standing of its functioning. The second is a challenge in terms of designing market alternatives. The third represents the area of controversy which represents a real opportunity to the economist as he strives to provide information that will be of value in decision-making on social problems.

We return again to a point made earlier. Even though the market is rejected as a means of allocating certain goods and services, it may still provide data and criteria of value in dealing with extra-market problems. The role of the market in generating relevant information for decision-makers has not been given the explicit treatment it deserves. The generation and communication of information is an automatic function of the market. When the market is displaced, some substitute for the choice indicator—i.e., price—must be provided. The amount of information summarized by price-quantity-quality relationships is certainly rather considerable. Obviously, when non-market organizations are relied upon, a different hierarchy of values and subsequent incentives may be developed. As an example, the stated objective found in many statements on educational policy is to provide opportunity for the *complete* development of human potential. Such an objective would stand the test neither of market performance nor economic logic. We do not argue for complete dominance of the market; we do argue for the kind of rationality that market logic can bring to social decision-making.

vention throughout the history of economic thought. He concludes that only recently have we acquired the measurement tools to answer the questions economists have been posing, but answering inadequately, for generations.

The Market Mechanism, Externalities, and Land Economics[*]

EMERY N. CASTLE[**]

The literature on external economies, diseconomies, and indivisibilities is related to past, present, and emerging land management problems. A definition of externalities and indivisibilities is provided and applied to problems of quality, common property resources, and outdoor recreation. Criteria for the evaluation of land management institutions are suggested and discussed. Current and past research efforts are examined in light of the perspective provided by the article. It is suggested that both the tools of neoclassical economics and the relevance of institutional economics might be combined profitably in the study of land economics problems. It was concluded that historical research efforts have tended to be polarized: the production economics-oriented group has been heavily oriented toward the internal aspects of individual firm theory; traditional land economists, while working on relevant problems, have not always made the best of existing theory in the evaluation of land management institutions.

LAND economics has long existed as an area of specialization within agricultural economics although the efforts of land economists have extended beyond agricultural economics. Recently land economics has experienced a new wave of popularity and considerable activity is underway on natural resource-related investigation.[1]

Yet land economics has come in for its share of professional criticism. Salter[2] found much of the research in the field unproductive. In his significant work on production economics, Heady[3] questioned the basic logic underlying land economics as an area of study. He conceded, however, that knowledge of "legal, historic and property rights aspects of resource tenure" is important.[4] T. W. Schultz has also had his say about land. He has not concerned himself about the content of a particular specialization within agricultural economics but rather has written extensively about the role of land in economic development.[5] It was in this context that Schultz advanced his locational matrix hypothesis. Writing more recently, Raup[6] argued that economists have too long treated natural resources as being fixed in supply and have not recognized the importance

[*] Tech. paper 1970, Oregon Agr. Expt. Sta. Supported by grant WP-00107 of the U. S. Public Health Service.

[**] I am very much indebted to Herbert Stoevener and John Edwards for their suggestions. The JFE reviewers also contributed greatly to whatever clarity, rigor, and relevance the article may have.

[1] Land is used here in the classical sense and encompasses that part of the natural environment that is relevant from an economic point of view. Used in this way

JOURNAL OF FARM ECONOMICS, 1965, Vol. 47, pp. 542-556.

of increasing human knowledge and the effectiveness with which it is applied. This is quite consistent with Schultz' earlier writings on the subject. Milton Friedman says,

> There may still be some problems for which it is important to distinguish land from other resources, but for most problems it hardly seems important to do so. In most contexts now important, land, in any economically relevant sense, is indistinguishable from other forms of capital. The productive power of the soil can be produced at a cost by drainage, fertilization, and the like, and is clearly not permanent.[7]

Despite these writings by respected economists, land economics has persisted and is growing more rapidly than the whole of agricultural economics. Surprisingly, there has been little serious effort made to answer the criticisms that have been made of the field or to provide any logic for the specialization beyond that of administrative convenience.[8]

In this paper, the position is developed that there are some compelling reasons arising from the process of economic development and associated decisions for the longevity of land economics. It is further contended that these reasons have not been clearly identified; the consequence has been that some of our research has not focused on problems faced by society. By identifying the root of the economic questions relative to natural resource management, a framework is provided for viewing such widely divergent efforts in land economics as the study of simulation techniques applied to river basin planning, and the examination of such economic institutions as water law and zoning ordinances.[9]

After the rather ambitious objectives of the above paragraph, perhaps a

---

there is no difference between land and natural resource economics. The emphasis is placed on traditional land economics problems in this country. The relation of land tenure issues to economic growth and problems of community development are not treated explicitly.

[2] Leonard Salter, *A Critical Review of Research in Land Economics*, University of Minnesota Press, 1948.

[3] E. O. Heady, *Economics of Agricultural Production and Resource Use*, Prentice Hall, 1952, pp. 24-25.

[4] *Ibid.*, p. 563.

[5] T. W. Schultz, *The Economic Organization of Agriculture*, McGraw-Hill Book Company, Inc., 1953. Also "A Framework for Land Economics," *J. Farm Econ.*, Vol. 33, May 1951.

[6] Phillip Raup, "Rural Resource Development in an Urban Society: Some Research Priorities," *J. Farm Econ.*, Vol. 45, December 1963.

[7] *Price Theory: A Provisional Text*, Chicago, Aldine Publishing Co., 1962, pp. 199, 200.

[8] An exception to the above statement is a recent note by Fredrick O. Sargent entitled "The Resource Allocation Process: A Distinguishing Characteristic of Land Economics," *Land Econ.*, Vol. 40, August 1964, p. 315.

[9] In preparing this paper I have had the benefit of reading an unpublished paper by Walter E. Chryst and W. B. Back entitled "Scope, Content and Methodological Problems of Land Economics."

delimiting paragraph is now in order. It is not maintained that land economics deserves to grow or even that it should necessarily survive. The answer to such questions can be obtained only by comparing the productivity of intellectual effort in land economics with that of comparable effort in other areas. Such questions are important and should be asked; our objective, however, is more modest. In summary, this is not an attempt either to bury or to praise land economics but rather to make its natural life somewhat more pleasant and productive.[10]

Specifically, the paper has the following objectives:

1. To relate natural resource management to overall economic policy issues and decisions
2. To suggest a framework which may be helpful in judging the adequacy of institutions used in the allocation, transfer, and tenure of natural resources
3. To identify questions relevant to group decision making on land resource issues
4. To relate past and prospective research efforts to the first three objectives.

Natural Resources and the Market Mechanism

Milliman[11] has argued that the market should be relied upon to a much greater extent in natural resource management. The purpose of this paper will not be served by debating this normative issue. But the underlying positive proposition that our economy has seen fit to rely upon many institutions other than the market for the management of natural resources does need to be established. This is the implicit assumption of Milliman's article.

In agriculture, public intervention in the factor markets is an old story. Although the literature on agricultural policy is preoccupied with commodity marketing and pricing programs, a case can be made that public policy pertaining to the factor markets is of equal or greater significance. We have followed a policy of abundance for every factor of production in agriculture. Public intervention has, on balance, made the inputs in agriculture more abundant than would have been the case if allocation had been left to the market. It is true, of course, that the abundance of certain commodities has led to land retirement programs but the impact of such action has been offset by reclamation and "conservation" activi-

---

[10] Neither is there any intent here to take credit for concepts and research approaches that are consistent with the viewpoint outlined herein. An effort has been made to cite relevant literature at appropriate points in the manuscript. The paper has value mainly to the extent it provides perspective.

[11] J. W. Milliman, "Can People Be Trusted with Natural Resources?" *Land Econ.*, Vol. 38, August 1962.

ties. The policy of abundance has been followed with capital (government-sponsored credit programs), labor (foreign labor, discouragement of unions for agriculture workers), management (agricultural education programs), and technology (government-sponsored research). The economist, of course, is aware of this deep and fundamental inconsistency in U. S. agricultural policy. Yet there have been only a few scattered research efforts to measure the extent and impact of the inconsistency; furthermore, only a relatively small number of citizens seem to be aware of it.

While government intervention in all of the agricultural factor markets has long existed, such intervention undoubtedly has been greater for land than for other factors when one views the entire economy. Public intervention ranges from complete socialization of certain natural resources to laws which permit certain property rights to be restricted or curtailed when property is transferred.[12] This public involvement is not likely to diminish in the future; in fact, most informed people believe even greater involvement is likely to occur.

This public participation has resulted in a large number of questions being posed to land economists that stem from "felt difficulty" situations. Had the market been relied upon and had it then achieved satisfactory results, the same kinds of questions would not have been raised. It is not surprising that many questions relating to land have been asked and that public funds have been made available to support systematic intellectual investigation of such questions. The past popularity of land economics can be at least partially explained on these grounds; such questions are likely to become relatively more important in the future. The market mechanism is put to a different kind of test as economic development proceeds, and the most desirable institutional alternatives also change.

Conceptual Considerations

The market mechanism, as a tool of natural resource management, has been abandoned in this country on pragmatic rather than doctrinaire grounds. The fact that both public and private activity prevail suggests a willingness to use either if the situation seems to warrant it. Yet the absence of preconceived ideas as to what institutional arrangement will prove superior is not the same as the absence of criteria which may be used to evaluate institutional arrangements. Indeed, the uniqueness of the economist's contribution is related directly to the extent that he has criteria which may be used to evaluate both market and nonmarket institutions without bias.

---

[12] One might argue that the remarkable feature of U. S. land policy, when compared to other countries, has not been the extent of market intervention but rather the lack of it. As relevant as this comparison may be for certain problems, it is not the issue at hand here.

Specification of objectives is necessary for the evaluation of any mechanism. There has been a tendency to treat income distribution and resource allocation as separate issues in much work in economics. There is no doubt that both objectives are important in natural resource management. However, their separation for some purposes is questionable; it has been demonstrated that "optimum" resource allocation cannot be separated from a distribution of income consistent with a theoretical social optimum.[13] Because both issues have historically been important in land economics, it is interesting to consider whether their separation has always been justified. In any case it is clear that both matters must be dealt with in the evaluation of institutions.

What appears to be needed are criteria against which a given situation may be judged to determine whether public or private decision making is more likely to lead to "desirable" results. The criteria need not be absolute, they need only supply a hypothesis rather than a final answer. The hypothesis will supply a base for empirical work but should not be used to anticipate the results of an investigation of an actual situation. Recent literature in general economies may be helpful in establishing such criteria.[14] It is beyond the scope of this paper to review in depth all of the relevant literature. Nevertheless an attempt will be made to identify those elements of this literature that are crucial to the matter at hand. Our search is for criteria useful in judging the adequacy of market or nonmarket institutions that may be used for natural resource management. Any such criteria must be capable of treating two important characteristics of natural resources which complicate their management. One such characteristic is the fact that natural resource use frequently gives rise to externalities. The other is the existence of indivisibilities.[15]

[13] See F. M. Bator, "The Simple Analytics of Welfare Maximization," *Am. Econ. Rev.*, Vol. 47, March 1957, p. 39, for a review. Buchanan and Tulloch in *The Calculus of Consent*, University of Michigan Press, 1962, p. 198, make the point that redistributional externalities may exist in addition to allocational externalities.

[14] F. M. Bator's "The Simple Analytics of Welfare Maximization" has already been noted. His companion article "The Anatomy of Market Failure," *Quar. J. Econ.* is relevant (Vol. 72, August 1958). Buchanan and Tulloch's *Calculus of Consent* has been cited. The following are also identified: James M. Buchanan, "Politics, Policy and Pigovion Margins," *Economica*, Vol. 29, February 1962; James M. Buchanan and William Craig Stubblebine, "Externality," *Economica*, Vol. 29, November 1962; Otto A. Davis and Andrew Winston, "Externalities, Welfare and the Theory of Games," *J. Pol. Econ.*, Vol. 70, June 1962; Ralph Turvey, "On Divergences Between Social Cost and Private Cost," *Economica*, Vol. 30, August 1963; R. H. Coase, "The Problem of Social Cost," *J. Law and Econ.*, Vol. 3, 1960; and Stanislaw Wellisz, "On External Diseconomies and the Government-Assisted Invisible Hand," *Economica*, Vol. 31, November 1964.

[15] Bator, *Quar. J. Econ., op. cit.*, cites externalities as being one of the main reasons for market failure. He then classifies externalities as ownership, technical, and public goods. We are not altogether comfortable with Bator's broad definition of exter-

External economies and diseconomies have a long history in economics literature. An attempt is made here to outline some of the main considerations.[16] Externalities, of course, may appear either in consumption or production, although there is symmetry between the treatment of the two.[17]

We utilize production relationships to illustrate externalities:

(1) $$Y_A = F(X_1, X_2 \cdots X_n)$$

(2) $$X_n = F(Y_B)$$

where Y_A is the output of producer A, Y_B is the output of producer B, and $X_1 X_2 \ldots X_n$ are inputs. Partial derivatives are helpful in defining externalities. When

(3) $$\frac{\partial Y_A}{\partial X_n} < 0 \quad \text{and} \quad \frac{\partial X_n}{\partial Y_B} < 0 \quad \text{or} \quad \frac{\partial Y_A}{\partial X_n} > 0 \quad \text{and} \quad \frac{\partial X_n}{\partial Y_B} > 0$$

external economies exist. If the inequality signs above go in opposite directions, external diseconomies prevail. All consuming and producing units are, of course, interdependent in a market sense. The distinguishing characteristics of the diseconomies being treated here is that they are nonpecuniary; they do not enter the decision-making framework through the stimuli provided by a decentralized pricing system. Externalities, of course, can go both ways. A's production may also be a variable in B's production. By the same token this type of interdependence may be reflected between production and consumption functions as well as be-

nalities although he is certainly correct in his position in citing all three as being possible reasons for the failure of decentralized decision making. In this article we define externalities as being the same as Bator's first category of externalities, namely, ownership. Indivisibilities are the same as Bator's technical externalities. Public good externalities (Bator's terminology) are not treated separately here because it appears that the management conclusions which flow from the treatment which follows would cover most of the land management problems which are likely to arise. In the event this is not the case, the treatment could be extended to cover Bator's public goods.

[16] A thorough review of the literature on external economies and diseconomies and a careful application of the theory to natural resource situations would be an exceedingly valuable addition to the literature of land economics. A companion review to identify the varied means of providing for externalities in the law would be of equal or greater value. For an excellent article in this tradition see L. M. Hartman and D. A. Seastone, *Welfare Goals and Organizations of Decision Making for the Allocation of Water Resources*, Conference Proceedings Committee on the Economics of Water Resource Development of the Western Agricultural Economics Research Council, December 18-20, 1963. Other articles in this vein are noted subsequently. Also see Coase, *op. cit.*

[17] Stubblebine, *op. cit.*

tween consumption functions. These interrelationships may be illustrated by the following diagram. Assume four decision-making units—two producers, P_A, P_B, and two consumers, C_A, C_B.

Interdependencies between producers and consumers may exist as follows:

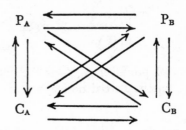

With the four decision-making units outlined above, the possibility of 12 external relationships exists.[18]

Physical interdependence is the main reason for the importance of externalities in the economics of land. Society has long been aware of externalities as they affect land management; the wide variety of institutional arrangements that have evolved to deal with them are testimony to this fact. As economic development proceeds, externalities become important in different contexts than was previously the case.

The traditional textbook case of pollution as an example of externalities is now assuming increased relevance. The producer who changes the quality of the natural environment may affect either the production or consumption function of others in a way that is not reflected by a system of relative prices. For example, the upstream polluter may affect the production function of the downstream commercial fisherman as well as the consumption function of the downstream sport fisherman. Air pollution provides another example. Neighborhood effects of land development as well as the intense utilization of the atmosphere which results in such external effects as the creation of "noise" provide other examples. The economics of quality of the environment is emerging as a problem of major importance. Even so, the land economist's traditional interest in zoning and water rights can be traced back to the same basic economic phenomena. The traditional land economist studied institutional techniques for handling the kinds of externalities that have long existed.

The difficulty of coming to grips with "quality" management stems not so much from the inability to discover a shadow price (although this may be a major undertaking) as from the development of an institutional ar-

---

[18] The number of possible externalities is n^2-n where n is the number of decision-making units.

rangement that can generate and utilize such information. This kind of situation may be described by utilizing the information of equation (3):

$$(4) \qquad \frac{\partial Y_A}{\partial X_n} < 0; \quad \frac{\partial X_n}{\partial Y_B} > 0$$

where Y_A is the output of the downstream producer and Y_B is the output of the upstream polluter. X_n is the polluting material which results from B's output and enters A's production function against his will. In the above case, producer A is suffering an external diseconomy. If C_T is the cost of pollution control, and if

$$(5) \qquad \frac{\partial C_T}{\partial Y_B} < \frac{\partial Y_A}{\partial X_n} \cdot P_A,$$

uncontrolled pollution will reduce the net social product. (We have abstracted here from decision-making costs which are introduced later.) If the inequality goes in the other direction, the value of the diseconomy does not warrant internalizing it. An equity problem exists in both cases, of course.

Other examples of physical interdependence may be found with common property resources. The oil pool, the ground water aquifer, and the ocean fishery all provide examples. When private ownership of natural resources prevail, the entrepreneur has a production function of the following form:

$$(6) \qquad Y_A = F(X_1 \cdots X_{n-1}, \,|\, X_n)$$

where X_n is the natural resource. To maximize returns to X_n he will

$$\frac{\partial Y_A}{\partial X_1} \cdot P_Y = P_{X_1}$$
$$\vdots$$
$$(7) \qquad \frac{\partial Y_A}{\partial X_{n-}} \cdot P_Y = P_{X_{n-1}}.$$

With a common property resource his production function is of the form:

$$(8) \qquad Y_A = F(X_1 \cdots X_{n-1}, X_n)$$

and B has a function of the form:

$$(9) \qquad Y_B = F(X_n, X_{n+1}, \cdots X_{n+m})$$

and

$$(10) \qquad X_{na} + X_{nb} = k.$$

For a social optimum each should take into consideration the effect of his action on the other. In this case A's decision model should be of the form:

(11)
$$\frac{\partial Y_A}{\partial X_1} \cdot P_{Y_c} + \frac{\partial Y_B}{\partial Y_A} \cdot P_{Y_B} = P_{X_1}$$

$$\frac{\partial Y_A}{\partial X_{n-1}} \cdot P_{Y_A} + \frac{\partial Y_B}{\partial Y_A} \cdot P_{Y_B} = P_{X_{n-1}}.\text{[19]}$$

Unrestricted entry and decentralized pricing may lead to producing in Stage III for common property resources.

Another characteristic of natural resources which is important in policy affairs is the existence of indivisibilities. When indivisibilities exist, the marginal social cost of usage will be zero over a wide range and any toll or price will tend to misallocate the output of the "lumpy" resources. In welfare economics jargon, lumpiness violates the convexity assumption. The ultimate result of decentralization will be private monopoly. It is probable that for fairly long periods in our history much outdoor recreation belonged to this category of externalities. It is also possible that this time has passed for some outdoor recreation and that some type of pricing would not necessarily lead to misallocation. The marginal social cost of use is no longer zero. Equilibrium in usage will be reached either by "crowding" which will result in a deterioration in the quality of the resource or by some form of price or nonprice rationing.

Because of space limitations, we cite only a few examples. Nevertheless, it appears the kinds of problems that have been illustrated are very common in land management. The variety of institutional arrangements that have emerged in response to problems of natural resource externalities and indivisibilities have already been noted. They are testimony to the pragmatism and imagination of man. They range from complete socialization to an essentially unregulated market. There are numerous examples of varying kinds of joint public and private participation in decision making. The results, however, are not equally satisfactory. We probably are operating in Stage III on the production function for the salmon fishery in the Pacific Northwest, which results from the failure to restrict entry. The quality of some of our outdoor recreational resources may be declining in an uneconomic fashion despite public ownership of many outdoor recreation resources.

Perhaps the most striking feature of the recent literature in general

---

[19] With a common property resources one would expect $\partial Y_B/\partial Y_A$ to have a negative sign.

economics on externalities is the agreement which has emerged on the proposition there is no single institutional technique, centralized or de-centralized, which is ideal in the management of externalities. Such techniques may range from private bargains (mergers) to government prohibition of certain activities to complete government ownership (socialization). The traditional approach of tax subsidy schemes may still have application although the problem is considerably more complex than Pigou originally believed it to be.[20] But the complexity of the theoretical problem and the variety of institutional forms existing and that might be developed provide opportunity and challenge for the economist. The search for generalization should go on but an intellectual basis for pragmatism exists. Doctrinaire prescription will become unattractive relative to empirical investigation.

Certain elements have been identified, however, which both the generalist and the case investigator must take into consideration. Buchanan and Tulloch's analysis of decision-making costs becomes relevant.[21] They point out that the costs of collective decision making with regard to externalities may well exceed the value of the external loss. If C_D refers to decision-making costs of internalizing the diseconomy, then inequality (5) will read:

$$(12) \qquad \frac{dC_T}{dY_B} + \frac{dC_D}{dY_B} < \frac{dY_A}{dX_n} \cdot P_A.$$

This condition must hold for a change in institutional arrangements to be economic. Decision-making costs will rise as the number of participants increase. Nevertheless it can be demonstrated that private bargains are less likely to be workable when the number of parties become large.[22] This line of reasoning suggests that the economist has a key role to play in the design of institutions. Landlord-tenant relations, for example, have long commanded the attention of land economists. Their analyses of the issues have contributed substantially to our understanding of the bargaining processes and served to identify the types of institutions which facilitate internalizing the externalities in question. Because of the small number of people involved, collective decision making has not been required for stable decision-making patterns to develop. Land reform, of course, changes bargaining power and may or may not involve collective bargaining with regard to contractual rent on land. Even so, it appears these kinds of issues lie at the heart of traditional land economics.[23]

---

[20] A. C. Pigou, *The Economics of Welfare*, 4th ed., London, Macmillan and Company, 1932.

[21] *op. cit.*, chap. 8.

[22] See Wellisz, *op. cit.*, p. 354 for a summary.

[23] Time has not been entered into the above analysis. Furthermore, conservation

Research Issues

There are many classifications of research efforts that would be consistent with the analysis of the previous section. It appears that relevant research efforts will need to come to grips with questions of the type listed below:

1. How can one best describe and evaluate the consequences of resources allocations, transfer, and tenure as brought about by alternative market and nonmarket institutions?
2. What criteria are to be used to judge the adequacy and performance of institutions used to allocate, transfer, and hold land resources?
3. Within any particular institutional complex what are the consequences of particular decisions?

How does one decide if the market mechanism is adequate or inadequate for a particular factor or product? The question is a loaded one. "Adequate" or "inadequate" in a relative rather than in an absolute sense implies that there is a superior alternative. It is not sufficient to compare the performance of either the market or a nonmarket mechanism against an "ideal," "optimum," or theoretical standard and conclude it is inappropriate for policy purpose.[24] Market "failure" in some abstract sense does not mean that a nonmarket alternative will not also fail in the same or in some other abstract sense. Conversely, it will not do to compare the results of public investment in water resources development with some theoretical ideal and conclude the market would have done better.[25] Even so, an implicit assumption of benefit-cost analysis is that values from the economy can be used, with minor adjustment, as a standard for public performance. It has always seemed to this writer to be a very neat trick to be able to use the values from the economy as data for benefit-cost analysis and then assume that the market was perhaps inadequate for the particular natural resource investment being considered.[26]

The existing theory of resource allocation is of value in outlining the conditions which should be met for maximum welfare. The absence of

---

problems have always been important in land economics. A major conservation problem, however, has related to the adequacy of the market in achieving "conservation." Externalities over time become relevant in such matters. Even so, the matter is much too complex to treat here and has been treated thoroughly and adequately elsewhere. See S. V. Ciriacy-Wantrup, *Resource Conservation Economics and Policies, infra.*

[24] E. N. Castle, "Criteria and Planning for Optimum Use," *Land and Water Use,* American Association for the Advancement of Science, Washington, D.C., 1964.

[25] Edward Renshaw, *Toward Responsible Government,* Chicago, Idyia Press, 1957.

[26] Otto Eckstein, *Water Resources Development,* Harvard University Press, 1958.

these conditions suggests a hypothesis. But the theory is much less adequate in providing help in devising a test for the hypothesis. The development of alternative institutions and their comparison with the market appears to be a rather fundamental kind of investigation which might well occupy land economists.

A superficial view of the institutions common in natural resource management suggests they cope rather well with certain kinds of externalities but really do not help much with others. It appears that third party effects have been very important in the development of water laws. It is even possible that they have been given more attention than their economic importance warrants. It is not valid, however, to conclude that these laws are inefficient unless third part effects are at least considered. Yet other externalities are provided for much less satisfactorily. Water and air pollution and common property resources such as fisheries and ground water have been cited as examples. The external effects associated with urban expansion provide many additional examples.

If one of the inadequacies of the decentralized market is in its failure to reflect externalities, then some technique is needed that will register the repercussion resulting from various economic decisions. The Leontief input-output technique is ideally suited to showing the second and third round effects of a change in a particular sector of the economy. There are two ways such techniques might be used. One would be to use the results as a direct tool of management. The other would be to diagnose the weaknesses and strengths of alternative institutional arrangements in reflecting costs and benefits throughout the economy in decision making. A study at Oregon State on the economics of water pollution control reflects an attempt to make this latter type of application of the technique.[27] In view of the formidable problems involved and the rather substantial resources required, the indirect type of use has considerable appeal.

The "bread and butter" work of land economists involves predicting the consequences of particular decisions within a particular institutional complex. Agency economists are working almost entirely in this area. It is here that the interesting work in simulation will have its greatest influence. Of course, the more imaginative and fundamental work will not accept institutions as fixed and will have an impact on the future of these social mechanisms. There is considerable research underway which attempts to estimate the extra-market values associated with outdoor

[27] Herbert H. Stoevener, "Water Use Relationships as Affected by Water Quality on the Yaquina Bay," *Proceedings,* Water Resources Conference, University of Colorado, July 1964; and also "An Economic Evaluation of Water Pollution Control Alternatives," *Water Resources and Economic Development of the West,* Rept. No. 12, Western Agricultural Economics Research Council, December 1963.

recreation.[28] The complex problems associated with the use of such estimates in social decision making have not really been faced in our research.[29]

An Evaluation

Considerable research in land economics has been consistent with the analysis presented herein. Wantrup's classic book on conservation gives explicit recognition to those instances where private and public objectives in resource management may not coincide.[30] He has suggested that greater attention be devoted to those instances where price signals fail to communicate the ends of society.[31] Mason has written an excellent article in the same vein.[32] Kneese's work on water quality gives explicit recognition to the problem and uses the basin-wide firm as a technique for internalizing diseconomies.[33] Other examples could be cited.

Yet the treatment of externalities has not been a central part of traditional land economics. One searches in vain for a treatment of externalities in land economics texts.[34]

Authors of land economics texts seem to proceed on the assumption that there must be at least one chapter on economic principles. But, after tradition has been served, there is little subsequent application of such principles. Given the particular economic principles chosen for development, their decision to minimize their use is appropriate. Agricultural economists have apparently become so immersed in the internal workings of the theory of the firm that they have failed to study carefully the means by which the firm relates to its environment. In the absence of ex-

---

[28] For examples see Marion Clawson, *Methods of Measuring the Demand for and Value of Outdoor Recreation*, Reprint No. 10, Washington, D.C., Resources for the Future, Inc., February 1959; William G. Brown, Ajmer Singh, and Emery N. Castle, *An Economic Evaluation of the Salmon Steelhead Sport Fishery*, Tech. Bul. 78, Agr. Expt. Sta., Oregon State University, September 1964.

[29] Emery N. Castle and William G. Brown, *The Economic Value of a Recreational Resource*, Proceedings Number 13 of the Western Agricultural Economics Research Council's Committee on the Economics of Water Resources Development, December 9, 10, 11, 1964, San Francisco, California.

[30] S. V. Ciriacy-Wantrup, *Resource Conservation Economics and Policies*, University of California Press, Berkeley, 1952.

[31] *Economics of Watershed Planning*, G. S. Tolley and F. E. Riggs (eds.), Iowa State University Press, 1961, chap. 1.

[32] Edward S. Mason, "The Political Economy of Resource Use," *Perspectives in Conservation*, Henry Jarrett (ed.), Johns Hopkins Press, 1958.

[33] Allen V. Kneese, *Water Pollution: Economic Aspects and Research Needs*, Resources for the Future, Inc., 1962; also *The Economics of Regional Water Quality Management*, Baltimore, Johns Hopkins Press, 1964.

[34] This statement is based on three commonly used texts in the field: Richard T. Ely and George S. Wehrwein, *Land Economics*, New York, The Macmillan Company, 1940; Raleigh Barlowe, *Land Resource Economics*, Englewood Cliffs, New Jersey, Prentice Hall, Inc., 1958; and Roland R. Renne, *Land Economics*, New York, Harper & Brothers, rev. ed., 1958.

ternal economies and diseconomies, this is done through the demand function for factors and the supply function for products. Even when we have given explicit recognition to supply we have often failed to recognize that the sum of the marginal cost curves will not necessarily equal the supply function for the industry. This results from failure to recognize the importance of pecuniary diseconomies. As noted earlier, nonpecuniary diseconomies are of primary importance in land economics. In land economics the relationship of the firm to the external world or its environment is the core of the problem. It is with such problems that society is constantly grappling. And it is the existence of such problems that accounts for the continuing popularity of land economics research. But whether land economists have really attempted to discover those relationships relevant to a solution of such problems is another matter. With the exception of the few such as Wantrup and others noted above, the record has not been particularly outstanding.

The same underlying factors also explain the preoccupation of land economists with institutions. Economic research on institutions has frequently been highly descriptive and has often seemed to have little relevance to the economic functions the institution is being called upon to perform. But the evaluation of institutions does require analytics; it is not a job to be undertaken with one's bare hands. To what can the land economist turn for help? A ready-made answer is not available but an adequate answer will require intellectual effort of the highest order.[35]

The principles that are associated with the treatment of externalities and indivisibilities in the literature can be helpful in identifying those instances where nonmarket institutions may be appropriate.[36] But it is not enough to reject the market; it must be replaced by something. The functions the market performs or fails to perform should be provided for by alternative institutions. We need to come to grips with questions of criteria for the evaluation of both market and nonmarket institutions. A study of this type which holds the prospect of being quite durable is Wantrup's article on water law.[37] The production economics-oriented group in land economics has tended to concentrate too intensely on firm theory without being sufficiently concerned with how the firm related to its environment. At the other extreme, another group has industriously

---

[35] We have reference to explicit treatment of such a question. As indicated above, these relationships have always been implicit in the work of land economists.

[36] It is recognized that the market is not an immutable institution. The performance of the market may vary widely depending upon the constraints and rules of the game within which it functions. Furthermore, it has been assumed that markets and other institutions are means rather than ends. To the extent particular institutions become ends in themselves, the above analysis will miss the mark.

[37] See *Economics and Public Policy in Water Resource Development*, Stephen C. Smith and Emery N. Castle (eds.), Iowa State University Press, 1964, chap. 15.

examined, compared, and described institutional devices for natural resource management without relating those institutions to the economic functions they must perform. Internal firm problems are farm management. Land economics must consider nonmarket institutions, but description and classification in the absence of an explicit theory is an obvious indication of immaturity.

Conclusions

This article suggests the literature on external economies, diseconomies, and indivisibilities may be useful in researching the market and nonmarket institutions which may be used for natural resource management. It is not suggested that this theory be used as a basis for searching for a utopian quantitative optimum as defined in modern welfare economies, it is rather that such theory may be useful in judging the adequacy of certain decision-making institutions. There is substantial difference in solving for an optimum and establishing a framework which will permit alternative lines of action to be evaluated in the decision-making process. The formulation also indicates that the motivation and findings of the traditional land economists with their emphasis on institutions are still appropriate. The approach suggested may be useful both to those who are attempting to apply quantitative techniques to land economics problems as well as to those who are studying the institutions that affect the management of land resources.

Market Solutions to Externality Problems:
Theory and Practice*

The concept of market solution to externality problems has received the favorable attention of many economic theorists. Yet, policy practitioners and the general public seem less enthusiastic. Theoretical studies and available empirical work have effectively demolished Coase's doctrine of the allocative neutrality of liability rules. In reality, a full liability law will result in a greater degree of abatement of external diseconomies than will zero or intermediate liability laws. It is suggested that market solutions can be seriously considered in a world with pervasive externalities only if something approaching a full liability rule is established. Even then, excessive transactions costs may limit the success of market solutions.

AGRICULTURAL economists are directly and immediately concerned with externalities in agricultural settings, such as the problems of pesticide residues and animal waste disposal. But their concern with externalities is much wider than these. All forms of pollution from industrial and municipal sources in both urban and rural areas, externalities associated with consumption activities such as driving automobiles for pleasure, the whole range of externalities arising from land zoning, subdivision, and provision of utilities and community services, and so on, are of interest to the agricultural economist because they influence the geographic distribution and the urban-suburban-rural mix of the population.

An externality is said to exist wherever the utility of one or more individuals is dependent upon, among other things, one or more activities which are under the control of someone else. Buchanan and Stubblebine [2] have defined a Pareto-relevant externality as one which may be modified in such a way as to make the externally affected party better off without making the acting party worse off. A Pareto-relevant externality is characterized by the existence of potential gains from trade between the affected and acting parties. In what follows, the term externality may be taken to mean Pareto-relevant externality. An external diseconomy is an externality in which the affected party is made worse off by the activities of the acting party.

Many of society's environmental quality problems, particularly those types of problems which are referred to in the popular literature as spillover effects, are the result of external diseconomies. Improvement of environmental quality requires a modification of the behavior of acting parties who produce these external diseconomies.[1]

The Theory

Economic theory is based on the premise that if one wishes to modify the behavior of an economic unit, one must modify the incentives facing that unit so that the preferred behavior becomes more appealing to it (i.e., more pleasant, more profitable, or both). Economic literature on environmental quality externalities considers three broad classes of methods of solution of environmental quality problems, each designed to make the creation of Pareto-relevant externalities less profitable to acting parties. They are (1) market solutions, following establishment of a liability rule to serve as a starting point for negotiations; (2) systems of per unit taxes, charges, fines, or subsidies; and (3) systems of standards, enforced by the threat of fines or jail sentences. While (1) relies on private negotiation and (2) and (3) on government intervention, the three classes represent a clear progression from more to less reliance on market forces to determine the equilibrium output of externality.

The logical underpinnings of the suggestion that the market may be relied upon to achieve solutions to externality problems are presented by its supporters as follows: A Pareto-relevant externality is, by definition, characterized by the existence of potential gains from trade be-

* Journal Article 409, New Mexico Agricultural Experiment Station, Las Cruces. This article has benefited from the helpful comments of an anonymous reviewer.

ALAN RANDALL *is assistant professor of agricultural economics at New Mexico State University.*

[1] Mishan [11] and an anonymous reviewer suggest that the adverse effects of a degraded environment on people may in some cases be minimized by evasive action taken by the affected party. However, this type of solution would not strictly improve environmental quality.

AMERICAN JOURNAL OF AGRICULTURAL ECONOMICS, 1972, Vol. 54, pp. 175-183.

49

tween the acting and affected parties. Surely, then, self-interest can be relied upon to ensure the realization of these potential gains through exchange between the involved parties. As always, efficient exchange requires precisely defined and rigidly enforced property rights. In the case of external diseconomies, these property rights include some specification of the laws of liability for damages associated with the diseconomy. If liability rules are specified in a particular manner—allowing a specified amount of externality to be created with impunity and that amount to be exceeded only if the affected party is willing to agree—they serve as the starting point for negotiations to realize the potential gains from trade. The two extreme examples of such liability rules are the zero liability rule, L^z, and the full liability rule, L^f; an infinite number of intermediate rules could be conceived. L^z specifies that external diseconomies in any amount may be created with impunity; under such a rule, the affected party would have an incentive to offer a bribe to induce the acting party to reduce his output of external diseconomy. L^f specifies that absolutely no externality may be created without the consent of the affected party; under such a rule, the acting party would have an incentive to offer compensation to induce the affected party to accept a positive amount of externality.

Coase [5] perceived that regardless of which liability rule is in operation one or another party has an incentive to modify a Pareto-relevant externality. Given perfect competition and zero transactions costs,[2] negotiations will continue until all gains from trade have been exhausted. Coase argued that all gains from trade will be exhausted at the same Pareto-efficient outcome, regardless of which liability rule is in operation. In other words, the market solution to a particular externality problem is

allocatively neutral with respect to the assignment of liability. Of course, the specification of liability influences the final distribution of income at the completion of the exchange, since an L^z rule would result in the affected party making payments to the acting party and an L^f rule would result in the opposite flow of payments.

It is understandable that such an approach to externalities would be attractive to academic economists. It relies upon the market to establish the price of an externality. All the society has to do is to establish a liability rule, and it does not matter too much what that rule is since any rule will result in the same Pareto-efficient equilibrium solution. If society is concerned with income distribution, it may either attempt to choose a liability rule which will lead to a satisfactory distribution of income or use any other income redistribution method to attempt to restore a situation of equity.

Of the three broad groups of methods of solving externality problems listed above, it is noticeable that academic economists usually prefer market solutions or systems of fines, charges, taxes, or subsidies. There is a group of academic economists who remain fervent supporters of the market solution method. However, politicians, administrators, and the general public seem to have more faith in systems of standards. This divergence of opinion between academic economists on the one hand and the public and its representatives on the other motivated the preparation of this paper, which focuses on market solutions in theory and practice and offers some speculations on their future.

The Coasian analysis of externality was rapidly enshrined in the economic literature. Whereas Coase's analysis concentrated entirely on the case where both the acting and the affected parties were single firms engaged in production, Davis and Whinston [7] in 1965 extended the analysis to the case where both parties were single consumers. Their results duplicated those of Coase in all respects, including the finding of allocative neutrality of liability rules. Calabresi [4] spoke for the proponents of market solutions in 1968: all externalities can be internalized and all misallocations can be remedied by the market except to the extent that transactions cost money.[3]

[2] It is worthwhile to define transactions costs carefully, since they play an important part in the analysis to follow. Transactions costs are the costs of making and enforcing decisions. Included are the costs of obtaining information, establishing one's bargaining position, bargaining and arriving at a group decision, and enforcing the decision made. Any method of modifying externalities will involve some transactions costs. The size of the transactions costs and the type of transactions services used are likely to vary with the use of different types of solution methods and with the actual solution obtained. Transactions costs may be so large that they become a major factor in the selection of an efficient method of solution of any particular externality problem.

[3] This line of reasoning culminated in Demsetz's argument [8] that where a market for an external diseconomy does not exist it should not exist, since the benefits from

Beginning in 1966, the Coasian analysis came under attack from at least two quarters. One group claimed that Coase's assumptions were so far removed from the real world that his analysis was irrelevant for prescriptive purposes; and another group accepted Coase's static-perfect competition assumptions for the sake of argument. Even so, they were able to demolish Coase's claim of allocative neutrality of liability rules. Dolbear [9], Randall [13, 14], and Mishan [11], using static-perfect competition analysis of two-party cases, have made varying degrees of progress toward circumscribing the claimed generality of Coase's allocative neutrality doctrine. Here summarized is the treatment in Randall [14], in which the following propositions are proven mathematically.

In an external diseconomy situation where both the acting and affected parties are consumers, a change in liability rules will change the budget constraint faced by both. Under the L^z rule, the affected party would offer the acting party a bribe. Under the L^f rule, the acting party would offer compensation to the affected party. The relevant budget constraints are under L^z, for the affected party,

$$(1) \quad \overline{Y}_1 - \bar{p}_1 q_{11} - \cdots - \bar{p}_m q_{m1} \\ - p_n^*(q_{n2}{}^o - q_{n2}) = 0$$

and for the acting party,

$$(2) \quad \overline{Y}_2 - \bar{p}_1 q_{12} - \cdots - \bar{p}_m q_{m2} - \bar{p}_n q_{n2} \\ + p_n^*(q_{n2}{}^o - q_{n2}) = 0$$

under L^f, for the affected party,

$$(3) \quad \overline{Y}_1 - \bar{p}_1 q_{11} - \cdots - \bar{p}_m q_{m1} + p_n^* q_{n2}{}^o \\ - p_n^*(q_{n2}{}^o - q_{n2}) = 0$$

and for the acting party,

$$(4) \quad \overline{Y}_2 - \bar{p}_1 q_{12} - \cdots - \bar{p}_m q_{m2} - \bar{p}_n q_{n2} \\ - p_n^* q_{n2}{}^o + p_n^*(q_{n2}{}^o - q_{n2}) = 0$$

such a market clearly cannot exceed the costs of its operation. The absence of an observable market is, in itself, a market solution. This argument would seem to lead to the conclusion that any externalities which are observed to exist unmodified should not be modified, since transactions costs must therefore be so high that modification is unprofitable. However, the fallacy is obvious. The unprofitability of market solution does not prove that solution by any other method must also be unprofitable. If some other method of solution involves lower transactions costs, solution by that method may be preferable to no solution at all.

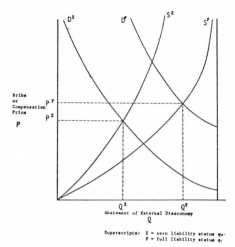

Figure 1. Market solutions to externality in consumption

Source: Randall [13, 14]

where the affected party suffers an external diseconomy from the acting party's consumption of the good n,

$\overline{Y}_j$ is the income of Mr. j,

q_{ij} is the consumption of the good i by Mr. j,

$\bar{p}_i$ is the competitive market price of the good i,

p_n^* is the unit bribe or compensation price,

and $q_{n2}{}^o$ is the amount of the good n which would be consumed by the acting party if $p_n^* = 0$.

These changes in budget constraints associated with changes in liability rules are sufficient to induce shifts in the resultant demand and supply curves for abatement of the external diseconomy. This is true for all cases, except the very special case where the affected party has an income elasticity of demand for abatement equal to zero and the acting party has a zero income elasticity of demand for the commodity associated with the externality. Figure 1 shows the situation. The L^f rule results in a greater level of abatement of an external diseconomy than does the L^z rule. Where any consumers are involved in an externality situation, the demand or supply curves of abatement associated with those consumers will shift with a change in

51

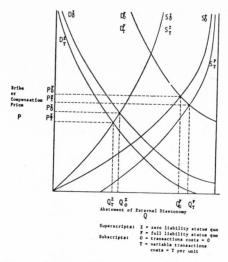

Figure 2. Market solutions to externality in consumption: the effect of transactions costs

Source: Randall [13, 14]

liability rules, resulting in different equilibrium levels of abatement.

In the case of externality in production, a change in liability rules will result in a change in equilibrium output of externality whenever (a) there is an inflexible capital constraint or (b) the use of capital has a positive price. The analysis is similar to that for externality in consumption: a change in liability rules changes the capital constraints affecting both parties. Again, an L^f rule will result in a greater level of abatement than an L^z rule.

Where transactions costs are greater than zero, the party who must pay makes an offer. However, the party who receives payment receives only the amount remaining after transactions costs have been subtracted. As a change in liability rules from L^z to L^f results in the former payer becoming the receiver of payment and vice versa, the assignment of liability affects the equilibrium output of externality when transactions costs are positive. In fairness, it must be noted that Coase [5] recognized that allocative neutrality is predicated upon zero transactions costs.

Figure 2 shows the effect of positive transactions costs on the equilibrium output of externality under the L^z and L^f rules. As unit transactions costs increase, the disparity between the equilibrium solutions under different liability rules increases. It is conceivable, and

may often be the case in practice, that transactions costs may be so great that movements away from the starting point defined by the liability law are impossible. In such cases, an L^z law results in zero abatement while an L^f law results in complete abatement of an external diseconomy.

In summary, allocative neutrality with' respect to liability rules can be accepted only in situations where all of the involved parties are producers, the use of capital is a free good, and transactions costs are zero. In cases other than these (i.e., in almost every significant externality problem), an L^f rule will result in a market solution specifying a higher degree of abatement of external diseconomies than will an L^z rule.

Mishan [11] makes one further observation, which, although unproven in his article, seems plausible: the incentives for strategies to reduce the effects of external diseconomies are greater under a full liability law. The effects of pollution, for example, can be reduced by emission-reducing technological improvements, or by location of the externality producing business in an out-of-the-way place, or by various other means. Mishan also argues for a full liability rule on the grounds of equity. If polluters are likely to be more prosperous than the affected parties, he argues that a full liability rule would be more equitable than a zero liability rule.

If, following the arguments of Buchanan and Tullock [3] and Olson [12], transactions costs are likely to be larger when negotiations must be initiated by a large and diffuse group of individuals rather than by a much smaller group of individuals who are more vitally interested in this particular issue, it follows that in cases of pollution from industrial sources, an L^z rule is more likely than is the L^f rule to result in transactions costs too high for the achievement of a solution other than the status quo.

The current situation in the theory of market solutions to externality problems can be summarized as follows: A Pareto-relevant externality, being characterized by potential gains from trade, will generate incentives for one or the other of the involved parties to initiate negotiations aimed at modifying that externality. A solution different from the status quo situation may be achieved and, if perfect competition prevails in all relevant industries including the transactions industry, that solution may be Pareto-efficient. However, the resource allocation and income distribution characteristics of the solution achieved are not neutral to the choice of liability rules. In comparison with a

52

zero liability rule, a full liability rule will result in (1) a higher degree of abatement of an external diseconomy such as pollution, (2) a reallocation of resources toward pollution control and production of commodities which can be produced by low pollution processes, and (3) an income redistribution in favor of the affected party. The effective demolition of the doctrine of allocative neutrality of liability rules removes one of the prime advantages which has been claimed for market solutions to externality problems. The role of the body politic and the bureaucracy in setting the operative liability rule is now known to include the power to affect allocation of resources in production and allocation of budgets in consumption. In a macroeconomic sense, if externalities are as pervasive as is now believed, the power to set liability rules therefore implies the power to affect resource allocation in the whole economy, aggregate production and consumption, and relative and aggregate prices.

Economic Analyses of Observed Market Solutions

Economic analyses of market solutions to externality in practice, unfortunately, seem mostly confined to casual empiricism. As noted above, Demsetz [8] found several externality situations where no market transactions were observed. He attributed this to transactions costs so high that the operation of the market was unprofitable. Alexander [1] mentioned cases involving aluminum refining industries. In some cases market solutions have occurred where the aluminum industry pays compensation to agriculturalists and orchardists on nearby farms. In other cases, the aluminum industry has purchased the land affected by its emissions, creating a merger between acting and affected parties. However, parties less directly affected (e.g., citizens who may suffer some unpleasantness but no loss of agricultural productivity or future generations who may lose the assimilative power of the environment) may not feel that these externalities have been fully internalized.

In a notable exception to this trend of casual empiricism, Crocker [6] presented a reasonably careful regression analysis of market solutions over a time period during which the liability rule effectively changed. He examined a situation in which inorganic fertilizers were produced from locally mined phosphate rock in Polk County, Florida. Damage was observed to local citrus and beef cattle industries over an area of approximately 400 square miles. Prior to 1957, a liability rule not very different from the zero liability rule of the theories presented here was in effect. The only recourse available to the affected parties was civil suit for damages. In such suits, the burden of proof of liability for these damages lay with the plaintiff. The burden of proof had been extremely onerous and no plaintiff had been successful in recovering any damages from the polluting fertilizer companies. Then, in 1957, an Air Pollution Control District was established. Fertilizer companies were in effect advised to buy the affected land or face the prospect of imposition of emission standards.

Crocker obtained and analyzed land sales data for a 20-year period, including 10 years before and 10 years after this effective change in the liability rule. In the earlier period there was a downward trend in land prices, correlated with the decreasing agricultural productivity of the land. However, after the establishment of the Air Pollution Control District, land prices began to rise as the fertilizer companies bought up land in order to avoid the imposition of emission standards. It was also observed that along with a rise in prices of affected land and a gradual but continuous increase in the amount of agricultural land in the ownership of the phosphate companies, the output of polluting emissions by the fertilizer companies was reduced gradually and consistently over the years. Crocker interpreted this reduction in emissions as the result of internalization of the externalities. When the companies owned most of the affected land, their optimum economic strategy was to maximize total returns from both the use of the land and the production of phosphate. No longer could they regard the land and the air above it as a cost-free waste disposal resource.

Crocker's empirical result was that the effective change in liability rules changed the allocative efficiency in the phosphate fertilizer, citrus, and beef industries. He was able to demonstrate that transactions costs were very much higher in the period when the liability situation was essentially L^s than in the later period when the fertilizer companies faced the threat of emissions standards. The change in the liability situation shifted the burden of initiating negotiations from the affected party to the acting party (which group had significantly fewer numbers). Also, the affected party was relieved of the burden of proving damage. Crocker was able to correlate a change in resource allocation with a change in liability rules and a concurrent change in transactions costs.[4] Significantly, the only detailed empirical study of market solutions to externality which has been completed has demonstrated that a change in liability rules changes resource allocation and the output of pollution emissions.

The Future of Market Solutions

What can be said, then, about market solutions to externality in practice? The theoretical and empirical demonstration that market solutions to externality problems are not allocatively neutral with respect to liability rules may provide some explanation of what has been the major practical objection to market solutions—they are very seldom observed in practice. In the past, laws with respect to externalities such as environmental pollution have been lenient, seldom and ineffectively enforced, or both. In a majority of cases, something approaching a zero liability rule has been in operation. The author's analyses have demonstrated that the zero liability rule is more likely than any positive liability rule to result in zero or low levels of abatement. If market solutions are to be used effectively to ensure environmental quality, the task seems to be that of converting liability rules to L^f, full liability, or to some intermediate position. The important policy question then becomes: are market solutions based on a full or intermediate liability rule preferable to solutions forced by systems of fines and subsidies or standards?

Kneese [10] argues vigorously against reliance upon market solutions on the grounds that market solutions are best adapted (or are adaptable only) to the two-party case, while the environmental quality problem arises from the disposal of wastes into common property resources. One, or a relatively small number of acting parties dumps wastes into a common property resource (e.g., air or water), reducing the welfare of many affected parties. This question can be considered now by briefly examining the operation of market solutions to a pollu-

tion problem under a full liability rule. The process of negotiating and enforcing a market solution can be divided into three major steps. It is possible to identify a number of alternative ways these steps can be carried out.

1. The *first step* is enforcement of recognition of the status quo established by an L^f rule. Firms polluting without having obtained the permission of the affected parties must be made to either cease polluting or obtain that permission. This could be done in several ways: 1A: A public agency could ascertain that some emissions are being released[5] and then, 1A$_1$, directly impose a very high penalty on the offender unless he ceases polluting or demonstrates he has obtained permission from the affected party, or, 1A$_2$, ask a court to do the same; or, 1B: The affected parties could initiate litigation to prove that emissions are being released and seek court enforcement of the L^f rule. Organization could occur in several ways: 1B$_1$, unanimous action by the affected parties, or, 1B$_2$, "unanimous" action by a leader or committee after a majority vote of the affected parties; or, 1B$_3$, a class action initiated by one individual on behalf of the affected parties[6]; or, 1B$_4$, a series of individual actions by affected parties.

2. The *second step:* The acting party has an incentive to initiate negotiations to induce the affected parties to accept a certain amount of emissions in exchange for compensation. The affected parties must be organized in some way in order to conduct their side of the negotiations. Possibilities are: 2A: A public agency could bargain on behalf of the affected parties, or, 2B: The affected parties could bargain in several ways: 2B$_1$, unanimous action by the affected parties, or, 2B$_2$, take a "unanimous" position and appoint a representative or committee to bargain, following a majority vote, or, 2B$_3$, each individual affected could deal separately with the acting party.

3. The *third step* is the policing and enforcement of the agreement made. Compensation payments must be made as agreed and the agreed emission limit must not be exceeded. The possible types of organization of the affected party for this purpose parallel those in 1.

---

[4] Crocker interpreted this change in output of pollutants and resource allocation with the change in liability rules as being entirely attributable to the change in transactions costs. The theoretical work by Randall would suggest that the change in liability rules would result in a different solution with respect to pollution emissions and resource allocation even if transactions costs were unchanged. But this is a relatively minor quibble.

[5] Note: A full liability rule requires proof only that emissions are being released. This is a much simpler matter than proving that (a) damage is occurring and (b) the defendant is responsible.

[6] It would be necessary to change the law in most states to allow this.

It seems reasonable that different methods of organization of affected parties may lead to solutions which are different in terms of resource allocation and income distribution. The next few pages are devoted to speculation about these differences.

(a) The $1B_1$–$2B_1$–$3B_1$ procedure is most unlikely to occur widely, relying as it does on unanimity. Transactions costs required to achieve unanimity may be extremely high [3, 12].

(b) Decision procedures relying on $2B_3$, a series of bargains between the acting and the affected parties one-by-one, would suffer from the "holdout problem" familiar to urbanologists,[7] if the law required that agreement be reached with all affected parties. Also, since different affected individuals have different demand curves for abatement, while the firm has a single supply curve, individual bargains are likely to result in permission for different amounts of emission. Yet, the amount of emissions into a common property resource at any one time must necessarily be unique. So, extensive contracting and recontracting would be required to arrive at agreements with all parties allowing the same amount of emission. Transactions costs would be extremely high. The situation could conceivably be improved by a modification of the L' rule so that once, say, 60 percent of the affected individuals had agreed upon a particular permissable amount of emissions and a unit compensation rate, the remainder must accept that agreement or go without compensation.

(c) The $1B_3$–$2B_2$–$3B_3$ and the $1B_2$–$2B_2$–$3B_2$ procedures would seem likely to involve lower transactions costs than the other procedures which rely on direct bargaining with the affected parties without the help of a governmental agency. These procedures reduce transactions costs because they allow the affected party to make decisions on the basis of less than unanimous consent. Too little is known about transactions costs to venture a guess on the relative costs of these kinds of direct bargaining methods versus bargaining by a public agency on behalf of the affected parties.

(d) The 1A–2A–3A pattern has been seen elsewhere. It is the system of charges advocated

by Kneese [10]. Kneese's proposal is really a type of market solution where the L' rule is applied and a public agency bargains on behalf of the affected parties to arrive at the unit compensation price and undertakes to distribute the income from charges among the affected parties or to spend it on their behalf (e.g., on environmental projects). If the charge income simply goes into the general fund, the similarity of this type of solution to market solutions is more tenuous.

(e) It seems worthwhile to point out that any market solution relying on the help of a public or governmental agency (i.e., the 1A–2A–3A procedure) or on less than unanimous action by the affected parties, voluntarily organized for that purpose (i.e., the $1B_3$–$2B_2$–$3B_3$ and $1B_2$–$2B_2$–$3B_2$ procedures), would result in a unique amount of waste being dumped into a common property resource and a unique amount of compensation. This solution will not be optimal for all of the individuals and firms involved in an externality situation. (If it was optimal for all, unanimous agreement would have been reached.) So, some parties may regard the group agreement as simply a new starting point for further negotiations aimed at exhausting all possible gains from trade.

If this occurred, the group agreement would not be sabotaged. Further negotiations could not result in individual agreements to allow the quantity of emissions specified in the group agreement to be exceeded. Enforcement procedures for the group agreement would be adequate to prevent this. On the other hand, there may be some members of the affected party who feel so strongly about improvement of environmental quality that they would offer bribes to induce polluters to reduce emissions even more. The author fails to see any harm in such private agreements resulting, as they would, in reduced total emissions into the common property resource. On the other hand, the theory of common property resources does not lead him to expect such agreements to occur frequently.

(f) Decision procedures based on $2B_1$ or $2B_2$ introduce a bilateral monopoly situation. It is known that exchange in bilateral monopoly situations can achieve a unique solution in quantities but price is not uniquely determined. Rather, price depends upon relative bargaining strength. An L' rule would give the affected parties the upper hand and therefore allow

---

[7] Once word is out, for example, that a firm is buying all houses on a block in order to demolish them and build a single large structure, one or more homeowners may hold out in order to obtain a very high price (i.e., to obtain most of the economic surplus for themselves).

them to gain the maximum possible compensation.

From this sketchy examination of the various decision and enforcement procedures which could conceivably be used to facilitate market solutions, it seems that procedures other than those which use 2A or 2B$_2$ (i.e., public agencies or committees) to facilitate the second step, the negotiations, have severe practical limitations. In cases of pollution in urban areas where there are many sources of pollution, each affecting different but overlapping geographical areas, reliance in 2B$_2$ may require a huge number of committees to be set up, each dealing with a single polluter. Alternatively, one committee would bargain with all polluters. If this latter alternative was chosen, the amount of expertise required of committee members and the amount of their time used would tend to grow so large that the committee would take on the characteristics of a public agency.

In summary, it seems that market solutions could in many cases achieve substantial improvement in environmental quality[8] if (1) the liability rules were changed to L' or something approaching it and (2) the affected parties were legally required to either set up their own bargaining committee to make *binding* bargains or accept the help of a governmental agency to do it for them.

In the absence of institutional changes of this

nature, it seems that market solutions to externality problems are limited in practice.[9] However, market solutions based on the suggested institutional changes seem to deserve serious consideration and empirical analysis, if only because market solutions promise less institutional rigidity and inefficiency than, say, a system of nationwide emissions standards.

Conclusion

This article has attempted to examine market solutions to externality in theory and practice. It has not attempted to compare rigorously (1) market solutions with (2) systems of per unit fines, charges, taxes or subsidies, and (3) standards enforced by the threat of penalty. It is clear, nevertheless, that transactions costs are a crucial variable in the selection of suitable institutional mechanisms for the modification of externality. Unless ways can be found to reduce the transactions costs associated with market solutions, market solutions, even under an L' rule, will remain the plaything of academic economists, largely ignored by policy makers and the general public.

Standards, although inefficient but not necessarily very inefficient, are simple decision rules, at least partially enforceable at low cost. Market solutions will be preferable to, for example, standards only if the gains in efficiency (*ceteris paribus* transactions costs) exceed the additional transactions costs of using the market solution method. The onus to develop ways in which market solutions can be made to work lies squarely on the shoulders of academic supporters of market solutions. An essential step is to generate institutional forms which minimize transactions costs.

---

[8] The allocative effects of a change to L' have not received detailed consideration in this paper. In industrial pollution situations, a change to L' would result in lower production of higher-priced commodities and lower industrial employment in a first-step adjustment. After the first stage of adjustment, a longer term adjustment may result in lower wages. Unless the practice was forbidden, some less sensitive people would move into the affected area to gain compensation; this may also drive wages down. A reduction in wages would lead to some lowering of costs of production. The final situation would lie somewhere between the initial situation and the first-stage adjustment.

[9] Crocker's paper suggests one workable method of market solution in some externality situations: a full liability rule (or something similar) and the purchase of affected property by the acting party. This "merger" solution is more likely to take place under a full liability rule.

References

[1] ALEXANDER, ROBERT M., "Social Aspects of Environmental Pollution," *Agr. Sci. Rev.* 9:9–18, 1971.

[2] BUCHANAN, JAMES M., AND WILLIAM CRAIG STUBBLEBINE, "Externality," *Economica* 29:371–384, Nov. 1962.

[3] ———, AND GORDON TULLOCK, *The Calculus of Consent. Logical Foundation of Constitutional Democracy,* Ann Arbor, University of Michigan Press, 1962.

[4] CALABRESI, G., "Transactions Costs, Resource Allocation and Liability Rules," *J. Law & Econ.* 11:66–73, 1968.

[5] COASE, R. H., "The Problem of Social Cost," *J. Law & Econ.* 3:1–44, Oct. 1960.

[6] CROCKER, T. D., "Externalities, Property Rights and Transactions Costs: An Empirical Study," Program in Environmental Economics, Working Paper No. 2, Department of Economics, University of California, Riverside, 1971.

[7] DAVIS, OTTO A., AND ANDREW B. WHINSTON, "Some Notes on Equating Private and Social Cost," *Southern Econ. J.* 32:113–126, Oct. 1965.

[8] DEMSETZ, H., "The Exchange and Enforcement of Property Rights," *J. Law & Econ.* 7:11–26, 1964.

[9] DOLBEAR, F. TRENERY, JR., "On the Theory of Optimum Externality," *Am. Econ. Rev.* 57:90–103, March 1967.

[10] KNEESE, ALLEN V., "Environmental Pollution: Economics and Policy," *Am. Econ. Rev.* 61:153–166, May 1971.

[11] MISHAN, E. J., "The Post-War Literature on Externalities: An Interpretative Essay," *J. Econ. Lit.* 9:1–28, March 1971.

[12] OLSON, MANCUR, JR., *The Logic of Collective Action.*

Public Goods and the Theory of Groups, Cambridge, Harvard University Press, 1965.

[13] RANDALL, A., "Liability Rules, Transactions Costs and Optimum Externality," unpublished Ph.D. thesis, Oregon State University, 1971.

[14] ——, *On the Theory of Market Solutions to Externality Problems*, Oregon Agr. Exp. Sta. Special Rep. 351, 1972.

EXTERNALITIES, INFORMATION AND ALTERNATIVE COLLECTIVE ACTION

BY OTTO A. DAVIS and MORTON I. KAMIEN

Otto A. Davis and Morton I. Kamien are both Professors of Economics at Carnegie-Mellon University.

One of the reasons why the operation of an unfettered market system may fail to serve the public interest is the inability of markets to accommodate certain kinds of side effects. Another reason for market failure is that buyers and sellers often lack the quantity and the quality of information necessary for them to choose effectively when engaging in market transactions. The authors of this paper deal with both the problem of side effects or spillovers which are not accommodated in markets, and with the problem of inadequate market information. In dealing with the problem of inadequate information, they cite drug products as an example of a commodity whose distribution requires collective or governmental action as a supplement to the market place. The problems of air and water pollution are employed to illustrate the market failure entailed by side effects or externalities. In the case of spillovers, the authors point out that a number of collective solutions to market failure are available. They discuss solution by prohibition, by directive, by voluntary action, by taxes and subsidies, by regulation, by payment, and by direct public action.

Introduction

Awareness that an action often entails subsidiary as well as direct consequences is commonplace. In choosing an occupation we consider not only the direct monetary remunerations involved but also the security, power and prestige associated with the various endeavors. When purchasing wearing apparel we take into account its attractiveness as well as the protection and comfort which it affords. In the use of drugs we should be acutely conscious of their possibly harmful side effects as well as of their direct curative powers. When purchasing a house we are likely to take into account in addition to the size and age the quality of the neighborhood in which it is located, its proximity to good schools, and public transportation facilities.

In everyday parlance we refer to these secondary attributes of products or actions as "side-effects," "fringe-benefits," or "occupational disease." Our concern with these matters is not wasted on the advertising industry which promotes many products by stressing their desirable side-benefits. Witness the number of advertisements that allude to the masculinity, femininity, youthfulness, and glamour that are to be derived from the use of this or that product. Indeed, some products and occupations have become better known by their side effects than by their direct benefits.

Of course, concern with secondary consequences is not confined to the advertising industry alone. This regard for side-effects finds expression in the selection of products or occupations and the amounts we are willing to pay or sacrifice to avoid or incur them. In other words, many kinds of side effects are accommodated by the market sys-

THE ANALYSIS AND EVALUATION OF PUBLIC EXPENDITURE: THE PPB SYSTEM, (U.S. Government Printing Office: Washington, D.C.) 1969, Vol. 1, pp. 67-86.

tem. For example, a desire to live in a "better" neighborhood manifests itself by a willingness to pay more for a house in the preferred neighborhood than for a comparable house elsewhere. Likewise, a strong preference for a relatively secure occupation is satisfied by a willingness to sacrifice potentially higher monetary gains in other occupations. Businessmen find it profitable to be responsive to these desires of consumers. Though the primary function of an automobile is transportation, manufacturers provide a wide variety of models to satisfy the secondary features desired by purchasers. Drug producers attempt to develop new drugs that possess the same beneficial properties as existing ones while reducing undesirable side-effects. Moreover, the responsiveness of producers is spurred by the knowledge that competitors will cater to the preferences of customers. It is for this reason that competition among producers is thought to be desirable. Similarly, competition among buyers assures that goods and services will be allocated in conformity with the relative desires and abilities of the participants to pay.

From the above argument one might be tempted to conclude that a freely competitive economy should provide the goods and services desired by consumers in such a way as to preclude the possibility that another allocative mechanism (such as government) might be judged to be more appropriate for given situations. Given certain conditions and a plausible criterion, one of the major contributions of modern economic theory is the confirmation of this conclusion. Yet, even the most casual observation of the real world discloses that our society often takes recourse to collective governmental action for the provision of certain goods and services. One could allow such a casual observation to bring one to the conclusion that modern economic theory must be either wrong or irrelevant for the real world. While there probably is considerable sympathy for such a conclusion in some circles, it is taken here to be an obviously incorrect deduction. An alternative explanation of this apparent divergence between theory and reality is that collective decisions are necessarily bad and that governments act in a nonsensical manner. This conclusion too is rejected here. Of course, the rejection of this alternative does not imply that governments always make the wisest or best decisions. Instead, the view adopted here is that the governmental decision process can be improved and that we should do what we can to improve it. Another explanation of the apparent divergence between theory and reality—and this one is accepted here—is that the conditions or assumptions upon which the above conclusion about the efficiency of a market system is based are not always satsified in reality. According to this viewpoint, there may be some advantage in the study of particular aspects of economic theory since such a study might produce considerable insight into the detection of situations where market systems cannot be expected to work very well. The mere existence of such situations raise the problem of selecting the proper institutional arrangement under which the activity under consideration may be conducted, and one would be foolish to believe that this problem can be solved at this time in a way which might produce a consensus. Yet, there is considerable advantage in merely knowing where markets might, and where they might not, work tolerably well.

Given the above discussion, the plan of this essay is to present informally the major conclusion of modern welfare economics; a theorem about the allocation of resources by a market mechanism.

Particular attention will be paid to certain of the assumptions upon which this theorem is based. Examples will be used to help make the major points clear. Neither will the problem of selecting proper criteria for institutional choice be overlooked. It is hoped that the outcome of the discussion will be a better understanding of some of the issues and difficulties involved in selecting institutional mechanisms which are capable of attaining an acceptable allocation of limited resources.

THE CRITERION, THE MARKET, AND OPTIMALITY

Obviously, if one is to talk meaningfully about a choice among alternatives, one must have in mind some kind of method for ordering or weighing the various possibilities. Economists have been rather explicit in their choice of an abstract criterion. It is the notion of efficiency or, to use the more technical term, the concept of Pareto optimality. The basic idea is that a situation is inefficient or non-optimal if it is possible to make at least one member of a society better off without making any other member worse off. In other words, a situation is Pareto optimal if it is impossible to make anyone better off without the same time making someone else worse off. It is worth while pointing out that this criterion of efficiency or Pareto optimality need not lead to an unambiguous ordering of alternatives since, theoretically speaking, there exists at least an infinity of positions which are Pareto optimal. On the other hand, there is good reason to insist within the limits of practicality that all solutions be efficient since, by definition, a non-Pareto optimal solution means that someone can be made better off without making anyone else worse off. The qualifying phrase "within the limits of practicality" is used here to denote the fact that although the theoretical possibility of improving at least one person's position without inflicting harm on anyone else must be admitted whenever the situation is not Pareto optimal, the practical means of actually accomplishing such an improvement need not be at all obvious to the frail minds of humans.

The notion of Pareto optimality probably would be neither interesting nor useful were it not for some of the developments of modern welfare economics. The most important of these developments can be viewed as one of the central theorems of economics. It can be stated informally as follows: Given certain assumptions about the technology, the availability of information, the characteristics of goods and services, and the absence of monopoly power, then there exists a set of market prices such that profit maximizing firms and utility maximizing consumers which respond to those prices will automatically cause the economic system to attain a Pareto optimum position. This theorem is, of course, a powerful argument for the organization of our society so that exchange takes place through the mechanism of competitive markets. If the assumptions of the theorem were universally satisfied, then the Government could limit itself largely to programs aimed at the attainment of a desirable distribution of income and be rather certain that the vehicle of competition would cause the system to be efficient.

There is little, if any, need to review the entire set of assumptions which appear to be required for the above theorem to obtain. Indeed, economists have long been searching for a minimal set of assumptions which will be sufficient for markets to attain Pareto optimality, and it is doubtful that the end of the search is anywhere in sight. Accordingly, it is appropriate to review here only those which seem to cause the greater part of the difficulty in the real world. Fortunately or unfortunately, it will be seen that these difficulties appear to be interrelated in ways that are not always obvious.

Consider first the technology, The assumption here is that all firms have convex production possibility sets. What this supposition means is that there must be an absence of increasing returns to scale. In other words, it must not be true that ever larger firms can produce the same product at a lower per unit cost than can relatively smaller ones. Of course, it is recognized that there can be increasing returns over a range as long as that range is not significant in terms of industry output.

A second consideration is the availablity of information. Producers are assumed to have knowledge of the available technology. Consumers are supposed to know whether particular goods and services are available as well as their characteristics. More will be said about this below, but it is obvious that this is a heroic assumption. Finally, both producers and consumers are presumed to know the relevant set of prices.

The third condition concerns the characteristics of the goods and services which are to be produced by the economic system. First, not only are there supposed to be no "public" goods—that is, goods such as radio waves or television signals which are noted for the fact that when one listener or viewer "uses" them via reception, the quantity available for use by other persons is not diminished—but the consumption of other goods and services (called "private" goods) is not supposed to directly affect decision units who are not doing the consuming. In other words, although the "side effects" mentioned in the introduction are allowed, there is supposed to be an absence of what in technical language goes under the name of nonpecuniary externalities. Since a large part of this essay is devoted to these external effects, a detailed discussion of the phenomena is postponed. One should note here, however, that the mere presence of externalities is not a sufficient reason for the market to avoid optimality but such a presence is a danger signal which should not go unnoticed.

A final condition worth noting is the absence of monopoly power. It is the competitive market which, under certain circumstances, is supposed to be capable of attaining Pareto optimality. Since relatively little discussion of monopoly will be presented in this essay, it is worthwhile to point out here that monopoly is often related to the other conditions under consideration. For example, it is acknowledged that one of the difficulties associated with increasing returns is that the logical consequence of attempted competition is the emergence of monopoly. Similarly, initial monopoly power can sometimes be maintained due to the fact that technological knowledge is not always available to all and, even when it is, there may be barriers in the form of difficulties in transmission and assimilation.

All of the above assumes that markets either do or can be made to exist. Unfortunately, such does not always seem to be the case.

The remainder of this essay will concentrate upon the dual considerations of information and externality with an emphasis upon the latter. However, the discussion itself will be testimony to the fact that all of these matters are interwoven and cannot always be separated.

PROBLEMS OF INFORMATION

While theoretical discussions traditionally have assumed, as was noted above, that participants in the economic system have full knowledge, there has been a widespread awareness that this assumption is never fully satisfied. Some recent works have taken cognizance of the fact that information is both scarce and costly. Obviously, some kinds of information are more easily acquired than other types and recognition of this continuum of costs is helpful in any attempt to understand the functioning of the market. As an illustration imagine a consumer faced with the problem of selecting a detergent. In the terminology of marketing such a purchase is called a "repeat sale" which emphasizes the fact that the consumer purchases this type of product on a weekly or monthly basis. Detergents and items that are purchased often offer a minimal informational problem for the consumer. There is little cost in "trying out" various brands until one is identified whose characteristics appear most suited for the individual task at hand. The advertising often gives information about the product's characteristics such as its cleaning power or sudsiness. Even here, however, it is clear that laws which promote truth in advertising can help the market perform its proper function since without such regulation advertising might not be a source of information with any reliability.

Items that are not purchased very often, such as consumer durables, offer a more difficult informational problem. Clearly, it is not always practical for the consumer to learn the characteristics of the brands in this class of products by simply trying out various items until one with the desired properties is identified. Even here, for relatively expensive items which are easily transported and which are sufficiently complex to make it desirable for a trained person to instruct the customer in the operating methodology, some companies find it profitable to allow potential customers to keep the item for a trial period during which he can learn at least some of the characteristics of the machine. When this practice is followed, however, salesmen seldom make it easy for the customer to make systematic comparisons among available brands. Hence, other sources of information must be relied upon.

Clearly, one source is often informal and casual conversations in which experiences with various brands are related from one person to another. Another source is advertising, and it would appear that regulations designed to prevent misleading claims from being made are even more important for this class of goods than for the one discussed above since the absence of frequent and periodic purchases make it less easy for the customer to gain comparative information from his own experience. A third source is independent "testing laboratories" such as Consumer's Union. Several points are relevant here. Any serious or casual reader of Consumer's Report knows that for every major product, with the possible exception of automobiles, the information which can be presented is so scanty and model specific, with many models not being examined, that there is simply not sufficient information for a careful comparison and choice among the models that might be available. Now this statement is not intended as a criticism of the management of Consumer's Union. The point is that knowledge of the characteristics of a product is very analogous to a public good. Once the characteristics are known, then the "consumption" of this knowledge by any one shopper in making his choice does not diminish either the availability or usefulness of that knowledge for any other shopper. All of the well-known difficulties of trying to market a useful public good are relevant here. Although there are obvious costs associated with the production of knowledge of a product's characteristics, the producer of that knowledge cannot hope to recoup anything even approximating its value to the consumer. Neither should one suggest that even if it were possible for him to do so—which is not possible since the information can be transmitted easily from one person to another—should he actually do it since the optimality conditions would require that the transmission take place at marginal cost which is trivially close to zero. This situation means, however, that the producer of this knowledge cannot afford to produce as much information as it would be socially optimal to provide both in terms of the quality of knowledge that could be produced and in terms of the range of coverage of models of the various products.

The above point should not be taken as a criticism of the provision of this class of goods, which is mainly durables, by the private sector. Even the governmental provision of this class of goods would not alter in any basic way the problem under consideration. What is suggested, however, is that a certain kind of governmental regulation can serve to improve the functioning of an otherwise unregulated market. Producers are certainly in a better position than anyone else to know the characteristics of their products. It would appear to be relatively simple to have groups of persons who are knowledgeable about the various products, and who know what characteristics one should consider in making a purchase, draw up a list of these features for each product category. Manufacturers would then be responsible for making this information available to those who deal with the public and these, in turn, could be required to furnish the information to prospective purchasers. Claims about products could be checked in the way that advertising is now regulated. Note that this proposal differs from the existing situation where producers are motivated to furnish the public only that information which is favorable to their product. No one would claim, of course, that information concerning all of the relevant characteristics can be made available. Even the manufacturer may not know, for example, the expected life of a new kind of machine.

There is another class of goods and services where the informational problems can be orders of magnitude greater than those discussed above. The salient features of this class are: (1) Information about the relevant characteristics, even when it is available, is difficult to understand, interpret, and evaluate without the benefit of special training; (2) the consequences of an incorrect choice can be serious to the extent that there is an order of magnitude difference in terms of real costs between this and previous cases. Probably, the best example of a product category belonging to this class is some of the drugs which are produced. The usual incentives of the marketplace operate here as elsewhere in the sense that consumers should be willing to pay more, ceteris paribus, for a drug which is safer than others which might be available. Consequently, manufacturers should have an incentive to produce safer drugs. The obvious informational difficulty here, however, is the very problem of identifying which drug is safer. It is difficult to consider seriously the possibility of consumers having to use various drugs in order to determine experimentally both their curative powers and their safety when possible side effects may not be immediate and may be irreversible.

While private "testing laboratories" might be relied upon for information, with all the difficulties previously discussed about this kind of institution, it is easy to see why our society has made the collective decision that the Food and Drug Administration should regulate this market under the law. Thus, given the fact that a drug is on the market, one can be certain that manufacturers have at least minimally tried to determine side effects and associated dangers. Of course, given the difficulties associated with the attempt to make such a determination, there obviously can be no certainty that there are no harmful side effects as is illustrated by the example of the Thalidomide case of a few years ago. This case happened under the additional safeguard which society has imposed of allowing particular drugs to be used only when a prescription certifies that one is under the care of a physician.

One rationale for allowing certain drugs to be sold only under prescription is, of course, informational costs. Supposedly, the physican has the necessary information at his fingertips and can exercise his professional judgment in administering any drug which is known to have undesirable side effects for some (unidentified) portion of the population. Presumably, there is little need to mention that the arrangement does not work perfectly, but one of the authors has been pointedly reminded several times of the imperfection when a serious attack of asthma while in a strange town has prompted visits to local physicians who had to be told not only of the available range of drugs but also advised as to which particular one had the properties which made it most desirable to be prescribed for the given condition. In addition, some of the institutional practices are not designed to stimulate price competition between drug manufacturers so that the market is certainly noncompetitive and may be monopolistic. Yet, one of the rationales of this particular institutional arrangement is the costs, which would be associated with the acquisition of information under alternative arrangements so that the monopolistic costs of the present arrangement must be weighed against the costs associated with the conceivable alternatives, which includes modifications, in making an institutional choice.

PROBLEMS ASSOCIATED WITH EXTERNALITIES

All of the above difficulties and the institutional arrangements which have been or might be designed to deal with them are related for the greater part to the impact or effect which given items might have upon the consumer who purchased them. Therefore, it is only natural to inquire about possible effects of the purchase and consumption of these given items upon other persons or decision units who were not parties to the exchanges. Effects upon those external to or not associated with specified purchases or activities appropriately are called externalities. Alternative terms are called spillovers, external effects, or social effects.

While the literature distinguishes many kinds of externalities, it is necessary for the purposes of this essay to identify only two types. These are technological (or nonpecuniary) and pecuniary externalities.

Let us first deal with the concept of the pecuniary externality. When deciding whether or not to purchase an item an individual will ordinarily take into account his own desire for the item, its price, and his budgetary situation. It will be rare indeed, and generally only in the case of a monopsony, that the individual might even consider that his decision to purchase can contribute to and maybe even increase the demand for that product and thereby cause its price to rise. Of course, in most instances the individual's purchase of a commodity is such a small fraction of the total amount sold that his decision has a negligible impact upon price, although the totality of decision is certainly of importance. Whenever an individual decision does have an effect upon price, it is important to note that not only does he, but also all other purchasers, have to pay the resulting increase or decrease. This change in price, caused by individual decisions, is termed a pecuniary externality. If the individual decision causes the price to rise, which is the usual case associated with an increase in demand, then the phenomenon is a pecuniary external diseconomy to other consumers. Whenever the decision causes the price to fall, which might be illustrated by a decision to join a group travel arrangement which is not yet at capacity, then the phenomenon is termed a pecuniary external economy to other consumers. Of course, by symmetry, a pecuniary external diseconomy to consumers, is a pecuniary external economy to sellers, while a pecuniary external economy to consumers is a diseconomy to sellers.

The important point to note here, however, is that pecuniary externalities, be they economies or diseconomies, pose no problem for the market economy. Indeed, they are the central ingredient of the marketplace. Changing demands cause prices to rise and fall, generally according to whether demand increases or decreases, and the resulting alterations on prices are the essential feature of a marketplace which rations the available goods and services to those whose willingness to pay indicates that they need them most.

Technological externalities are quite another matter. These refer to more or less direct effects, which are not priced, which one decision unit might impose on another. Technological externalities can, and in many instances do, prevent the marketing mechanism from functioning in such a manner as to lead the economic system to a position of Pareto optimality. In such instances, of course, there exists the theoretical possibility that action can be taken to improve the society in the sense that one or more citizens can be made better off without anyone being made worse off. Some examples may serve to illustrate what is at issue here.

Since both of the authors reside in Pittsburgh, it may be appropriate to begin with the example of the manufacture of steel. For the purpose of exposition, imagine that there is no smoke control ordinance. Then, according to the process which is employed, more or less smoke may be discharged into the atmosphere as a byproduct of steel production. Insofar as the manufacturer is interested in profits—and most are—there is motivation to choose that method of production which is most profitable without regard for the associated level of the discharge of smoke. The point is that the manufacturer can be thought of as envisioning the opportunity to dispose of smoke as another resource which contributes to the production of steel. The justification of viewing disposal as another resource is that a reduction in the discharge of smoke could only be achieved by either adopting an alternative and more expensive method of production which emits less smoke or by using the same process but with the addition of smoke control devices. Either alternative involves the use of additional resources such as labor and capital. While these additional resources are not free, there is no charge for the emission of smoke into the atmosphere so that there is little if any motivation to attempt to limit the usage of the resource which might be called smoke disposal.

Although the discharge of smoke into the atmosphere might be viewed as a free resource by the firm, it is certainly not without consequence to those residing within adjoining communities. Not only does smoke contribute to the more rapid deterioration of the exteriors of buildings and certain kinds of equipment—which will certainly mean that compensatory resources will have to be spent in more intensive cleaning, maintenance, and repair—but it certainly contributes to smog which probably has a direct, though not yet fully documented, effect upon the health of at least some of the residents of the community. In other words, to the community at large the discharge of smoke into the atmosphere is not a free resource. Instead, smoke disposal is costly. Pigou would say that such a situation, where the firm does not bear the full costs of its actions, is an instance where private costs diverge from social costs. The essential point to notice about the situation as it has been outlined here, however, is that without some kind of action the steel producer has nothing more than possible humanitarian concerns, which conflict with his interests in profits, to make him take into account the fact that the discharge of smoke imposes costs upon his neighbors. The discharge of smoke is a technological externality. Without some kind of adjustment the system will not be at a Pareto optimum so that there exists the theoretical possibility that at least one person may be made better off without making anyone else worst off.

Of course, smoke is not the only cause of smog. One of the most often mentioned contributors today is the automobile. In order to understand fully the nature of the relevant motivations, imagine the situation prior to the establishment of the regulation which requires that smog control devices be installed upon all new cars. It is obvious that if consumers demand and are willing to pay for smog control devices, the automobile industry would develop and sell these devices in much the same way that it develops and sells special conveniences and optional equipment. The competition among the various manufacturers, foreign and domestic, compels the producers to try to give the public what it wants. Would the public demand smog control devices? The answer can be found by examining the consumer's motivation.

Imagine for the sake of argument that the auto industry had developed an effective smog control device which it offered as optional equipment for all new cars. A person who was considering whether or not to order this optional for his new car might reason as follows: Suppose I purchase the smog control devices for my new car. If I purchase and everyone else also purchases, then we will have less smog in the city. On the other hand, my individual car can add only a negligible amount to the smog problem so that if everyone else purchases a device and I do not do so, then the smog will be diminished by almost exactly the same amount and I will have saved the cost of the device. Hence, if everyone else purchases a device, I will be better off if I do not get one installed on my car. Now presume that no one, with the possible exception of myself, purchases a device. Obviously, there will be a smog problem. However, if I purchase a device the problem will not be noticably different since my individual car contributes only negligibly to the situation and I will be out of the money which I paid for the smog control device. Hence, if no one else purchases, I should not purchase either. Obviously, the analysis is the same if some of the other people purchase and some do not. Conclusion: I will be better off, no matter what other people do, if I do not purchase a smog control device.

Since all potential new-car buyers will reason roughly as the representative individual above, the result is that there will be a zero demand for smog control devices. Hence, in the absence of some kind of regulation or collective decision, the automobile manufacturers will have no motivation to develop and market smog control devices. This conclusion holds even if—and it is an if—everyone would be better off if all cars were equipped with smog control devices. The point is that for each prospective purchaser of a device, the benefits from his purchase are widely dispersed while the costs accrue to him. Thus the technological externality associated with the exhaust of a car can prevent the unregulated market from leading the system to a Pareto optimum.

For the final example of this section, consider the problem of the pollution of Lake Erie. Biologists tell us that Lake Erie is dying and that it has "aged" 15,000 years in the past half century. The problem is complex. It was long believed that the major source of the pollution stemmed from the fact that raw sewage and industrial wastes are dumped into the lake. A major source of the raw sewage is antiquated systems, some of which are combined sanitary and storm sewers so that the overflow runs into the lake during periods of rain. For the moment, and for the purpose of discussion, imagine that the entire problem of pollution is caused by the raw sewage so that treatment, which could remove the organic material which otherwise is broken down in the lake by a biological process which consumes its oxygen, could solve the problem. The now familiar dilemma would act to frustrate a pure market solution. Each municipality or sewage district would reap but little of the benefits of its own efforts at treating the sewage, but it would bear the full costs of that treatment. Hence, similar to the above

67

case of a customer considering the purchase of a smog control device, each would come to the rational decision to continue to allow the raw sewage to flow into the lake even though all might be better off if all installed modern systems with treating devices. Thus the technological externality reflected in reverse in the failure to receive the full benefit of one's expenditure for treatment—the fact that the decisionmaking entity does not bear the full costs of its decision to forego treatment and allow a flow of raw sewage—results in a failure of a pure market solution where no financial incentive to come to the opposite decision is offered from a higher level of government.

In actuality the pollution of Lake Erie is a much more complex phenomenon than is indicated by the above discussion. Even after treatment to remove indigestible solids and to break down organic material so that the sewage is discharged as mostly inorganic products, the residual inorganic matter contains large amounts of nitrate and phosphate which, instead of being swept harmlessly to the sea, tend to remain in the lake long enough to fertilize monstrous growths of algae which use up to an estimated 18 times as much oxygen as the present flow of organic matter from inadequate sewage plants. Thus, the standard treatment of sewage, which is aimed at the organic matter, is not likely to solve the problem even if such treatment were accomplished. One might suggest that one of the "essential" nutrients such as the phosphate should be removed from the waste so that the algae would not grow, and this suggestion brings us to the economics of the situation. Some two-thirds of the phosphorus in municipal waste, which is roughly three-quarters of the total wastes, stems from detergents. Even if the housewife or commercial laundry knew that the detergent used for the wash contributed importantly to the pollution of the lake, which they probably do not know, would there be any incentive to economize on the use of detergents or demand a kind which contained less phosphorus? Again, the familiar dilemma appears. Even if they knew of their contribution to pollution, each could rationalize that their own contribution was negligible, that the benefits to be derived from an individual decision to try to perform the wash in such a manner as to contribute less phosphorus to the sewage was too small to be measured, that the costs of this kind of action was not negligible, so that the rational decision would be to ignore the entire situation.

Thus, the manufacturers of detergents would have no incentive to try to develop products which contain less phosphorus, the municipal sewage systems would have no more incentive than in the previous instance to attempt to remove the material, and the result is that the pure market solution would be to continue the pollution of the lake. Thus, the existence of this technological externality—the fact that those causing the pollution do not bear the full costs of their actions—can cause the market mechanism to lead the system to a situation which is not Pareto optimal.

THE POSSIBILITY OF A SOLUTION:

The above illustrations are indicative of the fact that the very existence of technological externalities can cause problems for the claims of the efficiency of the unregulated market mechanism. It must be admitted that the problems caused by these technological externalities are most perplexing. Although only a few years ago economists may have been of the opinion that an adequate solution was available, the consensus now has vanished. Instead, one finds that a variety of solutions have been suggested by various persons, many of whom are not economists, and a goodly number of these have even been tried or implemented in certain situations.

What seems to have been present in many of the discussions and analyses of technological externalities in the literature is a belief that a universal solution might be found. Thus, proposals are often treated as if they are supposed to be "the" solution to the problem of technological externalities. Unfortunately, this belief may turn out to be unfounded, which is the authors' own belief, and it may be that there is no simple and universally acceptable solution to the problem. It may be that, at least for the foreseeable future, our society may have no alternative but to seek pragmatic solutions to the problem.

In keeping with the above, the proper perspective requires that attention be devoted to a consideration of many of the suggested solutions to the problem. Accordingly, the remainder of this essay is devoted to an examination of some of the proposed solutions. It is desirable, of course, that the point of view which is adopted in this discussion be made explicit. The reader is thus warned that the authors view the situation as one which can be conceptually accommodated to cost-benefit analysis. All of the proposals have associated costs and benefits. The problem is to identify which is most suitable for a given situation. It is hoped that the following discussion may be helpful in this regard. The plan is to discuss the more popular of the proposed solutions. Examples will be used to illustrate all of the major points.

Solution by Prohibition

When one is convinced that collective action is necessary to try to improve the situation, or to correct the abuses caused by technological externalities, the first thought that one is likely to have is that action should be taken to prohibit the externalities. After all, if the externalities are prohibited, will not the market system then function so that our economy will be brought to a Pareto optimum position?

Although this course of action may seem appealing at first, it takes little thought to convince one that simple prohibition of activities causing the technological externalities is a poor approach. Obviously, one could not seriously propose that car owners stop driving, that steel manufacturers stop producing, or that municipalities stop disposing of their sewage. Some might think, however, that we should have perfectly clean water or perfectly clean air, so that full treatment is desired. Such a thought, however, misses the fundamental point. Optimality does not require that externalities be eliminated. Instead, optimality requires that externalities be present in the "right amount." Some examples may make this point more clear.

Consider the case of water pollution. Natural biological processes in both lakes and streams give them certain capability of cleaning themselves up. Thus if absolutely no wastes are allowed to flow into these waters, and if all sewage is made "perfectly" clean, this natural capability will not be used. The proper way of viewing this natural capability is as a resource and, as is true for all scarce and valuable resources, it should be used. In addition, it would be very expensive to make sewage perfectly clean, and benefits must always be balanced against the costs. The problem of pollution arises when so much wastes are dumped into a stream or lake that the capacity of the water to clean itself up without producing objectionable side effects is exceeded.

Air pollution affords a similar example. It would be prohibitively expensive to prevent any contaminants whatsoever from escaping into the air. Further, there is no reason not to use the natural absorbic capability of the atmosphere. The problem of air pollution arises when there are excesses.

The above examples should make clear the fact that strict prohibition of whatever causes a technological externality is insurance that the economic system cannot attain Pareto optimality. What is desired is just the right amount of the externality. So, for example, in the case of water pollution a Pareto optimal solution may in fact call for some deterioration of water quality in certain streams and may even mean complete deterioration of water quality in other streams.

SOLUTION BY DIRECTIVE

Having seen that part of the problem is to get just the right amount of the technological externality, it is tempting to say that the easiest procedure would be to let the Government decide how much of it should be produced. This procedure would involve, for example, governmental determination of just how well the municipalities bordering Lake Erie should treat their sewage in terms of, say, the percentage of organic matter removed and phosphorous content, and an absolute quantity limit above which the sewage would have to be treated until it was pure. Similarly, in the air pollution example the Government would have to specify just how much smoke each factory could emit.

There are several difficulties with this procedure. First, there is the problem of determining just how much of the externality is desirable. This might be called the problem of the overall standard. It is not to be dismissed as a trivial problem. There is, needless to say, a theoretically correct way to determine the standard. It should be set by a careful weighing of costs and benefits. To be specific, consider again the example of the pollution of Lake Erie. For the purpose of illustrating the main point, imagine that it would cost 50 billion dollars per year in operating costs alone to process the sewage in such a manner that the pollution in the lake would diminish from present levels. Now while there may be many benefits to be derived from an unpolluted Lake Erie, it is rather doubtful that they would be valued at anything near 50 billion dollars per year. Hence, in such a case the rational decision would be to tolerate an even higher level of pollution and the standard should be set in such a manner that there would be no increase in the level of processing the sewage. The costs would simply outweigh the benefits. On the other hand, imagine that all of the sewage could be processed if there were an increase in annual expenditures of only $5. Clearly, the yearly benefits from an unpolluted lake would exceed this figure so that the standard should be set so that all sewage would be treated. The benefits would outweigh

70

the costs. In between these extremes, however, the computations become very difficult. The difficulties of determining the benefits associated with various degrees of pollution are almost insolvable. Hence, there must be a great deal of arbitrariness in setting the overall standard. One of the difficulties here is that the tools for measuring benefits are rather crude. Another problem, which has been overlooked in the above discussion, is that relatively little is known about the ecology of lakes so that there is a great deal of uncertainty concerning what effects treatment might have upon pollution.

Even if the overall standard could be easily determined instead of involving the difficulties discussed above (the problem of measuring benefits is most crucial here), other difficulties would still remain. The overall standard must be translated into directives for each of the entities which emit pollutants. In principle the directives should be adjusted so that the marginal effectiveness of the last dollar spent upon the processing of wastes should be equated for all of the pollutors. In practice the marginal effectiveness of dollars spent for treating wastes probably cannot be determined since for any given pollutor, the effectiveness depends upon the policies which the other pollutor follow. In other words, there would be arbitrariness at this level, too.

If one takes another example, such as air pollution, the problems are even more difficult although the principles involved are the same. The overall standard should still be determined by weighing and comparing the benefits and the costs of the various possibilities. However, the uncertainties are even greater since one does not know, for example, the exact relationship between the level of pollution and the health of the residents. Also, there is the fact that in most urban areas the amount of pollutants which can be released into the atmosphere for any given standard depends upon the weather and especially the prevailing winds.

None of the above comments should be interpreted as meaning that the policy of controlling externalities by directives is to be dismissed as being obviously inappropriate. What is intended here is to point out that there are difficulties associated with the procedure. Further, one should observe that in addition to the above, this particular approach also involves an administrative cost of policing the directives, which cannot be ignored.

SOLUTION BY VOLUNTARY ACTION

Some argue that collective action is not needed to correct the market solution when there are technological externalities. It has often been pointed out that there is motivation for private parties to act to correct the situation by a variety of methods. Two which are often discussed are the methods of bribes and merger. These will be discussed in order.

Consider once more the example of a steel producer discharging smoke into the atmosphere unchecked by a smoke control ordinance. The previous discussion indicated that this situation potentially gives rise to a divergence between private and social cost or between the private and social benefit of steel production. To avoid the adverse effects

71

of smoke discharge the community might resort to bribing the steel producer to decrease or discontinue altogether the discharge of smoke. The rationale for this behavior is that as long as the amount of the bribe needed to induce the steel manufacturer to reduce smoke discharge is less than the damage inflicted on the community, then the community will on net be better off by paying the bribe. Of course, the community acting in its self-interest should never offer a bribe that exceeded the value of the damage inflicted via smoke discharge. The steel producer should in turn accept or reject the bribe in accordance with his best interests. Accordingly, if the bribe exceeded the amount he would have to spend on means to reduce smoke discharge, he should accept the bribe and effect the desired reduction; and if the costs were too great, he should not. In any case a quantitative measure of the damage suffered by the community from smoke would have been presented to the manufacturer and in such a way as to make him cognizant of this figure when deciding how much smoke to discharge.

Moreover, whatever the final level of smoke discharge is it could be Pareto optimal if there were such a thing as perfect bargaining. One can reason as follows: Acceptance of the bribe by the manufacture indicates that he is at least as well off as before, while payment of the bribe by the community indicates that it is at least as well off as before. Consequently, the situation is improved and if the bargaining were perfect any departure from the agreed upon position would only improve the position of one of the parties at the expense of the other. It is also true that rejection of the bribe by the manufacturer under perfect bargaining leads to a Pareto optimal solution. By rejecting the bribe the manufacturer would disclose that the value of this resource (release of smoke into the air) is of greater value to him than to the community.

The method for avoiding a divergence between private and social cost just described is purely voluntary and leads to a Pareto optimal allocation of resources when bargaining is perfect. It would, therefore, appear to the ideal way in which to resolve such problems. Unfortunately, bargaining is not perfect and there are several impediments to its widespread use. The first difficulty is associated with the valuation of smoke damage suffered by the community. The most direct way of estimating the damage is to ask each member of the community how much he would be willing to contribute to the bribe to be offered to the manufacturer. In principle, each individual should be willing to contribute the amount he would have to expend to avoid the damage from smoke by other means. Unfortunately, however, the individual may realize that if he contributes nothing toward the bribe while others contribute positive amounts and smoke abatement is effected, he will reap the benefits of smoke abatement at no cost to himself. If all members of the community adopt this attitude, no bribe will be offered and the scheme will fail. In other words, the public good nature of the benefit from smoke abatement impedes the realization of the necessary collective action by the community. The second difficulty with the bribe procedure is that it requires that the community know all the available methods for manufacturing steel, as these are related to smoke control, and the associated costs so that they might prevent the manufacturer from cheating. For suppose after the bribe has been accepted by the manufacturer, the demand for steel rises and output increases. The producer can now legitimately argue that a larger bribe is required for him to maintain the previously agreed upon level of smoke discharge. Unless the community is completely knowledgeable about steelmaking technology it cannot be sure that the manufacturer is not expanding his output more than would be optimal for him in the absence of the bribe. Thus, a seemingly ideal scheme for avoidance of a divergence between private and social cost is marred by difficulties in implementation.

Another voluntary scheme for interalizing nonpecuniary externalities free of some of the implementation difficulties mentioned above is the merger of the entities involved when this is possible. To illustrate how this procedure might work, consider the following situation: Suppose a firm discharges wastes into a stream which are harmful to fish life. Suppose, further, that a fishery operates downstream from the firm. In the absence of any governmental regulation the upstream firm will discharge waste into the stream without regard to the damage inflicted on the fishery in the way of smaller catches or tainted fish. Were the firm and the fishery to merge under a single ownership, then it would be in the new consolidated firm's best interest to take account of the losses incurred by its downstream subsidiary as a consequence of the actions of its upstream plant. The consolidated firm should balance the cost of disposing the waste at the upstream plant by means other than discharge into the stream against the costs incurred by the downstream fishery as a result of waste discharge into the stream in such a way as to maximize the combined profit from the two operations. Since in this example Pareto optimality corresponds to joint profit maximization by the two entities, merger will assure a Pareto optimal allocation of the resource in question;—viz, the stream. It might also be noted that the profit of the consolidated firm will always be at least as great as the combined profits of the two firms operating in isolation. The reason for this is that the merged firm always has the option of adopting the operating policies of the two firms working independently and consequently can achieve a profit level at least as large as the combined profit of the previously independent firms. The difference between the profits of the consolidated firm and the combined profits of the individual firms reflects the loss to society from the presence of a nonpecuniary externality.

Two difficulties with the merger solution can be pointed out. The first is the entities have to be firms. The second in that merger is feasible only when the number of entities involved is small. As the number of decision making units to enter into the consolidation increases the chances of effecting the merger decline. This is primarily due to the fact that it becomes increasingly more difficult to persuade potential participants that it is in their best interest to join the coalition. Individual units may find it profitable to postpone entry into the coalition so as to extract a larger portion of the joint profits from the merged entity. The third difficulty is that a merged entity might become so big as to cause a distortion in the allocation of resources via monopoly or monopsony power. In this case the losses from the presence of nonpecuniary externalities have to be weighed against the losses to society from the resource allocation distortions engendered by imperfectly competitive markets.

If voluntary arrangements among the entities effected by nonpecuniary externalities are impractical or not forthcoming, collective governmental action might be justified. In the economics literature the classic form of government intervention in this situation is the payment of a subsidy to units that by their actions confer external economies upon other units and the levying of taxes upon those entities that by their actions confer external diseconomies upon other units. In essence, the idea is to encourage those activities that contribute to the "common good" and discourage those that detract from the "common good".

To illustrate the working of this scheme, consider again the example of an upstream firm and a downstream fishery. Suppose now, however, that the waste discharged into the stream by the firm provides food for fish in the stream and is therefore beneficial to the fishery. Since by hypthesis voluntary negotiation by the parties involved is ruled out here, the fishery has no way of communicating the magnitude of the benefits it derives from the firm's discharge of waste into the stream. Consequently, the amount of food provided to the fish may not be ideal. In this case a government subsidy to the firm for the discharge of waste can in principle be devised to achieve the desired result. Likewise, if as in our earlier description of the situation the waste discharged is harmful to fish life, then in principle a tax can be imposed on the firm that reflects the damage imposed on the fishery.

We have stressed the "in principle" nature of these conclusions because of the immense informational requirements necessary for the implementation of this scheme. A little reflection will make it apparent that the governmental agency imposing a tax or offering a subsidy will need to know the production technologies of all the entities involved. In effect the governmental agency will have to solve the same problem that the directors of the merged firm discussed above solve. Instead of issuing orders regarding the quantities of each product that each of the subsidiaries should produce so as maximize joint profits, a practice that the executives of the merged firm might follow, the agency would attempt to achieve the same results via the payment of subsidies and/or the issuance of taxes. Suffice it to say the information that would be available to the directors of the merged firm is rarely available to an outside governmental agency. Bits of this information may of course be available and it may be possible at a cost to obtain additional information.

The amount of information required also depends on the nature of the productive technologies involved. Less information is required by the agency for the successful implementation of a tax-subsidy scheme if the underlying productive technologies are separable or additive than if they are not. For example, if the cost of producing the upstream firm's product and the cost of waste treatment are additive then the tax on waste discharge, if that is what is called for, simply depends on the amount of waste discharge. On the other hand if these costs are not additive then the tax must vary not only in accordance with the level of waste discharge but also with the amount of the firm's primary product. Of course the information requirements mount enormously as the number of economic entities involved increases. Despite all these difficulties an attempt to achieve optimal resource allocation via taxes and subsidies might be justified if the losses to society from the presence of nonpecuniary externalities is large enough. In essence what has to be balanced in this situation is the cost of acquiring the needed information against the losses to society if nothing is done or another of the imperfect policies is followed.

SOLUTION BY REGULATION

Another collective action which is often suggested is governmental regulation. For example, the official governmental response to the fact that cars contribute to air pollution in our cities has been to reduce the range of consumer choice by simply requiring that all new cars be equipped with devices which are supposed to reduce the level of pollutants that escape from the engine. Such a regulation obviously permits an escape from the dilemma described earlier where a rational calculation would cause the consumer to refrain from purchasing a control device.

Regulation also has problems associated with it. There is often uncertainty associated with the imposition of a regulation. In the case of automobiles, for example, there is uncertainty as to whether the devices will be effective in reducing the level of pollutants which are discharged, especially as the cars grow old. There are also problems of enforcement. For instance, there is speculation that if the devices are effective and the pollutants are kept in the engine rather than being spewed into the atmosphere, the life of the engine is likely to be shortened and repairs will have to be made more frequently. These are costs of the regulation which, along with the costs of the devices, have to be weighed against possible benefits which, as was discussed earlier, are rather difficult to compute. Note, however, that if the devices do have the anticipated effect upon engines, then each owner has an incentive to take action to render the devices ineffective and to allow the pollutants to escape into the atmosphere since by doing so he can increase the life of his engine and reduce his repair bills. Certainly, the owner cannot be expected to keep the device in good working order, or to repair it when it breaks, since such an action would not be in his own self-interest. Hence, the regulation cannot be expected to be successful in reducing air pollution, even if the devices work, unless it is accompanied by the practice of periodically inspecting all cars and requiring that the devices be maintained in good working order.

The above discussion should make clear the fact that solution by regulation is not as simple as might first seem to be the case. The administrative costs of enforcing the regulations are relevant and should not be overlooked. Regulation differs from solution by directive in that under the latter scheme government prescribes the possibly different activity level of each economic entity involved while under the regulation alternative uniform requirements are imposed upon all entities or only uniform permissible bounds on certain activities are set.

Neither should one ignore the fact that a regulatory solution is of necessity inflexible. This point too can be better understood by recourse to the above example. Many of our Nation's motor vehicles are operated for a considerable portion of their life in nonurban areas where air pollution is not thought to be a problem. Ideally, vehicles operating in these areas should not be required to have smog control devices so that the natural ability of the atmosphere to accommodate a certain level of pollutants could be utilized. Obviously, it is impossible to design regulations which would accomplish this ideal due to the very mobility of motor vehicles and the population. Hence, for many externalities solution by regulation is inherently incapable of bringing the system to a Pareto optimal solution because regulations are by nature inflexible.

SOLUTION BY PAYMENT

One of the obvious ways of trying to accommodate the system to the presence of technological externalities is to attempt to provide a financial incentive for the desired actions to be taken. In the pollution of Lake Erie, for example, one of the problems is supposed to be the fact that Cleveland has an archaic sewage system which combines storm and sanitary sewers. The capacity of the facilities for treatment is sufficiently limited that anything but modest rainfall is supposed to create such a flow that the capacity of treating facilities are exceeded, allowing raw sewage to flow directly into the lake. As was explained earlier, the citizens of Cleveland do not bear the full cost of their archaic sewage system since, although it certainly contributes to the pollution of Lake Erie, persons residing outside of Cleveland desire to use the lake for various purposes. These other persons thus bear part of the costs of pollution including that portion of the pollution which stems from Cleveland's sewage system. Of course, what is true for Cleveland is also true for many of the other cities and towns in the lake area. Since each does not bear the full costs of the results from its own system, none have full incentive to remedy the situation.

One possible policy step is for a higher level of government—for example, the Federal Government—to provide an incentive for a remedy. Such a provision can be accomplished, at least in part, by Federal subsidy for the capital costs of improving the sewage facilities. Such a subsidy is an incentive to the local community.

One difficulty with this measure of policy is its crudeness. It does not easily provide proper coordination for all of the relevant units in the system. Another limitation of this policy is that it is suited only for those kinds of externalities, such as the one discussed here, where the capital costs are the only really significant feature which prevents the situation from being improved.

SOLUTION BY DIRECT PUBLIC ACTION

It sometimes happens that there are simple direct actions which can be taken to ameliorate the effects of an externality. Probably the clearest example involves fishing. Consider a lake or stream where many people come to fish. Now at least after some level of activity, the catch begins to affect the future fish population. Thus, when a fisherman makes a catch, he can affect the future population of fish and thus lower the pleasure and profits of other fishermen. No individual fisherman, of course, has incentive to take into account the effect which his own activity has upon others. In extreme cases, of course, the population of fish could be exhausted.

An obvious remedy for this situation is for the Government to continually stock the lake or river so that the fish population is never diminished to the danger point. The externality is then more or less eliminated by this direct action.

Needless to say, there are obvious problems associated with this policy of direct action. Not the least of these is the fact that it is suitable only for very special situations.

Concluding Remarks

It should be obvious by now that there is a whole menu of policies which can be fashioned to deal with problems caused by technological externalities. None of these policies, at least at our present level of knowledge, appears to be perfect. Neither does it seem to the authors that any one clearly dominates in the sense that it would be the best of the imperfect lot for each and every technological externality. Thus it is argued here that policies must be designed with particular situations in mind and what is best for one externality may be inappropriate for another. Accordingly, it is appropriate to conclude this essay with a few remarks about what seems to be the appropriate procedure for the selection of policy.

The tools of cost-benefit analysis appear to provide the proper perspective. In a given situation, the policymaker should consider the problem and imagine the application of each of the alternative approaches to it. The principle of selection is simple. Each measure of policy (including that of doing nothing) will have costs and benefits associate with it. The policymaker should select that measure for implementation which produces the greatest net benefits.

On Divergences between Social Cost and Private Cost*

By Ralph Turvey

The notion that the resource-allocation effects of divergences between marginal social and private costs can be dealt with by imposing a tax or granting a subsidy equal to the difference now seems too simple a notion. Three recent articles have shown us this. First came Professor Coase's " The Problem of Social Cost ", then Davis and Whinston's " Externalities, Welfare and the Theory of Games " appeared, and, finally, Buchanan and Stubblebine have published their paper " Externality ".[1] These articles have an aggregate length of eighty pages and are by no means easy to read. The following attempt to synthesise and summarise the main ideas may therefore be useful. It is couched in terms of external diseconomies, i.e. an excess of social over private costs, and the reader is left to invert the analysis himself should he be interested in external economies.

The scope of the following argument can usefully be indicated by starting with a brief statement of its main conclusions. The first is that if the party imposing external diseconomies and the party suffering them are able and willing to negotiate to their mutual advantage, state intervention is unnecessary to secure optimum resource allocation. The second is that the imposition of a tax upon the party imposing external diseconomies can be a very complicated matter, even in principle, so that the *a priori* prescription of such a tax is unwise.

To develop these and other points, let us begin by calling A the person, firm or group (of persons or firms) which imposes a diseconomy, and B the person, firm or group which suffers it. How much B suffers will in many cases depend not only upon the *scale* of A's diseconomy-creating activity, but also upon the precise *nature* of A's activity and upon B's *reaction* to it. If A emits smoke, for example, B's loss will depend not only upon the quantity emitted but also upon the height of A's chimney and upon the cost to B of installing air-conditioning, indoor clothes-dryers or other means of reducing the effect of the smoke. Thus to ascertain the optimum resource allocation will frequently require an investigation of the nature and costs both of alternative activities open to A and of the devices by which B can reduce the impact of each activity. The optimum involves that kind and scale of A's activity and that adjustment to it by B which maximises the algebraic sum of A's gain and B's loss as against the situation where A

* I am indebted to Professor Buchanan, Professor Coase, Mr. Klappholz, Dr. Mishan and Mr. Peston for helpful comments on an earlier draft.
[1] *Journal of Law and Economics*, Vol. III, October, 1960, *Journal of Political Economy*, June, 1962, and *Economica*, November, 1962, respectively.

ECONOMICA, August, 1963, Vol. 30, pp. 309-313.

pursues no diseconomy-creating acti.ity. Note that the optimum will frequently involve B suffering a loss, both in total and at the margin.[1]

If A and B are firms, gain and loss can be measured in money terms as profit differences. (In considering a social optimum, allowance has of course to be made for market imperfections.) Now assuming that they both seek to maximise profits, that they know about the available alternatives and adjustments and that they are able and willing to negotiate, they will achieve the optimum without any government interference. They will internalize the externality by merger[2], or they will make an agreement whereby B pays A to modify the nature or scale of its activity.[3] Alternatively,[4] if the law gives B rights against A, A will pay B to accept the optimal amount of loss imposed by A.

If A and B are people, their gain and loss must be measured as the amount of money they respectively would pay to indulge in and prevent A's activity. It could also be measured as the amount of money they respectively would require to refrain from and to endure A's activity, which will be different unless the marginal utility of income is constant. We shall assume that it is constant for both A and B, which is reasonable when the payments do not bulk large in relation to their incomes.[5] Under this assumption, it makes no difference whether B pays A or, if the law gives B rights against A, A compensates B.

Whether A and B are persons or firms, to levy a tax on A which is *not* received as damages or compensation by B may prevent optimal resource allocation from being achieved—still assuming that they can and do negotiate.[6] The reason is that the resource allocation which maximises A's *gain less* B's *loss* may differ from that which maximises A's *gain less* A's *tax less* B's *loss*.

The points made so far can usefully be presented diagrammatically (Figure 1). We assume that A has only two alternative activities, I and II, and that their scales and B's losses are all continuously variable. Let us temporarily disregard the dotted curve in the right-hand part of the diagram. The area under A's curves then gives the total gain to A. The area under B's curves gives the total loss to B after he has made the best adjustment possible to A's activity. This is thus the direct loss as reduced by adjustment, plus the cost of making that adjustment.

If A and B could not negotiate and if A were unhampered by restrictions of any sort, A would choose activity I at a scale of OR. A scale of OS would obviously give a larger social product, but the optimum is clearly activity II at scale OJ, since area 2 is greater than area 1. Now B will be prepared to pay up to $(1a + 1b - 2a)$ to secure this result, while

[1] Buchanan-Stubblebine, pp. 380–1.
[2] Davis-Whinston, pp. 244, 252, 256; Coase, pp. 16–17.
[3] Coase, p. 6; Buchanan-Stubblebine agree, p. 383.
[4] See previous references.
[5] Dr. Mishan has examined the welfare criterion for the case where the only variable is the scale of A's activity, but where neither A nor B has a constant marginal utility of income; Cf. his paper " Welfare Criteria for External Effects ", *American Economic Review*, September, 1961.
[6] Buchanan-Stubblebine, pp. 381–3.

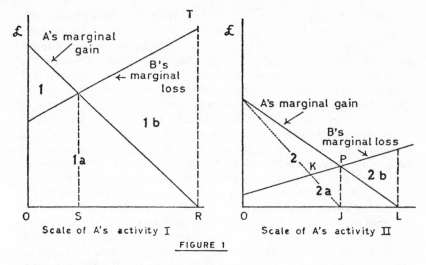

FIGURE 1

A will be prepared to accept down to $(1 + 1a - 2 - 2a)$ to assure it. The difference is $(1b - 1 + 2)$, the maximum gain to be shared between them, and this is clearly positive.

If A is liable to compensate B for actual damages caused by either activity I or II, he will choose activity II at scale OJ (i.e. the optimum allocation), pay $2a$ to B and retain a net gain of 2. The result is the same as when there is no such liability, though the distribution of the gain is very different: B will pay A up to $(1a + 1b - 2a)$ to secure this result. Hence whether or not we should advocate the imposition of a liability on A for damages caused is a matter of fairness, not of resource allocation. Our judgment will presumably depend on such factors as who got there first, whether one of them is a non-conforming user (e.g. an establishment for the breeding of maggots on putrescible vegetable matter in a residential district), who is richer, and so on. Efficient resource allocation requires the imposition of a liability upon A only if we can show that inertia, obstinacy, etc. inhibit A and B from reaching a voluntary agreement.[1]

We can now make the point implicit in Buchanan-Stubblebine's argument, namely that there is a necessity for any impost levied on A to be paid to B when A and B are able to negotiate. Suppose that A is charged an amount equal to the loss he imposes on B; subtracting this from his marginal gain curve in the right-hand part of the diagram gives us the dotted line as his marginal net gain. If A moves to point J it will then pay B to induce him to move back to position K (which is sub-optimal) as it is this position which maximises the *joint* net gain to A and B together.

There is a final point to be made about the case where A and B can negotiate. This is that if the external diseconomies are reciprocal, so

[1] Cf. the comparable argument on pp. 94–8 of my *The Economics of Real Property*, 1957, about the external economy to landlords of tenants' improvements.

that each imposes a loss upon the other, the problem is still more complicated.[1]

We now turn to the case where A and B cannot negotiate, which in most cases will result from A and/or B being too large a group for the members to get together. Here there are certain benefits to be had from resource re-allocation which are not privately appropriable. Just as with collective goods,[2] therefore, there is thus a case for collective action to achieve optimum allocation. But all this means is that *if* the state can ascertain and enforce a move to the optimum position at a cost less than the gain to be had, and *if* it can do this in a way which does not have unfavourable effects upon income distribution, then it should take action.

These two " ifs " are very important. The second is obvious and requires no elaboration. The first, however, deserves a few words. In order to ascertain the optimum type and scale of A's activity, the authorities must estimate all of the curves in the diagrams. They must, in other words, list and evaluate all the alternatives open to A and examine their effects upon B and the adjustments B could make to reduce the loss suffered. When this is done, if it can be done, it is necessary to consider how to reach the optimum. Now, where the nature as well as the scale of A's activity is variable, it may be necessary to control both, and this may require two controls, not one. Suppose, for instance, that in the diagram, both activities are the emission of smoke: I from a low chimney and II from a tall chimney. To induce A to shift from emitting OR smoke from the low chimney to emitting OJ smoke from the tall chimney, it will not suffice to levy a tax of PJ per unit of smoke.[3] If this alone were done, A would continue to use a low chimney, emitting slightly less than OR smoke. It will also be necessary to regulate chimney heights. A tax would do the trick alone only if it were proportioned to losses imposed rather than to smoke emitted, and that would be very difficult.

These complications show that in many cases the cost of achieving optimum resource allocation may outweigh the gain. If this is the case, a second-best solution may be appropriate. Thus a prohibition of all smoke emission would be better than OR smoke from a low chimney (since 1 is less than 1b) and a requirement that all chimneys be tall would be better still (giving a net gain of 2 less 2b). Whether these requirements should be imposed on existing chimney-owners as well as on new ones then introduces further complications relating to the short run and the long run.

There is no need to carry the example any further. It is now abundantly clear that any general prescription of a tax to deal with external diseconomies is useless. Each case must be considered on its own and

[1] Davis-Whinston devote several pages of game theory to this problem.
[2] Buchanan-Stubblebine, p. 383.
[3] Note how different PJ is from RT, the initial observable marginal external diseconomy.

there is no *a priori* reason to suppose that the imposition of a tax is better than alternative measures or indeed, that any measures at all are desirable unless we assume that information and administration are both costless.[1]

To sum up, then: when negotiation is possible, the case for government intervention is one of justice not of economic efficiency; when it is not, the theorist should be silent and call in the applied economist.

PART II. COMMON PROPERTY RESOURCES

THE ECONOMIC THEORY OF A COMMON-PROPERTY RESOURCE: THE FISHERY[1]

H. SCOTT GORDON

I. INTRODUCTION

THE chief aim of this paper is to examine the economic theory of natural resource utilization as it pertains to the fishing industry. It will appear, I hope, that most of the problems associated with the words "conservation" or "depletion" or "overexploitation" in the fishery are, in reality, manifestations of the fact that the natural resources of the sea yield no economic rent. Fishery resources are unusual in the fact of their common-property nature; but they are not unique, and similar problems are encountered in other cases of common-property resource industries, such as petroleum production, hunting and trapping, etc. Although the theory presented in the following pages is worked out in terms of the fishing industry, it is, I believe, applicable generally to all cases where natural resources are owned in common and exploited under conditions of individualistic competition.

II. BIOLOGICAL FACTORS AND THEORIES

The great bulk of the research that has been done on the primary production phase of the fishing industry has so far been in the field of biology. Owing to the

lack of theoretical economic research,[2] biologists have been forced to extend the scope of their own thought into the economic sphere and in some cases have penetrated quite deeply, despite the lack of the analytical tools of economic theory.[3] Many others, who have paid no specific attention to the economic aspects of the problem have nevertheless recognized that the ultimate question is not the ecology of life in the sea as such, but man's use of these resources for his own (economic) purposes. Dr. Martin D. Burkenroad, for example, began a recent article on fishery management with a section on "Fishery Management as Political Economy," saying that "the Management of fisheries is intended for the benefit of man, not fish; therefore effect of management upon fishstocks cannot be regarded as beneficial *per se*."[4] The

[1] I want to express my indebtedness to the Canadian Department of Fisheries for assistance and co-operation in making this study; also to Professor M. C. Urquhart, of Queen's University, Kingston, Ontario, for mathematical assistance with the last section of the paper and to the Economists' Summer Study Group at Queen's for affording opportunity for research and discussion.

[2] The single exception that I know is G. M. Gerhardsen, "Production Economics in Fisheries," *Revista de economia* (Lisbon), March, 1952.

[3] Especially remarkable efforts in this sense are Robert A. Nesbit, "Fishery Management" ("U.S. Fish and Wildlife Service, Special Scientific Reports," No. 18 [Chicago, 1943]) (mimeographed), and Harden F. Taylor, *Survey of Marine Fisheries of North Carolina* (Chapel Hill, 1951); also R. J. H. Beverton, "Some Observations on the Principles of Fishery Regulation," *Journal du conseil permanent international pour l'exploration de la mer* (Copenhagen), Vol. XIX, No. 1 (May, 1953); and M. D. Burkenroad, "Some Principles of Marine Fishery Biology," *Publications of the Institute of Marine Science* (University of Texas), Vol. II, No. 1 (September, 1951).

[4] "Theory and Practice of Marine Fishery Management," *Journal du conseil permanent international pour l'exploration de la mer*, Vol. XVIII, No. 3 (January, 1953).

JOURNAL OF POLITICAL ECONOMY, 1954, Vol. 65, No. 2, pp. 124-142.

great Russian marine biology theorist, T. I. Baranoff, referred to his work as "bionomics" or "bio-economics," although he made little explicit reference to economic factors.[5] In the same way, A. G. Huntsman, reporting in 1944 on the work of the Fisheries Research Board of Canada, defined the problem of fisheries depletion in economic terms: "Where the take in proportion to the effort fails to yield a satisfactory living to the fisherman";[6] and a later paper by the same author contains, as an incidental statement, the essence of the economic optimum solution without, apparently, any recognition of its significance.[7] Upon the occasion of its fiftieth anniversary in 1952, the International Council for the Exploration of the Sea published a *Rapport Jubilaire*, consisting of a series of papers summarizing progress in various fields of fisheries research. The paper by Michael Graham on "Overfishing and Optimum Fishing," by its emphatic recognition of the economic criterion, would lead one to think that the economic aspects of the question had been extensively examined during the last half-century. But such is not the case. Virtually no specific research into the economics of fishery resource utilization has been undertaken. The present state

of knowledge is that a great deal is known about the biology of the various commercial species but little about the economic characteristics of the fishing industry.

The most vivid thread that runs through the biological literature is the effort to determine the effect of fishing on the stock of fish in the sea. This discussion has had a very distinct practical orientation, being part of the effort to design regulative policies of a "conservation" nature. To the layman the problem appears to be dominated by a few facts of overriding importance. The first of these is the prodigious reproductive potential of most fish species. The adult female cod, for example, lays millions of eggs at each spawn. The egg that hatches and ultimately reaches maturity is the great exception rather than the rule. The various herrings (Clupeidae) are the most plentiful of the commercial species, accounting for close to half the world's total catch, as well as providing food for many other sea species. Yet herring are among the smallest spawners, laying a mere hundred thousand eggs a season, which, themselves, are eaten in large quantity by other species. Even in inclosed waters the survival and reproductive powers of fish appear to be very great. In 1939 the Fisheries Research Board of Canada deliberately tried to kill all the fish in one small lake by poisoning the water. Two years later more than ninety thousand fish were found in the lake, including only about six hundred old enough to have escaped the poisoning.

The picture one gets of life in the sea is one of constant predation of one species on another, each species living on a narrow margin of food supply. It reminds the economist of the Malthusian law of population; for, unlike man, the

[5] Two of Baranoff's most important papers— "On the Question of the Biological Basis of Fisheries" (1918) and "On the Question of the Dynamics of the Fishing Industry" (1925)—have been translated by W. E. Ricker, now of the Fisheries Research Board of Canada (Nanaimo, B.C.), and issued in mimeographed form.

[6] "Fishery Depletion," *Science*, XCIX (1944), 534.

[7] "The highest take is not necessarily the best. The take should be increased only as long as the extra cost is offset by the added revenue from sales" (A. G. Huntsman, "Research on Use and Increase of Fish Stocks," *Proceedings of the United Nations Scientific Conference on the Conservation and Utilization of Resources* [Lake Success, 1949]).

fish has no power to alter the conditions of his environment and consequently cannot progress. In fact, Malthus and his law are frequently mentioned in the biological literature. One's first reaction is to declare that environmental factors are so much more important than commercial fishing that man has no effect on the population of the sea at all. One of the continuing investigations made by fisheries biologists is the determination of the age distribution of catches. This is possible because fish continue to grow in size with age, and seasonal changes are reflected in certain hard parts of their bodies in much the same manner as one finds growth-rings in a tree. The study of these age distributions shows that commercial catches are heavily affected by good and bad brood years. A good brood year, one favorable to the hatching of eggs and the survival of fry, has its effect on future catches, and one can discern the dominating importance of that brood year in the commercial catches of succeeding years.[8] Large broods, however, do not appear to depend on large numbers of adult spawners, and this lends support to the belief that the fish population is entirely unaffected by the activity of man.

There is, however, important evidence to the contrary. World Wars I and II, during which fishing was sharply curtailed in European waters, were followed by indications of a significant growth in fish populations. Fish-marking experiments, of which there have been a great number, indicate that fishing is a major cause of fish mortality in developed fisheries. The introduction of restrictive laws has often been followed by an increase in fish populations, although the evidence on this point is capable of other interpretations which will be noted later.

General opinion among fisheries biologists appears to have had something of a cyclical pattern. During the latter part of the last century, the Scottish fisheries biologist, W. C. MacIntosh,[9] and the great Darwinian, T. H. Huxley, argued strongly against all restrictive measures on the basis of the inexhaustible nature of the fishery resources of the sea. As Huxley put it in 1883: "The cod fishery, the herring fishery, the pilchard fishery, the mackerel fishery, and probably all the great sea fisheries, are inexhaustible: that is to say that nothing we do seriously affects the number of fish. And any attempt to regulate these fisheries seems consequently, from the nature of the case, to be useless."[10] As a matter of fact, there was at this time relatively little restriction of fishing in European waters. Following the Royal Commission of 1866, England had repealed a host of restrictive laws. The development of steam-powered trawling in the 1880's, which enormously increased man's predatory capacity, and the marked improvement of the trawl method in 1923 turned the pendulum, and throughout the interwar years discussion centered on the problem of "overfishing" and "depletion." This was accompanied by a considerable growth of restrictive regula-

[8] One example of a very general phenomenon: 1904 was such a successful brood year for Norwegian herrings that the 1904 year class continued to outweigh all others in importance in the catch from 1907 through to 1919. The 1904 class was some thirty times as numerous as other year classes during the period (Johan Hjort, "Fluctuations in the Great Fisheries of Northern Europe," *Rapports et procès-verbaux, Conseil permanent international pour l'exploration de la mer*, Vol. XX [1914]; see also E. S. Russell, *The Overfishing Problem* [Cambridge, 1942], p. 57).

[9] See his *Resources of the Sea* published in 1899.

[10] Quoted in M. Graham, *The Fish Gate* (London, 1943), p. 111; see also T. H. Huxley, "The Herring," *Nature* (London), 1881.

tions.[11] Only recently has the pendulum begun to reverse again, and there has lately been expressed in biological quarters a high degree of skepticism concerning the efficacy of restrictive measures, and the Huxleyian faith in the inexhaustibility of the sea has once again begun to find advocates. In 1951 Dr. Harden F. Taylor summarized the over-all position of world fisheries in the following words:

Such statistics of world fisheries as are available suggest that while particular species have fluctuated in abundance, the *yield of the sea fisheries as a whole or of any considerable region has not only been sustained, but has generally increased with increasing human populations*, and there is as yet no sign that they will not continue to do so. No single species so far as we know has ever become extinct, and no regional fishery in the world has ever been exhausted.[12]

In formulating governmental policy, biologists appear to have had a hard struggle (not always successful) to avoid oversimplification of the problem. One of the crudest arguments to have had some support is known as the "propagation theory," associated with the name of the English biologist, E. W. L. Holt.[13] Holt advanced the proposition that legal size limits should be established at a level that would permit every individual of the species in question to spawn at least once. This suggestion was effectively demolished by the age-distribution studies whose results have been noted above. Moreover, some fisheries, such as the "sardine" fishery of the Canadian Atlantic Coast, are specifically for *immature* fish. The history of this particular fishery shows no evidence whatever that

the landings have been in any degree reduced by the practice of taking very large quantities of fish of prespawning age year after year.

The state of uncertainty in biological quarters around the turn of the century is perhaps indicated by the fact that Holt's propagation theory was advanced concurrently with its diametric opposite: "the thinning theory" of the Danish biologist, C. G. J. Petersen.[14] The latter argued that the fish may be too plentiful for the available food and that thinning out the young by fishing would enable the remainder to grow more rapidly. Petersen supported his theory with the results of transplanting experiments which showed that the fish transplanted to a new habitat frequently grew much more rapidly than before. But this is equivalent to arguing that the reason why rabbits multiplied so rapidly when introduced to Australia is because there were no rabbits already there with which they had to compete for food. Such an explanation would neglect all the other elements of importance in a natural ecology. In point of fact, in so far as food alone is concerned, thinning a cod population, say by half, would not double the food supply of the remaining individuals; for there are other species, perhaps not commercially valuable, that use the same food as the cod.

Dr. Burkenroad's comment, quoted earlier, that the purpose of practical policy is the benefit of man, not fish, was not gratuitous, for the argument has at times been advanced that commercial fishing should crop the resource in such a way as to leave the stocks of fish in the sea completely unchanged. Baranoff was largely responsible for destroying this

[11] See H. Scott Gordon, "The Trawler Question in the United Kingdom and Canada," *Dalhousie Review*, summer, 1951.

[12] Taylor, *op. cit.*, p. 314 (Dr. Taylor's italics).

[13] See E. W. L. Holt, "An Examination of the Grimsby Trawl Fishery," *Journal of the Marine Biological Association* (Plymouth), 1895.

[14] See C. G. J. Petersen, "What Is Overfishing?" *Journal of the Marine Biological Association* (Plymouth), 1900–1903.

approach, showing most elegantly that a commercial fishery cannot fail to diminish the fish stock. His general conclusion is worth quoting, for it states clearly not only his own position but the error of earlier thinking:

> As we see, a picture is obtained which diverges radically from the hypothesis which has been favoured almost down to the present time, namely that the natural reserve of fish is an inviolable capital, of which the fishing industry must use only the interest, not touching the capital at all. Our theory says, on the contrary, that a fishery and a natural reserve of fish are incompatible, and that the exploitable stock of fish is a changeable quantity, which depends on the intensity of the fishery. The more fish we take from a body of water, the smaller is the basic stock remaining in it; and the less fish we take, the greater is the basic stock, approximating to the natural stock when the fishery approaches zero. Such is the nature of the matter.[15]

The general conception of a fisheries ecology would appear to make such a conclusion inevitable. If a species were in ecological equilibrium before the commencement of commercial fishing, man's intrusion would have the same effect as any other predator; and that can only mean that the species population would reach a new equilibrium at a lower level of abundance, the divergence of the new equilibrium from the old depending on the degree of man's predatory effort and effectiveness.

The term "fisheries management" has been much in vogue in recent years, being taken to express a more subtle approach to the fisheries problem than the older terms "depletion" and "conservation." Briefly, it focuses attention on the quantity of fish caught, taking as the human objective of commercial fishing the derivation of the largest sustainable

catch. This approach is often hailed in the biological literature as the "new theory" or the "modern formulation" of the fisheries problem.[16] Its limitations, however, are very serious, and, indeed, the new approach comes very little closer to treating the fisheries problem as one of human utilization of natural resources than did the older, more primitive, theories. Focusing attention on the maximization of the catch neglects entirely the inputs of other factors of production which are used up in fishing and must be accounted for as costs. There are many references to such ultimate economic considerations in the biological literature but no analytical integration of the economic factors. In fact, the very conception of a *net economic yield* has scarcely made any appearance at all. On the whole, biologists tend to treat the fisherman as an exogenous element in their analytical model, and the behavior of fishermen is not made into an integrated element of a general and systematic "bionomic" theory. In the case of the fishing industry the large numbers of fishermen permit valid behavioristic generalization of their activities along the lines of the standard economic theory of production. The following section attempts to apply that theory to the fishing industry and to demonstrate that the "overfishing problem" has its roots in the economic organization of the industry.

III. ECONOMIC THEORY OF THE FISHERY

In the analysis which follows, the theory of optimum utilization of fishery re-

---

[15] T. I. Baranoff, "On the Question of the Dynamics of the Fishing Industry," p. 5 (mimeographed).

[16] See, e.g., R. E. Foerster, "Prospects for Managing Our Fisheries," *Bulletin of the Bingham Oceanographic Collection* (New Haven), May, 1948; E. S. Russell, "Some Theoretical Considerations on the Overfishing Problem," *Journal du conseil permanent international pour l'exploration de la mer*, 1931, and *The Overfishing Problem*, Lecture IV.

sources and the reasons for its frustration in practice are developed for a typical demersal fish. Demersal, or bottom-dwelling fishes, such as cod, haddock, and similar species and the various flat-fishes, are relatively nonmigratory in character. They live and feed on shallow continental shelves where the continual mixing of cold water maintains the availability of those nutrient salts which form the fundamental basis of marine-food chains. The various feeding grounds are separated by deep-water channels which constitute barriers to the movement of these species; and in some cases the fish of different banks can be differentiated morphologically, having varying numbers of vertebrae or some such distinguishing characteristic. The significance of this fact is that each fishing ground can be treated as unique, in the same sense as can a piece of land, possessing, at the very least, one characteristic not shared by any other piece: that is, location.

(Other species, such as herring, mackerel, and similar pelagic or surface dwellers, migrate over very large distances, and it is necessary to treat the resource of an entire geographic region as one. The conclusions arrived at below are applicable to such fisheries, but the method of analysis employed is not formally applicable. The same is true of species that migrate to and from fresh water and the lake fishes proper.)

We can define the optimum degree of utilization of any particular fishing ground as that which maximizes the net economic yield, the difference between total cost, on the one hand, and total receipts (or total value production), on the other.[17] Total cost and total production can each be expressed as a function of the degree of fishing intensity or, as the biologists put it, "fishing effort," so that a simple maximization solution is possible. Total cost will be a linear function of fishing effort, if we assume no fishing-induced effects on factor prices, which is reasonable for any particular regional fishery.

The production function—the relationship between fishing effort and total value produced—requires some special attention. If we were to follow the usual presentation of economic theory, we should argue that this function would be positive but, after a point, would rise at a diminishing rate because of the law of diminishing returns. This would not mean that the fish population has been reduced, for the law refers only to the *proportions* of factors to one another, and a fixed fish population, together with an increasing intensity of effort, would be assumed to show the typical sigmoid pattern of yield. However, in what follows it will be assumed that the law of diminishing returns in this pure sense is inoperative in the fishing industry. (The reasons will be advanced at a later point in this paper.) We shall assume that, as fishing effort expands, the catch of fish increases at a diminishing rate but that it does so because of the effect of catch upon the fish population.[18] So far as the argument of the next few pages is concerned, all that is formally necessary is to assume that, as fishing intensity increases, catch will grow at a diminishing rate. Whether this reflects the pure law of diminishing returns or the reduction

[17] Expressed in these terms, this appears to be the monopoly maximum, but it coincides with the social optimum under the conditions employed in the analysis, as will be indicated below.

[18] Throughout this paper the conception of fish population that is employed is one of *weight* rather than *numbers*. A good deal of the biological theory has been an effort to combine growth factors and numbers factors into weight sums. The following analysis will neglect the fact that, for some species, fish of different sizes bring different unit prices.

of population by fishing, or both, is of no particular importance. The point at issue will, however, take on more significance in Section IV and will be examined there.

Our analysis can be simplified if we retain the ordinary production function instead of converting it to cost curves, as is usually done in the theory of the firm. Let us further assume that the functional relationship between average production (production-per-unit-of-fishing-effort) and the quantity of fishing effort is uniformly linear. This does not distort the

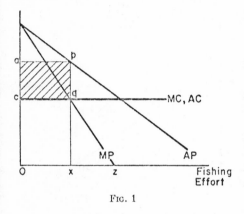

FIG. 1

results unduly, and it permits the analysis to be presented more simply and in graphic terms that are already quite familiar.

In Figure 1 the optimum intensity of utilization of a particular fishing ground is shown. The curves AP and MP represent, respectively, the average productivity and marginal productivity of fishing effort. The relationship between them is the same as that between average revenue and marginal revenue in imperfect competition theory, and MP bisects any horizontal between the ordinate and AP. Since the costs of fishing supplies, etc., are assumed to be unaffected by the amount of fishing effort, marginal cost and average cost are identical and

constant, as shown by the curve MC, AC.[19] These costs are assumed to include an opportunity income for the fishermen, the income that could be earned in other comparable employments. Then Ox is the optimum intensity of effort on this fishing ground, and the resource will, at this level of exploitation, provide the maximum net economic yield indicated by the shaded area $apqc$. The maximum sustained physical yield that the biologists speak of will be attained when marginal productivity of fishing effort is zero, at Oz of fishing intensity in the chart shown. Thus, as one might expect, the optimum economic fishing intensity is less than that which would produce the maximum sustained physical yield.

The area $apqc$ in Figure 1 can be regarded as the rent yielded by the fishery resource. Under the given conditions, Ox is the best rate of exploitation for the fishing ground in question, and the rent reflects the productivity of that ground, not any artificial market limitation. The rent here corresponds to the extra productivity yielded in agriculture by soils of better quality or location than those on the margin of cultivation, which may produce an opportunity income but no more. In short, Figure 1 shows the determination of the intensive margin of utilization on an intramarginal fishing ground.

We now come to the point that is of greatest theoretical importance in understanding the primary production phase of the fishing industry and in distinguishing it from agriculture. In the sea fish-

[19] Throughout this analysis, fixed costs are neglected. The general conclusions reached would not be appreciably altered, I think, by their inclusion, though the presentation would be greatly complicated. Moreover, in the fishing industry the most substantial portion of fixed cost—wharves, harbors, etc.—is borne by government and does not enter into the cost calculations of the operators.

eries the natural resource is not private property; hence the rent it may yield is not capable of being appropriated by anyone. The individual fisherman has no legal title to a section of ocean bottom. Each fisherman is more or less free to fish wherever he pleases. The result is a pattern of competition among fishermen which culminates in the dissipation of the rent of the intramarginal grounds. This can be most clearly seen through an analysis of the relationship between the

fishermen are free to fish on whichever ground they please, it is clear that this is not an equilibrium allocation of fishing effort in the sense of connoting stability. A fisherman starting from port and deciding whether to go to ground *1* or *2* does not care for *marginal* productivity but for *average* productivity, for it is the latter that indicates where the greater total yield may be obtained. If fishing effort were allocated in the optimum fashion, as shown in Figure 2, with *Ox* on

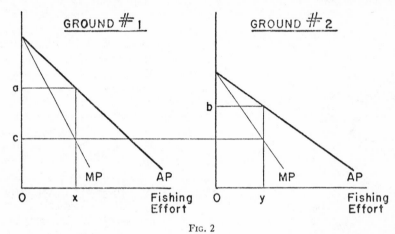

FIG. 2

intensive margin and the extensive margin of resource exploitation in fisheries.

In Figure 2, two fishing grounds of different fertility (or location) are shown. Any given amount of fishing effort devoted to ground *2* will yield a smaller total (and therefore average) product than if devoted to *1*. The maximization problem is now a question of the allocation of fishing effort between grounds *1* and *2*. The optimum is, of course, where the marginal productivities are equal on both grounds. In Figure 2, fishing effort of *Ox* on *1* and *Oy* on *2* would maximize the total net yield of *Ox* + *Oy* effort if marginal cost were equal to *Oc*. But if under such circumstances the individual

1, and *Oy* on *2*, this would be a disequilibrium situation. Each fisherman could expect to get an average catch of *Oa* on *1* but only *Ob* on *2*. Therefore, fishermen would shift from *2* to *1*. Stable equilibrium would not be reached until the average productivity of both grounds was equal. If we now imagine a continuous gradation of fishing grounds, the extensive margin would be on that ground which yielded nothing more than outlaid costs plus opportunity income—in short, the one on which average productivity and average cost were equal. But, since average cost is the same for all grounds and the average productivity of all grounds is also brought to equality by the free and competitive nature of fishing, this means that the intramarginal grounds also yield no rent. It is entirely possible that some grounds would be exploited at a level of *negative* marginal productivity. What happens is that the rent which the intramarginal grounds are capable of yielding is dissipated through misallocation of fishing effort.

This is why fishermen are not wealthy, despite the fact that the fishery resources of the sea are the richest and most indestructible available to man. By and large, the only fisherman who becomes rich is one who makes a lucky catch or one who participates in a fishery that is put under a form of social control that turns the open resource into property rights.

Up to this point, the remuneration of fishermen has been accounted for as an opportunity-cost income comparable to earnings attainable in other industries. In point of fact, fishermen typically earn less than most others, even in much less hazardous occupations or in those requiring less skill. There is no effective reason why the competition among fishermen described above must stop at the point where opportunity incomes are yielded. It may be and is in many cases carried much further. Two factors prevent an equilibration of fishermen's incomes with those of other members of society. The first is the great immobility of fishermen. Living often in isolated communities, with little knowledge of conditions or opportunities elsewhere; educationally and often romantically tied to the sea; and lacking the savings necessary to provide a "stake," the fisherman is one of the least mobile of occupational groups. But, second, there is in the spirit of every fisherman the hope of the "lucky catch." As those who know fishermen well have often testified, they

are gamblers and incurably optimistic. As a consequence, they will work for less than the going wage.[20]

The theory advanced above is substantiated by important developments in the fishing industry. For example, practically all control measures have, in the past, been designed by biologists, with sole attention paid to the production side of the problem and none to the cost side. The result has been a wide-open door for the frustration of the purposes of such measures. The Pacific halibut fishery, for example, is often hailed as a great achievement in modern fisheries management. Under international agreement between the United States and Canada, a fixed-catch limit was established during the early thirties. Since then, catch-per-unit-effort indexes, as usually interpreted, show a significant rise in the fish population. W. F. Thompson, the pioneer of the Pacific halibut management program, noted recently that "it has often been said that the halibut regulation presents the only definite case of sustained improvement of an overfished deep-sea fishery. This, I believe, is true and the fact should lend special importance to the principles which have been deliberately used to obtain this improvement."[21] Actually, careful study of the statistics indicates that the estimated recovery of halibut stocks could not have been due principally to the control measures, for the average catch was, in fact, greater during the recovery years than during the years of

[20] "The gambling instinct of the men makes many of them work for less remuneration than they would accept as a weekly wage, because there is always the possibility of a good catch and a financial windfall" (Graham, *op. cit.*, p. 86).

[21] W. F. Thompson, "Condition of Stocks of Halibut in the Pacific," *Journal du conseil permanent international pour l'exploration de la mer*, Vol. XVIII, No. 2 (August, 1952).

decline. The total amount of fish taken was only a small fraction of the estimated population reduction for the years prior to regulation.[22] Natural factors seem to be mainly responsible for the observed change in population, and the institution of control regulations almost a coincidence. Such coincidences are not uncommon in the history of fisheries policy, but they may be easily explained. If a long-term cyclical fluctuation is taking place in a commercially valuable species, controls will likely be instituted when fishing yields have fallen very low and the clamor of fishermen is great; but it is then, of course, that stocks are about due to recover in any case. The "success" of conservation measures may be due fully as much to the sociological foundations of public policy as to the policy's effect on the fish. Indeed, Burkenroad argues that biological statistics in general may be called into question on these grounds. Governments sponsor biological research when the catches are disappointing. If there are long-term cyclical fluctuations in fish populations, as some think, it is hardly to be wondered why biologists frequently discover that the sea is being depleted, only to change their collective opinion a decade or so later.

Quite aside from the *biological* argument on the Pacific halibut case, there is no clear-cut evidence that halibut fishermen were made relatively more prosperous by the control measures. Whether or not the recovery of the halibut stocks was due to natural factors or to the catch limit, the potential net yield this could have meant has been dissipated through a rise in fishing costs. Since the method of control was to halt fishing when the limit had been reached, this created a

[22] See M. D. Burkenroad, "Fluctuations in Abundance of Pacific Halibut," *Bulletin of the Bingham Oceanographic Collection*, May, 1948.

great incentive on the part of each fisherman to get the fish before his competitors. During the last twenty years, fishermen have invested in more, larger, and faster boats in a competitive race for fish. In 1933 the fishing season was more than six months long. In 1952 it took just twenty-six days to catch the legal limit in the area from Willapa Harbor to Cape Spencer, and sixty days in the Alaska region. What has been happening is a rise in the average cost of fishing effort, allowing no gap between average production and average cost to appear, and hence no rent.[23]

Essentially the same phenomenon is observable in the Canadian Atlantic Coast lobster-conservation program. The method of control here is by seasonal closure. The result has been a steady growth in the number of lobster traps set

[23] The economic significance of the reduction in season length which followed upon the catch limitation imposed in the Pacific halibut fishery has not been fully appreciated. E.g., Michael Graham said in summary of the program in 1943: "The result has been that it now takes only five months to catch the quantity of halibut that formerly needed nine. This, *of course*, has meant profit, where there was none before" (*op. cit.*, p. 156; my italics). Yet, even when biologists have grasped the economic import of the halibut program and its results, they appear reluctant to declare against it. E.g., W. E. Ricker: "This method of regulation does not necessarily make for more profitable fishing and certainly puts no effective brake on waste of effort, since an unlimited number of boats is free to join the fleet and compete during the short period that fishing is open. However, the stock is protected, and yield approximates to a maximum if quotas are wisely set; as biologists, perhaps we are not required to think any further. Some claim that any mixing into the economics of the matter might prejudice the desirable biological consequences of regulation by quotas" ("Production and Utilization of Fish Populations," in a Symposium on Dynamics of Production in Aquatic Populations, Ecological Society of America, *Ecological Monographs*, XVI [October, 1946], 385). What such "desirable biological consequences" might be, is hard to conceive. Since the regulatory policies are made by man, surely it is necessary they be evaluated in terms of human, not piscatorial, objectives.

by each fisherman. Virtually all available lobsters are now caught each year within the season, but at much greater cost in gear and supplies. At a fairly conservative estimate, the same quantity of lobsters could be caught with half the present number of traps. In a few places the fishermen have banded together into a local monopoly, preventing entry and controlling their own operations. By this means, the amount of fishing gear has been greatly reduced and incomes considerably improved.

That the plight of fishermen and the inefficiency of fisheries production stems from the common-property nature of the resources of the sea is further corroborated by the fact that one finds similar patterns of exploitation and similar problems in other cases of open resources. Perhaps the most obvious is hunting and trapping. Unlike fishes, the biotic potential of land animals is low enough for the species to be destroyed. Uncontrolled hunting means that animals will be killed for any short-range human reason, great or small: for food or simply for fun. Thus the buffalo of the western plains was destroyed to satisfy the most trivial desires of the white man, against which the long-term food needs of the aboriginal population counted as nothing. Even in the most civilized communities, conservation authorities have discovered that a bag-limit *per man* is necessary if complete destruction is to be avoided.

The results of anthropological investigation of modes of land tenure among primitive peoples render some further support to this thesis. In accordance with an evolutionary concept of cultural comparison, the older anthropological study was prone to regard resource tenure in common, with unrestricted exploitation, as a "lower" stage of development comparative with private and group property rights. However, more complete annals of primitive cultures reveal common tenure to be quite rare, even in hunting and gathering societies. Property rights in some form predominate by far, and, most important, their existence may be easily explained in terms of the necessity for orderly exploitation and conservation of the resource. Environmental conditions make necessary some vehicle which will prevent the resources of the community at large from being destroyed by excessive exploitation. Private or group land tenure accomplishes this end in an easily understandable fashion.[24] Significantly, land tenure is found to be "common" only in those cases where the hunting resource is migratory over such large areas that it cannot be regarded as husbandable by the society. In cases of group tenure where the numbers of the group are large, there is still the necessity of co-ordinating the practices of exploitation, in agricultural, as well as in hunting or gathering, economies. Thus, for example, Malinowski reported that among the Trobriand Islanders one of the fundamental principles of land tenure is the co-ordination of the productive activities of the gardeners by the person possessing magical leadership in the group.[25] Speaking generally, we may say that stable primitive cultures appear to have discovered the dangers of common-property tenure and to have de-

[24] See Frank G. Speck, "Land Ownership among Hunting Peoples in Primitive America and the World's Marginal Areas," *Proceedings of the 22nd International Congress of Americanists* (Rome, 1926), II, 323–32.

[25] B. Malinowski, *Coral Gardens and Their Magic*, Vol. I, chaps. xi and xii. Malinowski sees this as further evidence of the importance of magic in the culture rather than as a means of co-ordinating productive activity; but his discussion of the practice makes it clear that the latter is, to use Malinowski's own concept, the "function" of the institution of magical leadership, at least in this connection.

veloped measures to protect their resources. Or, if a more Darwinian explanation be preferred, we may say that only
those primitive cultures have survived
which succeeded in developing such institutions.

Another case, from a very different
industry, is that of petroleum production. Although the individual petroleum
producer may acquire undisputed lease
or ownership of the particular plot of
land upon which his well is drilled, he
shares, in most cases, a common pool of
oil with other drillers. There is, consequently, set up the same kind of competitive race as is found in the fishing
industry, with attending overexpansion
of productive facilities and gross wastage
of the resource. In the United States,
efforts to regulate a chaotic situation in
oil production began as early as 1915.
Production practices, number of wells,
and even output quotas were set by governmental authority; but it was not until
the federal "Hot Oil" Act of 1935 and
the development of interstate agreements
that the final loophole (bootlegging) was
closed through regulation of interstate
commerce in oil.

Perhaps the most interesting similar
case is the use of common pasture in the
medieval manorial economy. Where the
ownership of animals was private but the
resource on which they fed was common
(and limited), it was necessary to regulate the use of common pasture in order
to prevent each man from competing and
conflicting with his neighbors in an effort
to utilize more of the pasture for his own
animals. Thus the manor developed its
elaborate rules regulating the use of the
common pasture, or "stinting" the common: limitations on the number of animals, hours of pasturing, etc., designed
to prevent the abuses of excessive individualistic competition.[26]

There appears, then, to be some truth
in the conservative dictum that everybody's property is nobody's property.
Wealth that is free for all is valued by
none because he who is foolhardy enough
to wait for its proper time of use will only
find that it has been taken by another.
The blade of grass that the manorial
cowherd leaves behind is valueless to
him, for tomorrow it may be eaten by
another's animal; the oil left under the
earth is valueless to the driller, for another may legally take it; the fish in the
sea are valueless to the fisherman, because there is no assurance that they
will be there for him tomorrow if they
are left behind today. A factor of production that is valued at nothing in the business calculations of its users will yield
nothing in income. Common-property
natural resources are free goods for the
individual and scarce goods for society.
Under unregulated private exploitation,
they can yield no rent; that can be accomplished only by methods which make
them private property or public (government) property, in either case subject to
a unified directing power.

IV. THE BIONOMIC EQUILIBRIUM OF
THE FISHING INDUSTRY

The work of biological theory in the
fishing industry is, basically, an effort to
delineate the ecological system in which
a particular fish population is found. In
the main, the species that have been extensively studied are those which are
subject to commercial exploitation. This
is due not only to the fact that funds are
forthcoming for such research but also
because the activity of commercial fishing vessels provides the largest body of
data upon which the biologist may work.

[26] See P. Vinogradoff, *The Growth of the Manor*
[London, 1905], chap. iv; E. Lipson, *The Economic
History of England* [London, 1949], I, 72.

Despite this, however, the ecosystem of the fisheries biologist is typically one that excludes man. Or, rather, man is regarded as an exogenous factor, having influence on the biological ecosystem through his removal of fish from the sea, but the activities of man are themselves not regarded as behaviorized or determined by the other elements of a system of mutual interdependence. The large number of independent fishermen who exploit fish populations of commercial importance makes it possible to treat man as a behavior element in a larger, "bionomic," ecology, if we can find the rules which relate his behavior to the other elements of the system. Similarly, in their treatment of the principles of fisheries management, biologists have overlooked essential elements of the problem by setting maximum physical landings as the objective of management, thereby neglecting the economic factor of input cost.

An analysis of the bionomic equilibrium of the fishing industry may, then, be approached in terms of two problems. The first is to explain the nature of the equilibrium of the industry as it occurs in the state of uncontrolled or unmanaged exploitation of a common-property resource. The second is to indicate the nature of a socially optimum manner of exploitation, which is, presumably, what governmental management policy aims to achieve or promote. These two problems will be discussed in the remaining pages.

In the preceding section it was shown that the equilibrium condition of uncontrolled exploitation is such that the net yield (total value landings *minus* total cost) is zero. The "bionomic ecosystem" of the fishing industry, as we might call it, can then be expressed in terms of four variables and four equations. Let P represent the population of the particular fish species on the particular fishing bank in question; L the total quantity taken or "landed" by man, measured in value terms; E the intensity of fishing or the quantity of "fishing effort" expended; and C the total cost of making such effort. The system, then, is as follows:

$$P = P(L), \qquad (1)$$
$$L = L(P, E), \qquad (2)$$
$$C = C(E), \qquad (3)$$
$$C = L. \qquad (4)$$

Equation (4) is the equilibrium condition of an uncontrolled fishery.

The functional relations stated in equations (1), (2), and (3) may be graphically presented as shown in Figure 3. Segment *1* shows the fish population as a simple negative function of landings. In segment *2* a map of landings functions is drawn. Thus, for example, if population were P_3, effort of Oe would produce Ol of fish. For each given level of population, a larger fishing effort will result in larger landings. Each population contour is, then, a production function for a given population level. The linearity of these contours indicates that the law of diminishing returns is not operative, nor are any landings-induced price effects assumed to affect the value landings graphed on the vertical axis. These assumptions are made in order to produce the simplest determinate solution; yet each is reasonable in itself. The assumption of a fixed product price is reasonable, since our analysis deals with one fishing ground, not the fishery as a whole. The cost function represented in equation (3) and graphed in segment *3* of Figure 3 is not really necessary to the determination, but its inclusion makes the matter somewhat clearer. Fixed prices of input

95

factors—"fishing effort"—is assumed, which is reasonable again on the assumption that a small part of the total fishery is being analyzed.

Starting with the first segment, we see that a postulated catch of Ol connotes an equilibrium population in the biological ecosystem of Op. Suppose this population to be represented by the contour P_3 of segment 2. Then, given P_3, Oe is the effort required to catch the postulated landings Ol. This quantity of effort involves a total cost of Oc, as shown in segment 3 of the graph. In full bionomic

found. If the case were represented by C and L_1, the fishery would contract to zero; if by C and L_2, it would undergo an infinite expansion. Stable equilibrium requires that either the cost or the landings function be nonlinear. This condition is fulfilled by the assumption that population is reduced by fishing (eq. [1] above). The equilibrium is therefore as shown in Figure 5. Now Oe represents a fully stable equilibrium intensity of fishing.

The analysis of the conditions of stable equilibrium raises some points of general theoretical interest. In the foregoing we

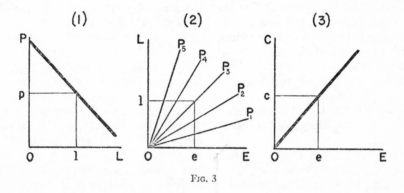

(1)   (2)   (3)

FIG. 3

equilibrium, $C = L$, and if the particular values Oc and Ol shown are not equal, other quantities of all four variables, L, P, E, and C, are required, involving movements of these variables through the functional system shown. The operative movement is, of course, in fishing effort, E. It is the equilibrating variable in the system.

The equilibrium equality of landings (L) and cost (C), however, must be a position of stability, and $L = C$ is a necessary, though not in itself sufficient, condition for stability in the ecosystem. This is shown by Figure 4. If effort-cost and effort-landings functions were both linear, no stable equilibrium could be

have assumed that stability results from the effect of fishing on the fish population. In the standard analysis of economic theory, we should have employed the law of diminishing returns to produce a landings function of the necessary shape. Market factors might also have been so employed; a larger supply of fish, forthcoming from greater fishing effort, would reduce unit price and thereby produce a landings function with the necessary negative second derivative. Similarly, greater fishing intensity might raise the unit costs of factors, producing a cost function with a positive second derivative. Any one of these three—population effects, law of diminishing re-

96

turns, or market effects—is alone sufficient to produce stable equilibrium in the ecosystem.

As to the law of diminishing returns, it has not been accepted per se by fisheries biologists. It is, in fact, a principle that becomes quite slippery when one applies it to the case of fisheries. Indicative of this is the fact that Alfred Marshall, in whose *Principles* one can find extremely little formal error, misinterprets the application of the law of dimin-

estingly enough, his various criticisms of the indexes were generally accepted, with the significant exception of this one point. More recently, A. G. Huntsman warned his colleagues in fisheries biology that "[there] may be a decrease in the take-per-unit-of-effort without any decrease in the total take or in the fish population. . . . This may mean that there has been an increase in fishermen rather than a decrease in fish."[29] While these statements run in terms of average

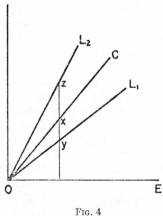

FIG. 4

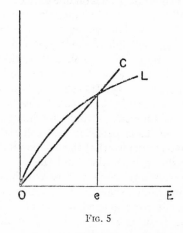

FIG. 5

ishing returns to the fishing industry, arguing, in effect, that the law exerts its influence through the reducing effect of fishing on the fish population.[27] There have been some interesting expressions of the law or, rather, its essential varying-proportions-of-factors aspect, in the biological literature. H. M. Kyle, a German biologist, included it in 1928 among a number of reasons why catch-per-unit-of-fishing-effort indexes are not adequate measures of population change.[28] Inter-

rather than marginal yield, their underlying reasoning clearly appears to be that of the law of diminishing returns. The point has had little influence in biological circles, however, and when, two years ago, I advanced it, as Kyle and Huntsman had done, in criticism of the standard biological method of estimating population change, it received pretty short shrift.

[27] See H. Scott Gordon, "On a Misinterpretation of the Law of Diminishing Returns in Alfred Marshall's *Principles*," *Canadian Journal of Economics and Political Science*, February, 1952.

[28] "Die Statistik der Seefischerei Nordeuropas," *Handbuch der Seefischerei Nordeuropas* (Stuttgart, 1928).

[29] A. G. Huntsman, "Fishing and Assessing Populations," *Bulletin of the Bingham Oceanographic Collection* (New Haven), May, 1948.

In point of fact, the law of diminishing returns is much more difficult to sustain in the case of fisheries than in agriculture or industry. The "proof" one finds in standard theory is not empirical, although the results of empirical experiments in agriculture are frequently adduced as subsidiary corroboration. The main weight of the law, however, rests on a *reductio ad absurdum*. One can easily demonstrate that, were it not for the law of diminishing returns, all the world's food could be grown on one acre of land. Reality is markedly different, and it is because the law serves to render this reality intelligible to the logical mind, or, as we might say, "explains" it, that it occupies such a firm place in the body of economic theory. In fisheries, however, the pattern of reality can easily be explained on other grounds. In the case at least of developed demersal fisheries, it cannot be denied that the fish population is reduced by fishing, and this relationship serves perfectly well to explain why an infinitely expansible production is not possible from a fixed fishing area. The other basis on which the law of diminishing returns is usually advanced in economic theory is the prima facie plausibility of the principle as such; but here, again, it is hard to grasp any similar reasoning in fisheries. In the typical agricultural illustration, for example, we may argue that the fourth harrowing or the fourth weeding, say, has a lower marginal productivity than the third. Such an assertion brings ready acceptance because it concerns a process with a zero productive limit. It is apparent that, ultimately, the land would be completely broken up or the weeds completely eliminated if harrowing or weeding were done in ever larger amounts. The law of diminishing returns signifies simply that such a zero limit is *gradually approached*, all of which appears to be quite acceptable on prima facie grounds. There is nothing comparable to this in fisheries at all, for there is no "cultivation" in the same sense of the term, except, of course, in such cases as oyster culture or pond rearing of fish, which are much more akin to farming than to typical sea fisheries.

In the biological literature the point has, I think, been well thought through, though the discussion does not revolve around the "law of diminishing returns" by that name. It is related rather to the fisheries biologist's problem of the interpretation of catch-per-unit-of-fishing-effort statistics. The essence of the law is usually eliminated by the assumption that there is no "competition" among units of fishing gear—that is, that the ratio of gear to fishing area and/or fish population is small. In some cases, corrections have been made by the use of the compound-interest formula where some competition among gear units is considered to exist.[30] Such corrections, however, appear to be based on the idea of an increasing catch-population ratio rather than an increasing effort-population ratio. The latter would be as the law of diminishing returns would have it; the idea lying behind the former is that the total population in existence represents the maximum that can be caught, and, since this maximum would be gradually approached, the ratio of catch to population has some bearing on the efficiency of fishing gear. It is, then, just an aspect of the population-reduction effect. Similarly, it has been pointed out that, since fish are recruited into the

[30] See, e.g., W. F. Thompson and F. H. Bell, *Biological Statistics of the Pacific Halibut Fishery, No. 2: Effect of Changes in Intensity upon Total Yield and Yield per Unit of Gear: Report of the International Fisheries Commission* (Seattle, 1934).

catchable stock in a seasonal fashion, one can expect the catch-per-unit-effort to fall as the fishing season progresses, at least in those fisheries where a substantial proportion of the stock is taken annually. Seasonal averaging is therefore necessary in using the catch-effort sta-

the fishery, nor is there any prima facie ground for its acceptance.

Let us now consider the exploitation of a fishing ground under unified control, in which case the equilibrium condition is the maximization of net financial yield, $L - C$.

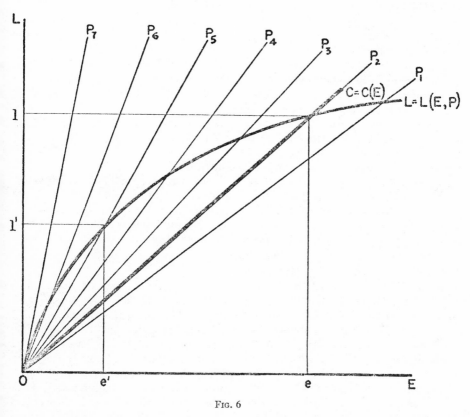

FIG. 6

tistics as population indexes from year to year. This again is a population-reduction effect, not the law of diminishing returns. In general, there seems to be no reason for departing from the approach of the fisheries biologist on this point. The law of diminishing returns is not necessary to explain the conditions of stable equilibrium in a static model of

The map of population contours graphed in segment 2 of Figure 3 may be superimposed upon the total-landings and total-cost functions graphed in Figure 5. The result is as shown in Figure 6. In the system of interrelationships we have to consider, population changes affect, and are in turn affected by, the amount of fish landed. The map of population contours does not include this roundabout effect that a population change has upon itself. The curve labeled L, however, is a landings function which accounts for the fact that larger landings reduce the population, and this is why it is shown to have a steadily diminishing slope. We may regard the landings function as moving progressively to lower population contours P_7, P_6, P_5, etc., as total landings increase in magnitude. As a consequence, while each population contour represents many hypothetical combinations of E, L, and P, only one such combination on each is actually compatible in this system of interrelationships. This combination is the point on any contour where that contour is met by the landings function L. Thus the curve labeled L may be regarded as tracing out a series of combinations of E, L, and P which are compatible with one another in the system.

The total-cost function may be drawn as shown, with total cost, C, measured in terms of landings, which the vertical axis represents.[31] This is a linear function of effort as shown. The optimum intensity of fishing effort is that which maximizes $L - C$. This is the monopoly solution; but, since we are considering only a single fishing ground, no price effects are introduced, and the social optimum coincides with maximum monopoly revenue. In this case we are maximizing the yield of a natural resource, not a privileged position, as in standard monopoly theory. The rent here is a social surplus yielded by the resource, not in any part due to artificial scarcity, as is monopoly profit or rent.

If the optimum fishing intensity is that which maximizes $L - C$, this is seen to

be the position where the slope of the landings function equals the slope of the cost function in Figure 6. Thus the optimum fishing intensity is Oe' of fishing effort. This will yield Ol' of landings, and the species population will be in continuing stable equilibrium at a level indicated by P_5.

The equilibrium resulting from uncontrolled competitive fishing, where the rent is dissipated, can also be seen in Figure 6. This, being where $C = L$, is at Oe of effort and Ol of landings, and at a stable population level of P_2. As can be clearly seen, the uncontrolled equilibrium means a higher expenditure of effort, higher fish landings, and a lower continuing fish population than the optimum equilibrium.

Algebraically, the bionomic ecosystem may be set out in terms of the optimum solution as follows. The species population in equilibrium is a linear function of the amount of fish taken from the sea:

$$P = a - bL . \qquad (1)$$

In this function, a may be described as the "natural population" of the species—the equilibrium level it would attain if not commercially fished. All natural factors, such as water temperatures, food supplies, natural predators, etc., which affect the population are, for the purposes of the system analyzed, locked up in a. The magnitude of a is the vertical intercept of the population function graphed in segment 1 of Figure 3. The slope of this function is b, which may be described as the "depletion coefficient," since it indicates the effect of catch on population. The landings function is such that no landings are forthcoming with either zero effort or zero population; therefore,

$$L = cEP . \qquad (2)$$

[31] More correctly, perhaps, C and L are both measured in money terms.

$\gamma\mu\gamma$

The parameter c in this equation is the technical coefficient of production or, as we may call it simply, the "production coefficient." Total cost is a function of the amount of fishing effort.

$$C = qE.$$

The optimum condition is that the total net receipts must be maximized, that is,

$$L - C \text{ to be maximized.}$$

Since q has been assumed constant and equal to unity (i.e., effort is counted in "dollars-worth" units), we may write $L - E$ to be maximized. Let this be represented by R:

$$R = L - E, \qquad (3)$$

$$\frac{dR}{dE} = 0. \qquad (4)$$

The four numbered equations constitute the system when in optimality equilibrium. In order to find this optimum, the landings junction (2) may be rewritten, with the aid of equation (1), as:

$$L = cE(a - bL).$$

From this we have at once

$$L(1 + cEb) = cEa,$$

$$L = \frac{caE}{1 + cbE}.$$

To find the optimum intensity of effort, we have, from equation (3):

$$\frac{dR}{dE} = \frac{dL}{dE} - \frac{dE}{dE}$$

$$= \frac{(1 + cbE)(ca) - caE(cb)}{(1 + cbE)^2} - 1,$$

$$= \frac{ca}{(1 + cbE)^2} - 1;$$

for a maximum, this must be set equal to zero; hence,

$$ca = (1 + cbE)^2,$$

$$1 + cbE = \pm \sqrt{ca},$$

$$E = \frac{-1 \pm \sqrt{ca}}{cb}.$$

For positive E,

$$E = \frac{\sqrt{ca} - 1}{cb}.$$

This result indicates that the effect on optimum effort of a change in the production coefficient is uncertain, a rise in c calling for a rise in E in some cases and a fall in E in others, depending on the magnitude of the change in c. The effects of changes in the natural population and depletion coefficient are, however, clear, a rise (fall) in a calling for a rise (fall) in E, while a rise (fall) in b means a fall (rise) in E.

COMMON PROPERTY RESOURCES AND
FACTOR ALLOCATION

J. A. CRUTCHFIELD

Two recent articles by Professors H. Scott Gordon and Anthony Scott present an interesting analysis of the conditions for economic maximization in a renewable resource industry the primary raw material for which is drawn from the public domain.[1] While their criticism of the concepts which now govern fishery conservation programmes will be generally accepted among the handful of economists dealing with the fishing industry, some aspects of the problem call for additional consideration. In this paper I should like to elaborate and modify the general outlines of the analysis, largely in terms of a specific and important case: the Pacific halibut fishery.[2]

I

As Gordon and Scott point out, the core of the "over-fishing" problem inheres in the fact that the basic resource is incapable of ownership in any meaningful sense.[3] When the demand for a given species exceeds the level at which supplies can be drawn from local waters at relatively constant costs, further exploitation of the fishery gives rise to higher costs at both intensive and extensive margins. The catch per unit of fishing effort will decline in the closer, more populous grounds as stocks are reduced, and greater costs must be incurred in pushing fishing activities to more distant grounds. If the grounds could be and were privately owned, the incremental income resulting from, say, secular growth in demand would, of course, accrue as rent in a purely Ricardian sense. Since they are not, and since there are no substantive barriers to the entry of new vessels, the increasing aggregate returns will simply be dissipated in excess capacity and higher monetary and real costs. If the reduction in stocks, viewed with grave alarm by biologist and legislator alike, now gives rise to restrictions on the catch designed to hold fish populations at some predetermined level or to rebuild them, the increases in price, aggregate returns, and excess capacity will continue. There is obviously no assurance that the final effect on economic output over time relative to total factor inputs is the same, better, or worse than in the absence of such restrictions. Moreover, if the industry group is defined, as I think it should be, to include at least waterfront buyers and processors as well as fishermen, the

[1]H. Scott Gordon, "The Economic Theory of a Common-Property Resource: The Fishery," *Journal of Political Economy*, LXII, April, 1954, 124–42; and Anthony Scott, "The Fishery: The Objectives of Sole Ownership," *Journal of Political Economy*, LXIII, April, 1955, 116–24.

[2]For a more general discussion of conservation measures affecting this and other Pacific Coast fisheries see James A. Crutchfield, "Conservation and Allocation in the Pacific Coast Fisheries," *Proceedings of the Western Economics Association*, 1955, 69–72.

[3]The only exceptions of importance are the shellfish "farming" operations in inshore waters, such as the oyster fisheries of the Pacific Northwest and Middle Atlantic areas.

CANADIAN JOURNAL OF ECONOMICS AND POLITICAL SCIENCE, 1956, Vol. 22, pp. 292–3(

economic repercussions go far beyond those sketched in Gordon's simplified model. The serious degree of distortion in the utilization of resources may be usefully illustrated by reference to the Pacific halibut fishery.

The Pacific halibut is a large, slow-growing demersal fish taken in quantity along the continental shelf of the North Pacific from Oregon to the Bering Sea. American and Canadian fishermen have exploited it intensively since the turn of the century largely because its excellent flavour, texture, and durability in cold storage enable them to sell it profitably in the national shipping markets centred in Chicago, New York, and Boston.

Landings reached a peak of 68,756,000 pounds in 1915, but never exceeded 57,000,000 pounds thereafter under unrestricted fishing despite a marked increase in the number, range, and efficiency of vessels engaged in the fishery.[4] By the middle twenties both Canadian and American authorities had become seriously concerned over reductions in the stocks of halibut, as evidenced by the declining average weight and age of the fish taken and the progressively lower yields per unit of fishing effort.[5] After prolonged negotiation, the two countries ratified a convention providing funds for intensive biological research. Later an international commission was established, vested with power to establish fishing seasons, closed "nursery" areas, and quotas by area, and to regulate the types of gear employed.[6] Since 1933, landings of halibut have been determined entirely by administrative orders of the Commission, and the full quota has been taken in each year, despite very wide variations in the prices paid to fishermen.[7]

The programme has been hailed as an outstanding success in the field of conservation. The Commission has allowed only gradual increases in total landings, but the catch per unit of fishing effort and the average weight and age of fish taken have shown a gratifying recovery. In this respect it seems likely that Gordon has under-estimated the potential economic benefits of this conservation programme. It is, unfortunately, limited entirely to the objective of maintaining the stock of fish, but at least it is soundly conceived in terms of that objective.[8] While I have reservations about resolving a controversy by counting heads on either side, I am assured by competent fishery biologists—including some not connected with the halibut programme—that current professional opinion leans heavily toward the view that stocks of slow-growing

[4]For a complete and recently revised series showing halibut landings, by area of origin, from 1888 to 1950, see *Report of the International Fisheries Commission*, no. 17 (Seattle, Wash., 1952), 10–11.

[5]In the Pacific halibut fishery, virtually all fish are taken on anchored ground lines or "skates" to which baited hooks are attached at intervals. The "unit of fishing effort" is therefore readily defined as a given fishing period for a standard skate of long-line gear.

[6]The International Pacific Halibut Commission exercises its powers subject, of course, to the approval of the Governor General in Council of Canada and the President of the United States.

[7]The Commission announces opening dates in advance of each season (usually in April or May). Closing dates for each regulatory area are announced when it appears that the quota will be filled by vessels then at sea. Weighted average prices of dressed halibut landed at Seattle ranged from $.075 per pound in 1934 to $.227 in 1952. Even in the post-war years annual prices fluctuated between $.207 and $.267.

[8]It may be contrasted, for example, with the Bristol Bay salmon programme, under which fishing was restricted to sailing craft only until very recently.

immobile bottom fish such as halibut can be seriously impaired by over-fishing. No convincing case has yet been made for the opinion that there were natural causes for the dramatic decline and subsequent recovery of the Pacific halibut populations. It is particularly difficult to explain on that basis the fact that stocks fell most rapidly and recovered most fully in precisely the areas where there was the most fishing. This matter aside, however, Gordon is quite correct in concluding that a programme designed to hold landings below levels which would be forthcoming on a free market will necessarily involve serious economic costs unless specific remedial measures are undertaken. In the case in point, the Commission clearly defines its role to exclude any consideration of such measures. Given the reasonable assumption that the demand for halibut will increase slowly over time, the types of "hidden costs" which result from the establishment of quotas may be elaborated as follows.

1. Since the total catch is fixed, the individual vessel's share will be largest if maximum fishing is maintained during the season permitted. Assuming a secular increase in the demand for halibut and stability in the general level of prices, the total proceeds will increase and the quota will be filled by successively larger numbers of vessels, each taking fewer fish in a shorter period of time. The effect is not only to waste resources in over-capacity, but to force the industry into combination vessels that can be used for other purposes. This simply generalizes over-capacity by forcing participants in other fisheries to diversify their operations. The net result is obviously duplication of gear, and a composite fleet less efficient in over-all terms than one including boats best adapted to each specialized operation.[9]

2. The shortening of the halibut season necessarily increases the aggregate costs of handling and marketing, since the proportion of the total catch that must be frozen and the average period of frozen storage will be greater. In addition, quality must suffer somewhat; at best, freezing can only arrest deterioration, and no frozen fish can be held more than a few months without some loss of flavour and texture. The problem of quality is accentuated further by the fact that each boat continues fishing as long as possible whenever the imminent closing of the season would preclude another trip to the grounds.

3. The geographic structure of the halibut operation, fairly typical of deep-sea fisheries, provides a further difficulty. The maximization of net returns to each primary producing unit depends primarily on the ability of each unit to secure the largest possible share of the total catch. Landings will therefore be concentrated in the ports nearest the fishing grounds whenever the net value of the additional poundage that can be secured from one or more extra trips to the grounds is sufficient to offset inter-port price differentials; and these differentials cannot exceed the cost of available transportation and handling. The concentration of landings also imposes greater peak loads on freezing and storage facilities, particularly since the peak periods for halibut are the same as for the other products in the Alaska ports to which the halibut landings are

---

[9]Flexibility in the use of fishing craft may well be desirable in so far as normal fishing conditions and relative price changes make some mobility among different fisheries essential. However, diversification in the Pacific Coast fisheries appears to have gone beyond these requirements.

being diverted. It is apparent that the present distribution of landings among ports would yield minimum total costs for the entire processing and marketing sequence only by sheer accident, and probably increases them significantly.

The seriousness of these practices is evident from the following figures. The number of vessels fishing primarily for halibut in season increased from 384 to 854 between 1933 and 1950, an increase of 122.4 per cent, while the total catch rose only 23.1 per cent. In terms of total fishing intensity, the effects were even more pronounced. No official figures are available, but it is estimated that the number of boats landing occasional fares of halibut increased more than 400 per cent from 1933 to 1949. Meanwhile the fishing season, 268 days in 1933, was reduced in 1953 to 24 days in one of the principal grounds and 55 days in the other. Landings in Alaska, 14.9 per cent of the total catch in 1934, reached 44.2 per cent in 1950. Landings in Prince Rupert, B.C., rose from 16.6 per cent to 26.6 per cent in the same period. Seattle, the principal entrepôt serving the national market, received directly only 12.9 per cent in 1949 as compared to 42.5 per cent in 1934. The additional burden on facilities for freezing is reflected in the fact that 82.9 per cent of the catch was frozen in 1950, in contrast to 45.3 per cent in 1933.[10] The huge increase in freezing cannot, of course, be attributed entirely to the conservation pro-gramme. Rapid technological progress in processing and marketing frozen fish, particularly in pre-packaged form, is partly responsible. Nevertheless, a very substantial majority of frozen halibut is marketed in bulk, in precisely the same form (except for freezing) as the fresh product: a fact which is widely deplored in the industry as contributing directly to higher costs and inferior quality in some of the markets served.

Thus the degree to which economic efficiency in the fishing industry is im-paired by the absence of the allocative function normally performed by implicit or explicit rent may be considerably greater than Gordon's brief statement implied. The readjustment of the entire marketing operation to an artificially shortened season is an inevitable result of the present technique of control. It is also apparent that mutual penetration of fisheries by under-employed factors tends quickly to generalize the problem of under-utilization. The combined effects on supply of increasing population, higher prices, and legal and biological restrictions have produced a high amount of over-capacity in the entire Pacific Coast fishing industry. The number of licensed boats and vessels rose from a low of 7,439 in 1934 to 11,496 in 1950 despite a slight decline in total landings.[11] The same tendency toward over-expansion is evident in each of the specialized fisheries for which data are available. It may be noted that these figures typically understate the seriousness of the problem in two respects. First, they include only licensed vessels, and thus ignore craft which are idle and therefore not licensed. Secondly, there is no

[10]James A. Crutchfield, "Conservation and Allocation in the Pacific Coast Fisheries," 70–1. Data are from annual yearbooks of the *Pacific Fisherman.*

[11]U.S. Dept. of the Interior, Fish and Wildlife Service, *Fishery Statistics of the United States, 1950* (Washington, D.C.: U.S. Government Printing Office, 1953). Total landings in 1950 were 2 per cent below those in 1934 largely because of sharply reduced stocks of pilchards, salmon, and mackerel. Only a continued increase in landings of tuna, most of which are caught in waters off Central America, has prevented a more marked decline.

ready way to measure changes in productivity. Yet it is clear that improvements in hulls, engines, auxiliary power units, and depth-finding and navigation gear have resulted in marked increases in the range and operating efficiency of Pacific Coast fishing vessels in the past two decades.

II

In addition to their implications for the efficient use of resources in the entire halibut operation, limitations on the supply of fish, whether legal or biological, exert a vital influence on price formation and price policy in dockside markets through their effect on the supply function of primary producers. Again taking the halibut fishery as a case in point, we may safely assume that the annual catch consistent with a sustained or increasing fish population is lower (in the short run) than that which would be taken in the absence of restrictions; otherwise no conservation problem would exist. The imposition of restrictions on the catch would thus imply creation of, or increase in, excess capacity in the fishing fleet. The number of vessels and men remaining in the fishery would be stabilized at a level where higher prices were sufficiently offset by under-utilization to equate returns (including an imputed return for leisure) in halibut fishing and alternative occupations. In the absence of barriers to entry, subsequent increases in demand, if in excess of the permitted annual increase in output, would result in continued increases in excess capacity.[12] In the case of a conservation programme restricting output of a renewable resource capable of private ownership, this result would not ensue, since a rental increment would accrue to the owner of the resource and would constitute an implicit or explicit cost to the individual harvester. In the case of the fisheries, the nature of the resource precludes private ownership and the effects on entry and capacity of increasing scarcity-returns could be forestalled only by some form of direct control.

It follows, therefore, that the imposition of an effective quota by the regulatory body implies the existence of a range within which supply is virtually inelastic to price: a range which would increase as the disparity between "free-market" short-run output and the quota increases. Any reduction in prices paid for fish would result ultimately in some egress, but the remaining vessels, at higher rates of utilization, would then receive necessary minimum earnings, and the quota would still be taken, though over a longer period of time.[13] The supply function could assume some degree of elasticity only if prices were reduced to the point where the alternatives of idleness or other occupations reduced the fleet below levels at which the quota could be taken by vessels fishing halibut on a full-time basis.

The present status of the halibut fishery suggests that the price elasticity of supply might be low over a rather wide range. The number of regular halibut boats has increased far more rapidly than the permitted catch. The secretary

12As a result either of new construction or the utilization of idle capacity in other fisheries which would otherwise be reduced in the long run.

13A longer period of time would, of course, be distinctly desirable from the standpoint of the buyer-shipper. Since deliveries must be spread over the full year, aggregate storage charges and deterioration in quality would be reduced by more equal distribution of landings.

of the Seattle Fishing Vessel Owners' Association estimates that approximately one-third of the regular halibut vessels are idle between seasons, while the remainder are largely under-utilized in fisheries for which they are imperfectly adapted, or on charter. Moreover, the principal alternative fisheries—bottom-fish trawling, albacore, and shark—have been relatively unprofitable during the post-war years, and could absorb only a few additional units. Since the initiation of rigid restrictions on the catch, the full quota has been taken every year despite substantial variations in year-to-year prices to fishermen.

The actual results of this type of supply situation cannot be discussed, even in qualitative terms, without explicit analysis of the nature and degree of competition in the markets for fresh fish at the dockside. If entry is unrestricted and dockside markets are perfectly competitive, dealers' margins will be held to a necessary minimum and the number of primary producers will increase until returns at the margin (including a valuation for leisure) are equated with those in alternative occupations. In addition to causing over-capacity in the fisheries proper, the tendency to shorten the fishing season would require larger freezing and storage capacity, higher unit costs to cover the longer average storage period, and some loss of quality in the product.

If the dockside markets were purely monopsonistic and the entry of new dealers could be forestalled completely, excessive profits would be retained by purchasers. Thus the effects on the distribution of income would be generally undesirable but the increase in real costs indicated above would be minimized. On the more realistic assumption that new entry could not be prevented entirely, excess capacity in the dealers' group, probably accompanied by higher prices to fishermen, would ensue. The development of factor monopoly, likely under these conditions if it were legally sanctioned, would leave price indeterminate, but probably at a level above that prevailing under monopsony or oligopsony. Its effects on capacity would depend on the willingness and ability of the producers' organization to restrict entry. Mal-allocation could be minimized, therefore, only under conditions which would give rise to unacceptably large monopoloid returns. Since neither producers nor dealers are likely to possess complete control over new entry, in practice conservation programmes limited to specification of a maximum catch are likely to be accompanied by somewhat higher returns to fishermen in the regulated fisheries, some excess capacity in both fishing and marketing sectors, and persistent unrest in relations among members of those sectors.

It is thus evident that some degree of divergence from optimum rates and methods of utilizing the fishery resource will result whenever the supply function of producers becomes inelastic, whether through natural or administrative limitation. But the nature and degree of mal-allocation of factors and/or mal-distribution of income cannot be determined except in terms of a rather detailed investigation of market structures and of competition in the waterfront markets. Only a few detailed studies of this sort have been undertaken, but these suggest strongly that the traditional assumption of atomistic behaviour in the fishing industry is untenable in most instances.[14] Though the number and

14Cf.: Donald J. White, *The New England Fishing Industry* (Cambridge, Mass., 1954); Federal Trade Commission, *Report on Distribution Methods and Costs*, Part VIII, *Cost of*

107

size of primary producers and processor-shippers is relatively large in total (even within semi-separate regional industry groups), waterfront markets for fresh fish are not coextensive with markets for final products. In the former, the pronounced immobility of fishermen, and the inefficiency of the average fishing boat as a carrier, limit fishermen to a handful of alternative ports and buyers' groups. Consequently, though processors and primary distributors of fish are rarely large-scale firms by conventional standards, they bulk very large in relation to aggregate purchases in individual dockside markets. Both the continued bitterness and unrest which characterize the relationships between dealers and fishermen on both coasts and a series of anti-trust actions against both groups attest the fact that these markets persistently deviate from purely competitive behaviour.

A detailed analysis of the nature and degree of these deviations is beyond the scope of this paper. In the halibut fishery, as a case in point, it may be noted that the concentration of purchases in each port is very high;[15] that only a portion of the halibut fleet can move freely among the ports; and that many of the same buyers operate in several of the ports extending from Seattle to westward Alaska. It is not surprising, therefore, to find that the Antitrust Division has twice brought actions against dealers for collusive buying practices.[16] While overt collusion in buying has presumably been abandoned, there remains considerable doubt about the independence of bidding on auctions where the four largest purchasers account for two-thirds or more of the total catch.

The rapid increase in the number of halibut vessels and fishermen after 1935 suggests that the dealers' group was unable or unwilling to enforce fully monopsonistic buying policies despite close association on the various fish exchanges, conventional bidding and costing, and effective control over entry in the major ports.[17] Undoubtedly fear of adverse public reaction and of possible union or co-operative action, as well as legal sanctions, have also restricted the implementation of co-ordinated purchasing. On the other hand, the evidence underlying the anti-trust action of 1941-2 indicates clearly that much of the tendency toward non-aggressive buying is not dependent upon explicit collusion, helpful though it might be. The moderate expansion in the number

---

Production and Distribution of Fish in New England (Washington, D.C.: U.S. Government Printing Office, 1945), 46–64; California C.I.O. Council, Research Division, *The Fisheries of California* (mimeo.) (San Francisco, Calif., 1947); Stuart Jamieson and Percy Gladstone, "Unionism in the Fishing Industry of British Columbia," this JOURNAL, XVI, no. 1, Feb., 1950, 1–11; and James A. Crutchfield, "The Economics of the Pacific Coast Fresh Market Fishing Industry" (unpublished doctoral dissertation, University of California, Dept. of Economics, 1954), chaps. v, vi, and viii.

[15]The four largest dealers in Seattle purchased 72.4 per cent of total landings between 1951 and 1953. In other ports the percentage ranged from 86.8 to 100.

[16]See particularly *United States* v. *Seattle Fish Exchange, Inc., et al.,* Civil 612 District Court of the United States for Western District of Washington, Northern Division 1941. Both this and an earlier case involving the same companies were settled by pleas o *nolo contendere* and acceptance of consent decrees.

[17]Only members of the exchange could bid for fish, and admission to the exchange required a two-thirds' vote of the membership. No new buyers were admitted to the Seattle exchange until it was reorganized on an open basis under the terms of the 1942 consent decree.

of waterfront bidders for halibut after the 1942 consent decree is probably an indication of the fact that over-capacity, resulting in part from the conservation programme, is distributed among both producers and dealers.

III

As is true of much marginal analysis, the formal conditions for economic maximization in the fisheries, though useful as an explanatory device, are not readily quantifiable. Moreover, from the standpoint of political economy, the legislative environment in which current measures of conservation are formulated will rarely permit more than a crude approximation to any idealized solution, however elegant its logic. We may therefore move more rapidly toward the goal of more economical use of the sea fisheries if our specific recommendations of policy fly less vigorously in the face of the biologist and can be advanced and defended in quantitative terms. If we assume—correctly, in my opinion—that the demand for Pacific halibut will continue to increase secularly, a programme limiting output to the level of maximum sustained physical yield might not deviate too far from the social optimum if entry could be curbed. Such a programme is at least within the realm of possibility in the halibut fishery. On the basis of present data, the International Pacific Halibut Commission can determine within reasonable limits the maximum physical output and the number of vessels, fully employed over the months in which weather conditions permit fishing, required to take that quota.

If the regulatory authority were also empowered to limit the number of primary producers, presumably to such a degree that the quota could be filled by fully utilized vessels within the period in which natural conditions permit fishing, the most serious allocation problem could be minimized. Since effective organization of this limited group for bargaining purposes would be fairly easy, even in a loose co-operative form, the bulk of the ensuing scarcity-returns would accrue to fishermen. Given this authority, however, it would also appear possible and desirable to restrict the effects on income of a rigid licensing policy by a licence tax or by competitive bidding for licences. The disposition of logging, grazing, and mineral rights in publicly owned land provides some precedent for this procedure.

Implementation of a programme of this sort would, of course, encounter formidable obstacles. From a purely technical standpoint, it would require very close co-operation among the variety of regulatory agencies sharing jurisdiction over the American and Canadian fisheries. Even where authority is centred in a single body, as is the case in the halibut fishery, concurrence of Canadian and American members on the number of licences to be allotted each country would be difficult to obtain, particularly since the Canadian catch has increased steadily since 1932. In other fisheries, carried on in waters subject to state and provincial authority, concurrence of all regulatory bodies would be even more essential, since the standards of the most liberal agency would tend to govern. The industry itself would also present problems arising largely out of interests specific to particular groups and localities. Alaska dealers, for example, would be loath to accept any proposal which would reduce the pressure to land halibut in ports closest to the fishing grounds.

Waterfront buyers in general would view with trepidation the obvious strengthening of the bargaining position of fishermen's organizations limited in numbers and free of potential entry under law. Producers excluded from the fisheries might object with some cogency that restrictive licensing would force them to liquidate investments in vessels and gear under highly unfavourable circumstances. However, these difficulties are perhaps less imposing today than in even the recent past. The Commission has demonstrated an impressive ability to harmonize conflicting sectional interests, and has thus earned a respect for its competence and impartiality that might be sufficient to keep the support of the industry should it be given the extended powers indicated. Though in the past the record of co-operation among state fishery conservation authorities has been spotty, in recent years co-ordination of research efforts, increasing awareness of the interrelationships among fishing activities in the several states, and mounting concern over depletion have increased the possibility of mutual action.

The difficulties involved in securing sufficient support from the industry for control measurers that go beyond the "purely biological aspects of conservation" are likely to be greater, but need not be considered insurmountable if the necessary restrictions are imposed in a manner that permits gradual and orderly disinvestment in equipment and minimizes forced occupational shifts of currently active fishermen. The critical state of the Bristol Bay salmon population has already resulted in the acceptance by industry and union of a drastic curtailment of operating units in that area, and a proposal that the United States Fish and Wildlife Service be empowered to limit the number of fishermen is being given serious consideration. Proposals made by the industry to extend the halibut fishing season by splitting fishing periods or by granting the Commission power to control the rates at which individual vessels can fish represent a limited attempt to solve the problems suggested in this study. Though they do not strike at the heart of these problems, they may be taken as indicative of a growing concern among fishermen, vessel owners, and marketers over the heavy economic costs of the present programme.

There appear, therefore, to be grounds for cautious optimism with respect to the prospects for gradual reduction of the costs associated with fishery conservation. One can only hope that the long-run benefits of such a programme to the industry as well as to the general public may be perceived before the distortions of the economic structure of the fisheries resulting from restrictions on the catch proceed as far as they have in the past. The analysis in this paper points inevitably to the conclusion that the basic difficulty is not self-correcting and is likely to become more pressing with the passage of time.

PART III.   RESOURCE CONSERVATION

PRINCIPLES OF RESOURCE CONSERVATION POLICY

Committee on Soil and Water Conservation of the Agricultural Board

Introduction

CONSERVATION means many things to many people. Its meanings include prevention of waste, maximum development, efficient use, sustained yield, preservation, and nonuse.

Today, production practices, income-increasing measures, and all forms of resource development often are bundled together under the cloak of conservation. Over the years, billions of dollars of public funds have been spent in a broad spectrum of activities bearing the conservation label. Though many desirable objectives have been achieved, there still remain many serious conflicts and confusions in conservation policies and programs.

Soil and water conservation is only a part of the larger field of resource development and management. The Committee holds the view that a unifying concept and a framework amenable to analysis are needed to evaluate research and policy in resource development. The present report is an attempt of a group which has had experience in the fields of soil science, engineering, plant science, hydrology, and economics to formulate a framework which can guide policy development and to provide a factual and logical foundation for sound conservation in the years ahead.

PRINCIPLES OF RESOURCE CONSERVATION POLICY WITH SOME APPLICATIONS TO SOIL AND WATER RESOURCES, Publication 885, Agricultural Board, National Academy of Sciences — National Research Council, Washington, D.C. 1961.

Nature and Objectives
of Conservation

MEANING OF CONSERVATION

PICTURE a field on a fertile but shallow soil. Under routine farming practices the crop yield may be adequate but not extraordinary. In any one season the yield could be materially increased by the application of more fertilizer, intensive weed control, moisture conservation, and other production practices derived from research.

If this field were allowed to erode over a period of years, the potential productivity of the soil could be seriously impaired. If, after such impairment, the practices mentioned above were exercised, the maximum productivity would be far less than before. This degeneration in productivity potential would result in decreased production under any particular set of farming practices. The deterioration deprives the operator of some yield potential in any particular season. It also results in higher product prices to consumers and restricts future productivity available for unknown contingencies. Prevention of this deterioration is one aspect of conservation.

Actions taken to prevent the deterioration of potential productivity would not necessarily increase the yield in the individual year during which such actions were taken. Investments in terracing, contour strip cropping, gully control, or conversion to permanent cover might not increase yields that year, or even perhaps within the next few years. These resource improvements would be aimed at the prevention of any long-term reduction of the soil resource productivity. In fact, current yields might decrease temporarily, but with the expectation of greater returns later.

One of the important principles of conservation as defined in this report is this distinction between "production practices" and "resource improvement" *preventing* long-term reduction of productivity. Management methods might also be adopted and investments made for the purpose of *increasing* the long-term productivity of the soil. To reverse a situation of declining productivity would not necessarily increase the yield that particular year. It would, however, over a period of time make the productivity greater and increase the choice of production practices which an operator could use to obtain a particular yield.

Thus conservation, in contrast to production practice, involves (1) the prevention of deterioration of productivity, or (2) the enhancement of productive potential. There remains one more principle before a definition of conservation is complete.

Prevention of decreases in yield requires expenditure of money and effort. The same applies to maintenance of productive potential. In other words, an investment is required—a present expenditure to obtain a future gain.

Before stating these concepts in the form of a definition of conservation it should be made clear that productive potential need not be limited to crop yield but could include the yield of any publicly desirable attribute, including aesthetic enjoyment. Further, investment need not mean only the immediate expenditure of cash but may include a decision against taking immediate returns for the purpose of maintaining or enhancing the possibility of gaining future returns.

For example, suppose that a particular valley is valuable because of its scenery, for wildlife propagation, for its historical interest, or as wilderness. Assume that it has been suggested to the proper authorities that this area be converted into a water reservoir, highway location, or industrial site, but the authorities must determine whether the valley in its present state provides a more important return in the long run than it will if converted to another use giving immediate monetary benefits.

The benefits lost by such a decision are equivalent to an investment of a like amount of the money value of these benefits. In this sense, therefore, the benefits not extracted measure the amount of the investment made by the decision to retain the present state of use.

With this background, conservation can now be defined as an *investment* (1) *in maintaining productive potential,* (2) *in decreasing the productivity deterioration or* (3) *in enhancing the productivity potential.* As used here productivity or productive potential refers to value. It may be either monetary or nonmonetary in nature. This meaning of conservation will be applied throughout this report. Some further examples may clarify this definition.

Maximum net value

A widely accepted goal of programs supported by public funds is to obtain the maximum net value from the program. In practice, the

113

measurement of net value presents difficulties. Net value should include all values, not only those appearing in the market place and represented only by monetary advantage. For example, a water-development project might yield salable products such as electricity and irrigation water, but the net value of such a project might include gains such as improved health from purer water supplies and recreation and even the protection of human life through the control of floods, all of which are difficult to measure in terms of money.

Many products and services have market prices. There are other values for which some people would be willing to sacrifice income or to forego other advantages. These values should be included on the benefit side in assessing the net benefit. For example, an attractive countryside might be considered a public asset and, therefore, be included as one aspect of net value. Likewise, all costs, whether incurred directly by monetary outlays or indirectly by foregoing opportunities for monetary or non-monetary values, should be included. Thus, the recreation offered by the impounded water in the reservoir of a water-development project may preclude enjoyment of stream fishing or canoeing by a different group of people. Hence, the stream fishing enjoyment relinquished represents an investment in the cost of the project.

In practice, there are serious technical problems in estimating benefits and costs of conservation programs. Two of these difficulties deserve special mention. They are the interest rate on investment and the differences in public and private rates of discounting future productivity.

Conservation implies an investment or outlay of money, effort or time, or some other human expenditure. Such an investment may and frequently does provide a delayed rather than an immediate return. In such circumstances an evaluation of the present net value requires the use of some sort of interest rate, or a time discount factor. It could be the interest rate of government borrowing or of private borrowing. It might be influenced by the size of the initial investment and by the time interval between the outlay and the value realized.

In general, the time span employed in an analysis of net value should be appropriate to the type of resources involved as well as to the cultural and economic setting. For example, a farmer investing in a sound land-water use program must consider the time span and time preference that is relevant for him. He would usually not invest in something that would yield no appreciable return within 50 years. Society, on the other hand, can afford to consider a longer time span, even for a similar program on the same land. Provision for unpredictable contingencies of population growth, war, and international demands for food and fiber may lower the discount rate to society on benefits from conservation expenditures.

Distribution of benefits

The net value of land and water conservation outlays is ultimately distributed among individuals, both those now living and those of future generations. It often happens, therefore, that some people pay the costs but the benefits are received by others. In other situations the group that pays the costs may obtain the benefits, but some individuals in the group may bear costs disproportionate to their share of the benefits. This problem becomes particularly vexing when people, operating through government or private groups, assume a major part of the direct financial costs of the program in return for only a general and diffused benefit.

The sharing of costs and benefits is often affected by the knowledge that these factors may be of different kinds. Farmers may get their portion of the benefits in cash, whereas benefits to the general public may be only in terms of the general economic health and security of the nation.

It is difficult to determine whether one pattern of benefit distribution is more or less desirable than some other pattern, since modern society has many different sets of values. Conflicting ideas and standards exist even if one set is dominant. A pattern of distribution of benefits desired by one group might be opposed by another.

An Analytical Framework for Appraising Conservation Programs

THE CHARACTER OF RESOURCES

SOME resources become available over time and others exist in fixed quantities. Some resources are renewable, others are not. Some can be stored, others cannot. A general classification is an aid in the analysis of these characteristics. There are two general categories of resources; namely, flow and fund, which vary in their renewability and storability characteristics.

	Flow Resources		*Fund Resources*	
Nonstorable		*Storable*	*Renewable*	*Nonrenewable*

Flow resources

Rainfall and sunlight do not depend upon the activity of man. They are available naturally in a certain quantity per day, per month, and per year. These resources can thus be considered to flow onward with respect to time without control or contribution by man. Such resources are designated as *flow resources.*

The use of flow resources in one time period has no effect upon their availability in another time period. The sunshine used by a field of corn in one year does not increase or decrease the amount of sunshine available the next.

Sunlight cannot be stored, at least in the form in which it exists naturally. The natural emission of atomic particles from radioactive elements is produced by a continuous process. Like sunlight, radioactivity also is a source of power and might be viewed similarly as a nonstorable flow resource. Rainfall is also a flow resource. The amount of rainfall coming in any one year is essentially independent of that used the year before. But water can be stored. Thus, flow resources can be of two types: storable and nonstorable.

Fund resources

Resources that are diminished by previous use might be called *fund resources.* They constitute a stock or reservoir of potential goods or services. Within limits, the use of such resources in one period lessens their availability in a later period.

Among fund resources some are exhaustible but renewable. Forests, fish, wildlife, and soil fertility are examples.

In contrast, some resources are exhaustible and nonrenewable. Examples are many of the minerals, petroleum, certain soil minerals, and some reserves of ground water.

Characteristics of resources are summarized in the following table.

Type of resource	Relation of use in one period of time to use in following periods	Possibility of increasing supply in later periods by man's present activities	Management alternatives	Examples
I. Flow resources				
a. nonstorable	none	none, or very little	use or nonuse	sunlight
b. storable	large, within limits of storage capacity	considerable	storage, nonstorage, unstoring	water stored in reservoirs or in soil
II. Fund resource				
a. exhaustible but renewable	large, within range of reversibility	large, if necessary present steps taken	maintain, decrease or increase availability over time	soil fertility, forests
b. exhaustible and nonrenewable	complete and inverse; use now exactly reduces use later, and vice versa	only by refraining from consumption now	rationing over time, substituting flow or renewable fund resources	petroleum, peats and mucks

SIGNIFICANCE OF RESOURCE CHARACTERISTICS

Few resources fit neatly into any one of the above classes. Nevertheless, the general scheme is useful in differentiating among resources with different characteristics. Exhaustible and nonrenewable resources can be extended by rationing or by substituting renewable resources for the nonrenewable ones. Availability of the exhaustible but renewable type may be maintained, decreased, or increased between various time periods. In dealing with a storable resource it is possible to choose among storing, not storing, or using previously stored quantities. Much remains to be learned from research concerning the probable consequences of these various alternatives.

PRINCIPLES FOR APPRAISING ALTERNATIVE CONSERVATION MEASURES

Public welfare

Many public investments in resources obtain support simply because they are called conservation. In deciding on such public investments there is a tendency to make no distinction between production practices and conservation practices and between resources with different characteristics.

Many of the benefits of conservation programs accrue to the public. It is, therefore, highly important to find a framework within which meaningful definitions can be accepted on a broad basis. It is hoped that the formulation of a framework will be an initial step toward increasing public gains from conservation programs.

Conservation is an investment which maintains, enhances, or reduces the rate of deterioration of the potential productivity of storable flow and renewable fund resources. Diagrammatic examples of this follow.

Identification of conservation investments

In figure 1, consider first 1-A. This graph shows the relation between input or cost (horizontal scale) and output or benefit (vertical scale). Let an investment or cost having the value I result in a benefit shown by the letter P. A somewhat larger investment of I_1 is assumed to yield a consequently higher benefit, P_1. Graph 1-A represents this relationship at the present time.

As a specific example, the expenditure of I dollars on fertilizer would yield P bushels of corn. A somewhat larger investment equal to I_1 in fertilizer would give a somewhat larger yield equal to P_1 bushels of corn.

For comparison, let the graph 1-B represent a similar relationship at some time in the future, and assume that an input or investment I yields a production benefit P_t as it did previously. A larger investment I_1 yields a benefit P'_t which may be larger or smaller than P_1.

The relationship between present and future gains in graphs 1-A and 1-B can be visualized in the single graph presented in 1-C. In 1-C there are three scales: time, cost, and benefit. Diagram 1-C is a three-dimensional graph and the reader should keep this in mind when viewing it.

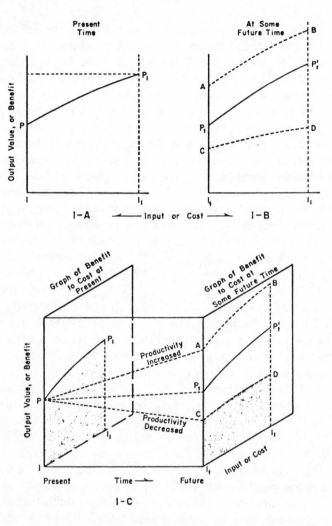

FIGURE 1. Conservation defined by the relation of investment to benefit at various times, present and future.

Curves lying in the plane oriented diagonally from the eye of the reader into the page represent the relation of input or cost to benefit. The curve lying in the plane of the paper represents the relationship of benefit to time.

In this diagram it can be seen that an investment I would yield a benefit P at the present time. But, it could yield benefits higher or lower than P at some time in the future. If in the future the situation were the same as at the present time, then the curve P_t-P'_t would be identical to that for the present time.

Using the previous example, if at a future time erosion should decrease the productivity of the field, the expenditure of I dollars on fertilizer would no longer give P bushels of corn, but a smaller value represented by C. Then, with the expenditure of I_1 dollars on fertilizer the output or value of the corn would no longer be P'_t, but only D.

Still referring to graph 1-C, consider an alternate position. Assume that between the present and future times the productivity of the resource had been enhanced, so that the expenditure of I dollars in fertilizer would actually give A return in corn. Further, the expenditure of I_1 dollars in fertilizer would yield a production equal to B bushels of corn. Now the change in production from P_t to A over the period between the present and future time represented could not have been accomplished without some investment in improving the production potential of the farmland. The investment to raise the input-output relation from P_t-P'_t to A-B is an expenditure for conservation. The investment would also be for conservation if it were for the purpose of preventing a deterioration in productivity. Thus, the investment necessary to prevent the productivity curve from falling from P_t-P'_t to C-D would also be a conservation investment. Minimum production expense for a given output is the expense incurred in the present production period if production conditions after the present period were neglected. Conservation expenditures are all expenses in excess of the minimum production expense.

It will be noted that in 1-C the line on the time scale from P to A is labeled "productivity increased" and the line on the time scale drawn between P and C is labeled "productivity decreased." In contrast, P-P_1 and P_t-P'_t relate the output to cost at any particular time and show the effect of production practices and not of conservation programs.

These curves do, however, tell us something about the success of past conservation programs. If the levels of successive curves are perennially higher than those preceding, it can be assumed that worthwhile conservation investments have been taking place. Such an upward shift in the expected level of a future production possibilities curve represents the definition of positive conservation as used in this report.

Determining needs for programs of conservation

Whenever a conservation program is proposed it is assumed that present conditions need improving. Justification for initiation of a conservation program should lie in the difference between conditions as they presently exist, and the conditions which are desired and toward which the program is to be directed.

It is important to estimate as accurately as possible the good to be accomplished by a program. Then the return obtainable can be compared with that which would be received from investment of the same effort or money in alternative uses.

There are few examples of objective and thorough analysis of present practices and of the possibility of improving them. Such examples are important because they show that an objective analysis can be made. Arguments against making such studies before a program is initiated usually include such statements as (a) that insufficient data are available, (b) a scheme of analysis acceptable to everybody concerned cannot be devised, or (c) the program is obviously beneficial and, therefore, no detailed analysis is necessary.

Under the auspices of the Iowa Agricultural Experiment Station and the former Bureau of Agricultural Economics, USDA, a study was made of soil erosion losses in the Ida-Monona Soil Association Area of western Iowa.[1] Public erosion control programs of the Soil Conservation Service, the Iowa Soil Conservation Districts, and the Agricultural Conservation Program had established a common goal for their erosion control activities, based on a permissible soil loss not to exceed 5 to 7 tons per year per acre. Experiments on plots and on fields had indicated that such annual soil loss would be physically permissible in terms of future productivity. Such an annual loss, though somewhat above the norm for geologic processes, would give reasonable assurance of continued productive use of the soil. This agreed-upon limit, however, has never been tested in terms of economic limitations, nor was there a test of how such a goal would compare with what the farmer desired and thought practical.

The study included the estimation of soil losses on a random sample of 144 farms in the Ida-Monona Soil Association Area.[2] The annual soil losses were estimated by using the "Browning Factors."[3] Losses for separate fields and parts of fields in each farm were determined in acres to give an annual (average) erosion loss for each farm.

In addition, each of the 144 farm operators was asked to list by fields the erosion control practices he believed were necessary on his farm to control erosion to the extent of maintaining productivity of the land. Through application of the Browning Factors, the researchers expressed these practices in terms of estimated. annual erosion losses.

There was a difference, of course, between farms and farmers. In order to present the variety of situations found in the study, the data are shown in figure 2 in the form of accumulative frequency distribution. The

[1] Frey, John C. Some obstacles to soil erosion control in western Iowa. Iowa Agr. Exp. Sta. Res. Bul. 391. 1952.
[2] *Ibid.*
[3] *Ibid.* See p. 953 ff. for discussion of Browning Factors.

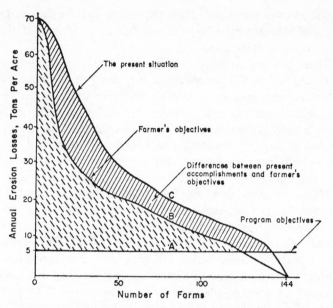

FIGURE 2. Cumulative frequency graph of soil losses equaled or exceeded on different numbers of farms, Ida-Monona Area, Iowa. Iowa Agricultural Experiment Station Research Bulletin 391.

vertical scale shows erosion losses in tons per acre. The horizontal scale indicates the number of farms in this sample, a total of 144. Considering first curve C, one farm was found to be losing soil at the rate of 70 tons per acre. Following curve C downward, 50 farms were found to be experiencing soil losses in excess of 31 tons per acre, 100 farms a loss of more than 17 tons per acre, and about 134 farms were sustaining losses greater than the permissible value of 5 to 7 tons per acre per year.

Curve B shows the annual erosion losses that would result from practices farmers reported necessary to maintain productivity. There was much variation in erosion loss goals reported by various farmers. For one farmer the acceptable erosion loss was 70 tons per acre per year; for 50 farmers it exceeded 21 tons; for 120 farmers, the acceptable soil loss exceeded the 5-ton loss used by the agricultural agencies as the goal for their programs.

The difference between line A, which is drawn at the proper objective value of 5 tons per acre, and the upper of the two curves represents the possibility of improvement due to an erosion control program. The single-hatched area between the upper and lower curved lines represents the amount of improvements desired by the farmers as a group. The broken-hatched area represents the difference between the farmers' goals and the programs' goals.

These data emphasize the need for studies to explain the differences in farmer and program goals of conservation. Research is continuing toward the objective of determining the value productivity of soil resources under the three levels of soil losses A, B, and C, shown in figure 2. Results of this research should provide guidelines for conservation programs in the area by (1) identifying public and private erosion control goals, and (2) suggesting the means for achieving each goal.

Comparison of alternative programs

To illustrate some of the principles that should govern decisions on how funds should be spent, figure 3 presents a theoretical picture of returns from investment made for conservation in two alternative problem areas. The problem areas are denoted as Areas X and Y. The graphs show on the vertical scale the return from the investment which is plotted along the horizontal scale. In Area X, for example, if an amount of money or effort represented by I_1 is invested at a particular time to which both graphs refer, the increased productivity is measured by the vertical value A_1. If, on the other hand, the funds invested had been in an amount equal to I_2, the productivity expected at the end of the same period of time would be A_2 on the vertical scale.

The same principle applied to Area Y is indicated on the diagram at the right. Because of the characteristics of the resources and their response to conservation programs, it can be seen that the investment I_1 in Area X will increase the value or productivity by the vertical value A_1, whereas the same investment in Area Y would give an increased productivity equal only to A'_1. In other words, the expenditure of I_1 funds would yield greater return by investment in Area X than in Area Y for the time period specified.

However, after an initial investment had been made in both areas equal to I_1, then the increase of the investment from I_1 to I_2 would give a greater increase in productivity in Area Y than in Area X, as can be seen by the fact that the vertical distance between A'_1 and A'_2 in Area Y is greater than between A_1 and A_2 in Area X.

These graphs illustrate that a unit of investment should be made in the area that gives the highest returns for that unit. For the first unit it was Area X but for the second unit of investment the return in Area Y would be highest even though the investment in Area Y yielded a much lower return than the first increment in Area X. It can be seen that if all investment in conservation were made so that the returns from the last unit

123

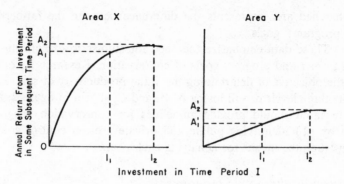

FIGURE 3. Relationship between investment in two alternative areas and returns in some subsequent time period.

of investment in all areas were equal, then the total return would be the highest it would be possible to achieve.

There are many instances in which conservation investment has been carried beyond this point in particular areas while in other areas that would yield higher returns there was little or no investment. When public funds are invested without regard to comparison of returns on the last unit of investment, the total returns may be seriously reduced from what could have been achieved. Probably the most important factor in causing over-investment in one area compared to another is the influence that proponents of developments in local areas have on the authorization of projects.

Allocation of conservation funds among various purposes

The allocation of conservation investment among purposes in a multipurpose activity should follow the same principles as its allocation among areas. However, there are additional complications. Those purposes that are independent and can be analyzed separately must be identified with their benefits and costs. Those purposes that are interdependent and have joint benefits and costs must also be identified. Otherwise, it is impossible to determine the effect of varying the amount of investment in an interdependent purpose. These effects might be called separable effects of interdependent purposes. Thus, there are three types of analyses: (1) independent purposes that have no joint relations with other purposes, (2) separable effects, and (3) joint effects that cannot be attributed to a single purpose.

To get the maximum return from the investment in conservation the various purposes should be analyzed in the same way as suggested in figure 3. That is, the returns from the last units of investment in independ-

124

ent, separable, or joint purposes should be equal. Often, because of legislative or political factors, investment in one purpose is carried too far in relation to returns that might be achieved in other purposes. Sometimes purposes with low returns in relation to cost are averaged in with other purposes with high returns. This "basin accounting" results in a program that yields less net benefits than if the program had been formulated according to above principles. Lack of consistency in cost-sharing arrangements is probably the most important factor in causing overinvestment in one purpose compared to another. Local proponents of projects are inclined to favor purposes that involve little local cost-sharing but have substantial local benefits. Thus, there is strong support for flood control reservoirs that require no local cost-sharing, but much less support for levees that require substantial local contributions. In the watershed program, purposes that are financed largely with federal funds seem to be favored over purposes that require large local contributions.[4] Sometimes "basin account," "interest component," and other devices are used to give the appearance of more reimbursement and cost-sharing than actually takes place.

The public cost of these misallocations of conservation investments can be estimated by comparing the returns with what they might have been if the conservation investment were made according to the above model.[5]

Scale of investment

There is another problem, different from that of allocating investment funds among practices or projects but closely allied to it. It concerns the amount of investment or scale of investment in some particular project. Principles of economic theory state that the amount of investment should not exceed the level at which marginal cost equals marginal revenue. To state this in other terms, no additional investment is justified when the additional increment of investment does not yield at least an equal increment of benefit.

Actually, from the standpoint of economics there are three different levels of investment of particular importance. These are illustrated in figure 4, which shows the relation between conservation benefits obtained from various amounts of effort or money invested. The benefits, stated in

[4] Examples from an analysis of various federal programs in the Missouri Basin are given in the report, Missouri: Land and Water. President's Missouri Basin Survey Commission. U. S. Govt. Print. Off., Washington, D. C. 1954. pp. 96-99.

[5] The use of programming to estimate the returns to investment in various purposes has been explored by Timmons and Pavelis. See: Pavelis, George A. and Timmons, John F. Programming small watershed development. Jour. Farm Econ. 42(2):225-240. May 1960.

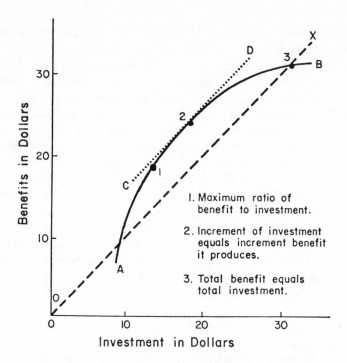

1. Maximum ratio of benefit to investment.

2. Increment of investment equals increment benefit it produces.

3. Total benefit equals total investment.

FIGURE 4. Relation of conservation benefit to amount of investment.

dollars, are plotted on the vertical scale. The investment in dollars necessary to gain those benefits is represented on the horizontal scale. The dashed line OX drawn at 45 degrees is a cumulative outlay of investment measured on the horizontal scale. The curved line AB represents the cumulative benefit measured on the vertical scale which arises from the associated outlay curve OX as measured on the horizontal scale.

The first point of interest is that labeled point "1," which represents the place where there is a maximum ratio of benefit to investment. In other words, point "1" indicates the level of investment that yields the highest benefit-cost ratio. As shown later, however, this point does not represent the maximum net benefits realizable from the project.

Point "2" indicates the level of investment at which an increment of investment yields an equal increment of benefit. Beyond this point each successive unit of investment yields a progressively smaller increment of benefit. This point is identified as the place where the line CD drawn parallel to the dashed line OX is tangent to the solid benefit line AB. This is the point at which net benefits are greatest and thus the point at which the maximum net results from conservation expenditures are realized.

At point "3" the benefit-cost ratio is unity. This point indicates the highest amount of total investment that will yield an equal amount of total benefit; that is, the highest investment possible that will give a unit benefit-cost ratio. It is identified as the place where the solid benefit line AB crosses the dashed line OX. Beyond this point, the total benefits are less than the total costs.

Each of these three levels of investment is important depending upon the nature of the benefits, the amount of available investment funds, the time period over which the benefits are expected to accrue, and the degree of public, as compared with private, concern. Federal flood-control legislation, for example, specifies that the benefits must exceed the cost. Under such a rule the construction agency may invest up to point "3" on the graph, even though economic logic cannot support an investment beyond point "2." But, unless and until legislation is changed, point "3" is relevant to scale of expenditures.

In retrospect, figure 4 illustrates an important criterion for conservation investments. It is this. The investment should be carried to point "2" but no further if it is desired to achieve maximum net benefits from conservation outlays.

It must also be recognized that the benefits derived from any given level of investment might be different if there were group participation in the investment rather than merely individual participation. That is, it may be profitable for a group as a whole to make a larger investment in some program than would be profitable for an individual.

Similarly, the public or governmental group might find it profitable to make a larger investment in a particular program than would either a small group or a private individual, because the larger the group the broader might be its scope of benefits.

Physical, Economic,
and Institutional Interrelationships
in Resource Conservation

THE PROCESS of making and implementing resource conservation decisions among the wide range of alternatives outlined in the previous section on resource classes necessitates the use of physical, economic, and what will be defined as institutional data. These data should be analyzed jointly because they are interrelated.[6] Such an analysis of conservation problems demands close working relationships among, as well as within, many disciplines in the physical and social sciences. Each discipline has important and necessary contributions to make, without which the working out of solutions to conservation problems would be limited or thwarted.

PHYSICAL AND BIOLOGICAL CONSIDERATIONS

Physical and biological scientists have the responsibility of appraising the kinds and ranges of possibilities for resource development and the probable consequences of particular developments. The appraisal should be in terms of definite physical units of resources, products, and services. The kinds and ranges of physical possibilities are continually being expanded through technological discoveries and developments. In short, scientists are chiefly concerned with finding answers to the limitless question, "What is *physically possible* in the use of natural resources?"

[6] For further elaboration of these interrelationships see: Timmons, John F. Integration of law and economics in analyzing agricultural land use problems. Jour. Farm Econ. 37(5):1126-1142. 1955; and Problems of water use and control. Iowa Law Rev. 41(2):160-180. 1956.

ECONOMIC CONSIDERATIONS

Effective decisions among conservation alternatives cannot be based on the knowledge of physical and biological possibilities alone. Conservation alternatives must be appraised in terms of what is *economically desirable*. "Economically desirable" is defined in terms of improved welfare; that is, reorganization of the use of resources toward the end of maximizing the net benefits from conservation investment. Determining the economic consequences of various physically possible alternatives is the province of the economist.

Economic consequences of particular alternatives change with changing numbers and tastes of people—the desires of the people as expressed in prices, votes, or other preference indicators. Changes in cost and in demand occur also with changing technology. Technology is dynamic and possible alternatives for decision may change greatly over time. Decisions must be based upon the knowledge of technology at hand and expectations of change for the future period over which the decision applies. As indicated earlier, individuals have different expectations regarding the future. Such differences in expectations may well lead to different decisions by different people and by society. These changing conditions and the uncertainty of the future demand flexibility in conservation policy.

INSTITUTIONAL CONSIDERATIONS

Although the economic as well as the physical consequences of various conservation alternatives must be considered in selecting a particular course of action, final decisions await data on what is *institutionally permissible*. Institutions mean social control over individual behavior in a formal or an informal manner. Zoning regulations and property rights are good examples of formal controls. Customary practices are informal controls.

Institutions may either facilitate or obstruct the achievement of conservation objectives.[7] Serving as facilitators, institutions help put conservation decisions into action. Serving as obstructors, institutions prevent conservation objectives from being realized. In this instance, either the institution must be (1) altered to function as a facilitating means or (2)

[7] For a more detailed development of this general idea see: Timmons, John F. Land institutions impeding and facilitating agricultural adjustment. Chap. 10. Problems and policies of American agriculture. Iowa State University Press, Ames, Iowa. 1959; and Chryst, Walter E. and Timmons, John F. The economic role of land resource institutions. Dynamics of land use: needed adjustment. Iowa State University Press, Ames, Iowa. 1961.

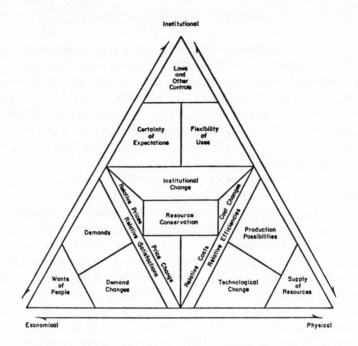

FIGURE 5.   Illustration of interrelationships between physical, economical, and institutional considerations in resource conservation.

the economic-physical alternative selected must be modified to permit the institution to operate as a facilitating means.

INTERRELATED CONSIDERATIONS

Figure 5 illustrates important interrelationships between physical, economical, and institutional considerations in resource conservation. The starting points are (1) wants of people, (2) supply of resources and existing technology for their utilization, and (3) controls over human behavior exerted by existing institutions.

Wants of people are exemplified in demands that change with population growth and changing preferences of individuals. These demands are expressed through preference indicators. Since markets exist for products and services, and since these products and services may be expressed in dollars, price constitutes the preference indicator in our form of society. However, for satisfactions not subject to cardinal measurement such as recreational satisfaction or furtherance of national security, alternative preference indicators are used. The voting mechanism is an example.

For physical sciences the starting point is the supply of resources and the production possibilities. Relative efficiencies of various alternative physical possibilities may be computed. When the factors are measurable by the market mechanism, relative costs and changes in costs are available to determine relative efficiencies. In the absence of adequate market value society has devised other means to indicate its preference.

Another starting point is the present status of laws and other factors exerting controls over human behavior. Institutions functioning as controls provide both a degree of certainty of expectation and a degree of flexibility of resource use. If these certainties and flexibilities are insufficient, or are not capable of bringing resources into maximum service of human wants, institutional change is in order. Institutions affecting resource use were made by man and are constantly being altered by man in the process of satisfying his wants more fully. Purposeful alteration of these institutions remains one of the more important as well as one of the more difficult aspects of resource conservation policy.

FIXING RESPONSIBILITY FOR CONSERVATION

Under our system of resource ownership the primary responsibility for conservation has rested with the resource owner. But both history and present trends indicate that individuals cannot always be depended on to make conservation investments that would meet public goals. In what situations are public actions to achieve conservation desirable?

Public action to achieve conservation is desirable: (1) when it would be economical for the individual resource owner to conserve but he fails to do so because of lack of knowledge or lack of capital, (2) when society can make conservation economical for both individual owners and society by adjusting institutions or incentive payments, (3) when conservation is economical for society but cannot be made economical for individuals, and (4) when intangible ends desired by a majority in a democracy can be achieved only by public action. These four situations are shown in figure 6. This chart illustrates that individuals have the primary responsibility in the first situation and that government—federal, state, and local— or group responsibility increases until the public is almost completely responsible for the fourth situation. Obviously, government is not the only avenue of group action. We do not rule out the possibility of nongovernment groups making substantial contributions in resource conservation, as did the Polio Foundation in another field of work.

131

When conservation is economical for individuals

Pursuing these ideas further, society could well expend funds for conservation so long as the expenditure resulted in increasing social net returns. But, ordinarily, society would need to take only limited action—such as research, education, technical service, or credit—to demonstrate that it would be profitable for individuals to conserve in this case.

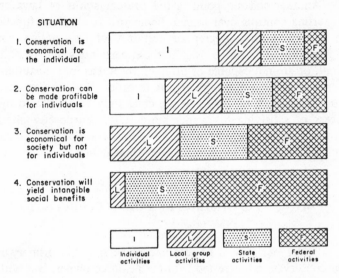

FIGURE 6. Hypothetical responsibilities for conservation.

Many farm conservation problems fall in this category. Often a farm conservation program will protect against erosion and at the same time yield the landowner enough increased production to pay for the program. If the landowner knows that this is true and has the capital and management skill to carry out the program he will probably do so. Assistance from society in the form of research, education, technical service, and credit would usually be sufficient to bring about initiation of this type of individual conservation program.

Making conservation profitable to individuals

Society can help make conservation economical for the individual by removing institutional obstacles, adjusting tenure arrangements, inducing cost-sharing arrangements, encouraging technological development, or by instituting regulatory or taxation measures that would motivate individual action toward conservation through a realignment of market values.

132

Examples of this type of program are cost-sharing on conservation and watershed programs, research to develop new techniques that make conservation economical, and adjusting property taxes on land removed from intensive crops. A large part of federal and state action in conservation programs falls into this category. Conservation programs that result in increased productivity may unavoidably add to the surplus problem. When this is true, public action may be designed to achieve conservation in such a way so as not to increase surplus production. The conservation reserve program is an attempt to take this kind of action.

Where conservation is economical for society but not for individuals

When conservation is economical for society but cannot be made economical for the individual, society must strive to achieve conservation through other means. Included would be developments that are needed for the long-run requirements of society but cannot be made profitable for the individual. The management of certain forest lands, the comprehensive development of river basins, and recreational development of natural resources are examples. In most cases, individuals or private corporations might profitably develop some part of the resource but could not develop or recover all of the private and public values involved.

Intangible social benefits from conservation

In many instances our market system does not provide a set of values that can measure the results of conservation. Also, there are situations in which individuals could not recover the benefits from a conservation investment. Decisions by society to undertake conservation depend upon returns that cannot be measured completely in the market place. Preservation of wilderness areas, the protection of migratory waterfowl, and the control of pollution of our soil, water, and air resources through fall-out and other forms of contamination are examples of conservation activities that are not completely measurable by market prices.

In our complex of resources and economic activity there is often such a mixture of these conditions that many types of private and public action are required to solve conservation problems.

CONSERVATION RECONSIDERED

By JOHN V. KRUTILLA*

"It is the clear duty of Government, which is the trustee for unborn generations as well as for its present citizens, to watch over, and if need be, by legislative enactment, to defend, the exhaustible natural resources of the country from rash and reckless spoliation. How far it should itself, either out of taxes, or out of State loans, or by the device of guaranteed interest, press resources into undertakings from which the business community, if left to itself, would hold aloof, is a more difficult problem. Plainly, if we assume adequate competence on the part of governments, there is a valid case for *some* artificial encouragement to investment, particularly to investments the return from which will only begin to appear after the lapse of many years."

A. C. PIGOU

Conservation of natural resources has meant different things to different people. But to the economist from the time of Pigou, who first took notice of the economics of conservation [10, p. 27ff], until quite recently, the central concerns have been associated with the question of the optimal intertemporal utilization of the fixed natural resource stocks. The gnawing anxiety provoked by the Malthusian thesis of natural resource scarcity was in no way allayed by the rates of consumption of natural resource stocks during two world wars occurring between the first and fourth editions of Pigou's famous work. In the United States, a presidential commission, reviewing the materials situation following World War II, concluded that an end had come to the historic decline in the cost of natural resource commodities [12, pp. 13-14]. This conclusion reinforced the concern of many that the resource base ultimately would be depleted.

More recently, on the other hand, a systematic analysis of the trends in prices of natural resource commodities did not reveal any permanent interruption in the decline relative to commodities and services in general [11]. Moreover, a rather ambitious attempt to test rigorously the thesis of natural resource scarcity suggested instead that technological progress had compensated quite adequately for the depletion of the higher quality natural resource stocks [1]. Further, given the present state of the arts, future advances need not be fortuitous occurrences;

* The author is indebted to all of his colleagues at Resources for the Future and to Harold Barnett, Paul Davidson, Otto Davis, Chandler Morse, Peter Pearse, and Ralph Turvey for many helpful suggestions on an earlier draft of this paper.

AMERICAN ECONOMIC REVIEW, 1967, Vol. 57, pp. 777-786.

rather the rate of advance can be influenced by investment in research and development. Indeed, those who take an optimistic view would hold that the modern industrial economy is winning its independence from the traditional natural resources sector to a remarkable degree. Ultimately, the raw material inputs to industrial production may be only mass and energy [1, p. 238].[1]

While such optimistic conclusions were being reached, they were nevertheless accompanied by a caveat that, while we may expect production of goods and services to increase without interruption, the level of living may not necessarily be improved. More specifically, Barnett and Morse concluded that the quality of the physical environment—the landscape, water, and atmospheric quality—was deteriorating.

These conclusions suggest that on the one hand the traditional concerns of conservation economics—the husbanding of natural resource stocks for the use of future generations—may now be outmoded by advances in technology. On the other hand, the central issue seems to be the problem of providing for the present and future the amenities associated with unspoiled natural environments, for which the market fails to make adequate provision. While this appears to be the implication of recent research,[2] and is certainly consistent with recent public policy in regard to preserving natural environments, the traditional economic rationale for conservation does not address itself to this issue directly.[3] The use of Pigou's social time preference may serve only to hasten the conversion of natural environments into low-yield capital investments.[4] On what basis, then, can we make decisions when we confront a choice entailing action which will have an irreversible adverse consequence for rare phenomena of nature? I investigate this question below.

Let us consider an area with some unique attribute of nature—a geomorphologic feature such as the Grand Canyon, a threatened species, or an entire ecosystem or biotic community essential to the survival of the threatened species.[5] Let us assume further that the area can be used

---

[1] The conclusions were based on data relevant to the U.S. economy. While they may be pertinent to Western Europe also, all of my subsequent observations are restricted to the United States.

[2] For example, see [7].

[3] It must be acknowledged that with sufficient patience and perception nearly all of the argument for preserving unique phenomena of nature can be found in the classic on conservation economics by Ciriacy-Wantrup [3].

[4] An example of this was the recent threat to the Grand Canyon by the proposed Bridge and Marble Canyon dams. Scott makes a similar point with reference to natural resource commodities [13].

[5] Uniqueness need not be absolute for the following arguments to hold. It may be, like Dupuit's bridge, a good with no adequate substitutes in the "natural" market area of its

for certain recreation and/or scientific research activities which would be compatible with the preservation of the natural environment, or for extractive activities such as logging or hydraulic mining, which would have adverse consequences for scenic landscapes and wildlife habitat.

A private resource owner would consider the discounted net income stream from the alternative uses and select the use which would hold prospects for the highest present net value. If the use which promises the highest present net value is incompatible with preserving the environment in its natural state, does it necessarily follow that the market will allocate the resources efficiently? There are several reasons why private and social returns in this case are likely to diverge significantly.

Consider the problem first in its static aspects. By assumption, the resources used in a manner compatible with preserving the natural environment have no close substitutes; on the other hand, alternative sources of supply of natural resource commodities are available.[6] Under the circumstances and given the practical obstacles to perfectly discriminating pricing, the private resource owner would not be able to appropriate in gate receipts the entire social value of the resources when used in a manner compatible with preserving the natural state. Thus the present values of his expected net revenues are not comparable as between the competing uses in evaluating the effciency of the resource allocation.

Aside from the practical problem of implementing a perfectly discriminating pricing policy, it is not clear even on theoretic grounds that a comparison of the total area under the demand curve on the one hand and market receipts on the other will yield an unambiguous answer to the allocative question. When the existence of a grand scenic wonder or a unique and fragile ecosystem is involved, its preservation and continued availability are a significant part of the real income of many individuals.[7] Under the conditions postulated, the area under the demand curve, which represents a maximum willingness to pay, may be significantly less than the minimum which would be required to compensate such individuals were they to be deprived in perpetuity of the opportunity

---

principal clientele, while possibly being replicated in other market areas to which the clientele in question has no access for all practical purposes.

[6] The asymmetry in the relation posited is realistic. The historic decline in cost of natural resource commodities relative to comomdities in general suggests that the production and exchange of the former occur under fairly competitive conditions. On the other hand, increasing congestion at parks, such as Yellowstone, Yosemite, and Grand Canyon, suggests there are no adequate substitutes for these rare natural environments.

[7] These would be the spiritual descendants of John Muir, the present members of the Sierra Club, the Wilderness Society, National Wildlife Federation, Audubon Society and others to whom the loss of a species or the disfigurement of a scenic area causes acute distress and a sense of genuine relative impoverishment.

to continue enjoying the natural phenomenon in question. Accordingly, it is conceivable that the potential losers cannot influence the decision in their favor by their aggregate willingness to pay, yet the resource owner may not be able to compensate the losers out of the receipts from the alternative use of the resource. In such cases—and they are more likely encountered in this area—it is impossible to determine whether the market allocation is efficient or inefficient.

Another reason for questioning the allocative efficiency of the market for the case in hand has been recognized only more recently. This involves the notion of *option demand* [14]. This demand is characterized as a willingness to pay for retaining an option to use an area or facility that would be difficult or impossible to replace and for which no close substitute is available. Moreover, such a demand may exist even though there is no current intention to use the area or facility in question and the option may never be exercised. If an option value exists for rare or unique occurrences of nature, but there is no means by which a private resource owner can appropriate this value, the resulting resource allocation may be questioned.

Because options are traded on the market in connection with other economic values, one may ask why no market has developed where option value exists for the preservation of natural environments.[8] We need to consider briefly the nature of the value in question and the marketability of the option.

From a purely scientific viewpoint, much is yet to be learned in the earth and life sciences; preservation of the objects of study may be defended on these grounds, given the serendipity value of basic research. We know also that the natural biota represents our reservoir of germ plasm, which has economic value. For example, modern agriculture in advanced countries represents cultivation figuratively in a hot-house environment in which crops are protected against disease, pests, and drought by a variety of agricultural practices. The energy released from some of the genetic characteristics no longer required for survival under cultivated conditions is redirected toward greater productivity. Yet because of the instability introduced with progressive reduction of biological diversity, a need occasionally arises for the reintroduction of some genetic characteristics lost in the past from domestic strains. It is from the natural biota that these can be obtained.

The value of botanical specimens for medicinal purposes also has been long, if not widely, recognized. Approximately half of the new drugs currently being developed are obtained from botanical specimens.[9] There is a traffic in medicinal plants which approximates a third

---

[8] For a somewhat differently developed argument, see [6].
[9] For an interesting account of the use of plants for medicinal purposes, see [8].

of a billion dollars annually. Cortisone, digitalis, and heparin are among the better known of the myriad drugs which are derived from natural vegetation or zoological sources. Since only a relatively small part of the potential medicinal value of biological specimens has yet been realized, preserving the opportunity to examine all species among the natural biota for this purpose is a matter of considerable importance.

The option value may have only a sentimental basis in some instances. Consider the rallying to preserve the historical relic, "Old Ironsides."[10] There are many persons who obtain satisfaction from mere knowledge that part of wilderness North America remains even though they would be appalled by the prospect of being exposed to it. Subscriptions to World Wildlife Fund are of the same character. The funds are employed predominantly in an effort to save exotic species in remote areas of the world which few subscribers to the Fund ever hope to see. An option demand may exist therefore not only among persons currently and prospectively active in the market for the object of the demand, but among others who place a value on the mere existence of biological and/or geomorphological variety and its widespread distribution.[11]

If a genuine value for retaining an option in these respects exists, why has not a market developed? To some extent, and for certain purposes, it has. Where a small natural area in some locality in the United States is threatened, the property is often purchased by Nature Conservancy,[12] a private organization which raises funds through voluntary subscriptions.[13] But this market is grossly imperfect. First, the risk for private investors associated with absence of knowledge as to whether a particular ecosystem has special characteristics not widely shared by others is enormous.[14] Moreover, to the extent that the natural environment will support basic scientific research which often has unanticipated practical results, the serendipity value may not be appropriable by those paying to preserve the options. But perhaps of greatest significance is that the preservation of the grand scenic wonders, threatened species, and the like involves comparatively large land tracts which are not of merely

[10] The presumption in favor of option value is applicable also to historic and cultural features; rare works of art, perhaps, being the most prominent of this class.

[11] The phenomenon discussed may have an exclusive sentimental basis, but if we consider the "bequest motivation" in economic behavior, discussed below, it may be explained by an interest in preserving an option for one's heirs to view or use the object in question.

[12] Not to be confused with a public agency of the same name in the United Kingdom.

[13] Subscriptions to World Wildlife Fund, the Wilderness Society, National Parks Association, etc. may be similar, but, of course, much of the effect these organizations have on the preservation of natural areas stems not from purchasing options, but from influencing public programs.

[14] The problem here is in part like a national lottery in which there exists a very small chance for a very large gain. Unlike a lottery, rather large sums at very large risk typically would be required.

local interest. Thus, all of the problems of organizing a market for public goods arise. Potential purchasers of options may be expected to bide time in the expectation that others will meet the necessary cost, thus eliminating cost to themselves. Since the mere existence or preservation of the natural environment in question satisfies the demand, those who do not subscribe cannot be excluded except by the failure to enroll sufficient subscribers for its preservation.

Perhaps of equal significance to the presumption of market failure are some dynamic characteristics of the problem suggested by recent research. First, consider the consumption aspects of the problem. Davidson, Adams, and Seneca have recently advanced some interesting notions regarding the formation of demand that may be particularly relevant to our problem [5, p. 186].

> When facilities are not readily available, skills will not be developed and, consequently, there may be little desire to participate in these activities. If facilities are made available, opportunities to acquire skill increase, and user demand tends to rise rapidly over time as individuals learn to enjoy these activities. Thus, participation in and enjoyment of water recreational activities by the present generation will stimulate future demand without diminishing the supply presently available. Learning-by-doing, to the extent it increases future demand, suggests an interaction between present and future demand functions, which will result in a public good externality, as present demand enters into the utility function of future users.

While this quotation refers to water-based recreation, it is likely to be more persuasive in connection with some other resource-based recreation activity. Its relevance for wilderness preservation is obvious. When we consider the remote backcountry landscape, or the wilderness scene as the object of experience and enjoyment, we recognize that utility from the experience depends predominantly upon the prior acquisition of technical skill and specialized knowledge. This, of course, must come from experience initially with less arduous or demanding activities. The more the present population is initiated into activities requiring similar but less advanced skills (e.g., car camping), the better prepared the future population will be to participate in the more exacting activities. Given the phenomenal rise of car camping, if this activity will spawn a disproportionate number of future back-packers, canoe cruisers, cross-country skiers, etc., the greater will be the induced demand for wild, primitive, and wilderness-related opportunities for indulging such interest. Admittedly, we know little about the demand for outdoor experiences which depend on unique phenomena of nature—its formation, stability, and probable course of development. These are important questions for research, results of which will have significant policy implications.

139

In regard to the production aspects of the "new conservation," we need to examine the implications of technological progress a little further. Earlier I suggested that the advances of technology have compensated for the depletion of the richer mineral deposits and, in a sense, for the superior stands of timber and tracts of arable land. On the other hand, there is likely to be an asymmetry in the implications of techno- ' logical progress for the production of goods and services from the natural resource base, and the production of natural phenomena which give rise to utility without undergoing fabrication or other processing.[15] In fact, it is improbable that technology will advance to the point at which the grand geomorphologic wonders could be replicated, or extinct species resurrected. Nor is it obvious that fabricated replicas, were they even possible, would have a value equivalent to that of the originals. To a lesser extent, the landscape can be manufactured in a pleasing way with artistry and the larger earth-moving equipment of today's construction technology. Open pit mines may be refilled and the surroundings rehabilitated in a way to approximate the original conditions. But even here the undertaking cannot be acccomplished without the cooperation of nature over a substantial period of time depending on the growth rate of the vegetal cover and the requirements of the native habitat.[16] Accordingly, while the supply of fabricated goods and commercial services may be capable of continuous expansion from a given resource base by reason of scientific discovery and mastery of technique, the supply of natural phenomena is virtually inelastic. That is, we may preserve the natural environment which remains to provide amenities of this sort for the future, but there are significant limitations on reproducing it in the future should we fail to preserve it.

If we consider the asymmetric implications of technology, we can conceive of a transformation function having along its vertical axis amenities derived directly from association with the natural environment and fabricated goods along the horizontal axis. Advances in technology would stretch the transformation function's terminus along the horizontal axis but not appreciably along the vertical. Accordingly, if we simply take the effect of technological progress over time, considering tastes as constant, the marginal trade-off between manufactured and natural amenities will progressively favor the latter. Natural environments will represent irreplaceable assets of appreciating value with the passage of time.

If we consider technology as constant, but consider a change in tastes progressively favoring amenities of the natural environment due to the learn-by-doing phenomenon, natural environments will similarly for this

[15] I owe this point to a related observation, to my knowledge first made by Ciriacy-Wantrup [3, p. 47].

[16] That is, giving rise to option value for members of the present population.

reason represent assets of appreciating value. If both influences are operative (changes in technology with asymmetric implications, and tastes), the appreciating value of natural environments will be compounded.

This leads to a final point which, while a static consideration, tends to have its real significance in conjunction with the effects of parametric shifts in tastes and technology. We are coming to realize that consumption-saving behavior is motivated by a desire to leave one's heirs an estate as well as by the utility to be obtained from consumption.[17] A bequest of maximum value would require an appropriate mix of public and private assets, and, equally, the appropriate mix of opportunities to enjoy amenities experienced directly from association with the natural environment along with readily producible goods. But the option to enjoy the grand scenic wonders for the bulk of the population depends upon their provision as public goods.

Several observations have been made which may now be summarized. The first is that, unlike resource allocation questions dealt with in conventional economic problems, there is a family of problems associated with the natural environment which involves the irreproducibility of unique phenomena of nature—or the irreversibility of some consequence inimical to human welfare. Second, it appears that the utility to individuals of direct association with natural environments may be increasing while the supply is not readily subject to enlargement by man. Third, the real cost of refraining from converting our remaining rare natural environments may not be very great. Moreover, with the continued advance in technology, more substitutes for conventional natural resources will be found for the industrial and agricultural sectors, liberating production from dependence on conventional sources of raw materials. Finally, if consumption-saving behavior is motivated also by the desire to leave an estate, some portion of the estate would need to be in assets which yield collective consumption goods of appreciating future value. For all of these reasons we are confronted with a problem not conventionally met in resource economics. The problem is of the following nature.

At any point in time characterized by a level of technology which is less advanced than at some future date, the conversion of the natural environment into industrially produced private goods has proceeded further than it would have with the more advanced future technology. Moreover, with the apparent increasing appreciation of direct contact with natural environments, the conversion will have proceeded further, for this reason as well, than it would have were the future composition of tastes to have prevailed. Given the irreversibility of converted natural

[17] See [2]; also [9].

environments, however, it will not be possible to achieve a level of well-being in the future that would have been possible had the conversion of natural environments been retarded. That this should be of concern to members of the present generation may be attributable to the bequest motivation in private economic behavior as much as to a sense of public responsibility.[18]

Accordingly, our problem is akin to the dynamic programming problem which requires a present action (which may violate conventional benefit-cost criteria) to be compatible with the attainment of future states of affairs. But we know little about the value that the instrumental variables may take. We have virtually no knowledge about the possible magnitude of the option demand. And we still have much to learn about the determinants of the growth in demand for outdoor recreation and about the quantitative significance of the asymmetry in the implications of technological advances for producing industrial goods on the one hand and natural environments on the other. Obviously, a great deal of research in these areas is necessary before we can hope to apply formal decision criteria comparable to current benefit-cost criteria. Fully useful results may be very long in coming; what then is a sensible way to proceed in the interim?

First, we need to consider what we need as a minimum reserve to avoid potentially grossly adverse consequences for human welfare. We may regard this as our scientific preserve of research materials required for advances in the life and earth sciences. While no careful evaluation of the size of this reserve has been undertaken by scientists, an educated guess has put the need in connection with terrestrial communities at about ten million acres for North America [4, p. 128]. Reservation of this amount of land—but a small fraction of one per cent of the total relevant area—is not likely to affect appreciably the supply or costs of material inputs to the manufacturing or agricultural sectors.

The size of the scientific preserve required for aquatic environments is still unknown. Only after there is developed an adequate system of classification of aquatic communities will it be possible to identify distinct environments, recognize the needed reservations, and, then, estimate the opportunity costs. Classification and identification of aquatic environments demand early research attention by natural scientists.

Finally, one might hope that the reservations for scientific purposes would also support the bulk of the outdoor recreation demands, or that substantial additional reservations for recreational purposes could be

[18] The rationale above differs from that of Stephen Marglin which is perhaps the most rigorous one relying on a sense of public responsibility and externalities to justify explicit provision for future generations. In this case also, my concern is with providing *collective consumption goods for the present and future,* whereas the traditional concern in conservation economics has been with provision of *private intermediate goods for the future.*

142

justified by the demand and implicit opportunity costs. Reservations for recreation, as well as for biotic communities, should include special or rare environments which can support esoteric tastes as well as the more common ones. This is a matter of some importance because outdoor recreation opportunities will be provided in large part by public, bodies, and within the public sector there is a tendency to provide a homogenized recreation commodity oriented toward a common denominator. There is need to recognize, and make provision for, the widest range of outdoor recreation tastes, just as a well-functioning market would do. We need a policy and a mechanism to ensure that all natural areas peculiarly suited for specialized recreation uses receive consideration for such uses. A policy of this kind would be consistent both with maintaining the greatest biological diversity for scientific research and educational purposes and with providing the widest choice for consumers of outdoor recreation.

REFERENCES

1. H. J. BARNETT AND C. MORSE, Scarcity and Growth: The Economics of Natural Resource Availability. Baltimore 1963.
2. S. B. CHASE, JR., Asset Prices in Economic Analysis. Berkeley 1963.
3. S. V. CIRIACY-WANTRUP, Resources Conservation. Berkeley 1952.
4. F. DARLING AND J. P. MILTON, ed., Future Environments of North America, Transformation of a Continent. Garden City, N.Y. 1966.
5. P. DAVIDSON, F. G. ADAMS, AND J. SENECA, "The Social Value of Water Recreation Facilities Resulting from an Improvement in Water Quality: The Delaware Estuary," in A. V. Kneese and S. C. Smith, ed., Water Research, Baltimore 1966.
6. A. E. KAHN, "The Tyranny of Small Decisions: Market Failures, Imperfections, and the Limits of Economics," Kyklos, 1966, 19 (1), 23-47.
7. A. V. KNEESE, The Economics of Regional Water Quality Management. Baltimore 1964.
8. M. B. KREIG, Green Medicine: The Search for Plants that Heal. New York 1964.
9. F. MODIGLIANI AND R. BRUMBERG, "Utility Analysis and the Consumption Function: An Interpretation of Cross-Section Data," in K. K. Kurihara, ed., Post-Keynesian Economics, New Brunswick 1954.
10. A. C. PIGOU, The Economics of Welfare. 4th ed., London 1952.
11. N. POTTER AND F. T. CHRISTY, JR., Trends in Natural Resources Commodities: Statistics of Prices, Output, Consumption, Foreign Trade, and Employment in the United States, 1870-1957. Baltimore 1962.
12. The President's Materials Policy Commission, Resources for Freedom, Foundation for Growth and Security, Vol. I. Washington 1952.
13. A. D. SCOTT, Natural Resources: The Economics of Conservation. Toronto 1955.
14. B. A. WEISBROD, "Collective Consumption Services of Individual Consumption Goods," Quart. Jour. Econ., Aug. 1964, 77, 71-77.

PART IV. BENEFIT-COST ANALYSIS

COST-BENEFIT ANALYSIS: A SURVEY[1]

By

A. R. PREST AND R. TURVEY

THE order of discussion in this survey article will be as follows: in I we shall outline the development and scope of the subject in general terms; II will be concerned with general principles; in III we shall survey particular applications of cost-benefit techniques, examining the uses made of them in a variety of fields—water-supply projects, transport, land usage, health, education, research, etc. We shall proceed to a general summing up in IV, and conclude with a bibliography.

I. INTRODUCTION

Cost-benefit analysis [2] is a practical way of assessing the desirability of projects, where it is important to take a long view (in the sense of looking at repercussions in the further, as well as the nearer, future) and a wide view (in the sense of allowing for side-effects of many kinds on many persons, industries, regions, etc.), *i.e.*, it implies the enumeration and evaluation of all the relevant costs and benefits. This involves drawing on a variety of traditional sections of economic study—welfare economics, public finance, resource economics—and trying to weld these components into a coherent whole. Although the subject of cost-benefit analysis has come into prominence among economists only in recent years, it has quite a long history, especially in France, where Dupuit's classic paper on the utility of public works, one of the most original path-breaking writings in the whole history of economics, appeared as long ago as 1844 [19]. In the present century cost-benefit analysis first came into prominence in the United States. Here, according to Hammond [32], it was " in origin an administrative device owing nothing to economic theory and adapted to a strictly limited type of Federal activity—the improvement of navigation " (*op. cit.*, p. 3).

The River and Harbor Act 1902 required a board of engineers to report on the desirability of Army Corps of Engineers' river and harbour projects, taking into account the amount of commerce benefited and the cost. Another

---

[1] The authors are respectively Professor of Economics and Public Finance in the University of Manchester and Chief Economist, The Electricity Council. They are indebted to M. E. Beesley, J. L. Carr, O. Eckstein, M. J. Farrell, M. S. Feldstein, C. D. Foster, R. N. McKean, E. Mishan, A. T. Peacock, M. H. Peston and C. S. Shoup for most valuable comments and suggestions on an earlier draft.
[2] Alternatively christened " investment planning " or " project appraisal."

THE ECONOMIC JOURNAL, Dec. 1965, Vol. 75, No. 300, pp. 683-705.
Reprinted with permission from St. Martin's Press, Inc., Macmillan & Co., Ltd.

Act further required a statement of local or special benefits as a means for charging local interests with part of the cost. So the Corps of Engineers worked out valuation techniques confined to tangible costs and benefits.

In the thirties, with the New Deal, the idea of a broader social justification for projects developed. The Flood Control Act of 1936 thus authorised Federal participation in flood-control schemes " if the benefits to whomsoever they may accrue are in excess of the estimated costs." The practice of making analyses then spread to the other agencies concerned with water-development projects. The purpose was not only to justify projects but also to help to decide who should pay.

By the end of the war, agencies had broadened their approaches by:

(a) bringing in secondary or indirect benefits and costs;
(b) including intangibles.

In 1950 an inter-agency committee produced the " Green Book " [40], an attempt to codify and agree general principles. It was noteworthy as bringing in the language of welfare economics.

Interest among economists in this technique has grown tremendously in the last few years, as can be seen from the number of references cited in the bibliography and the years in which these works appeared.[1] There seem to be several reasons for this. One has been the growth of large investment projects—absorbing a large amount of resources, having repercussions over a long period of time or substantially affecting prices and outputs of other products, etc. Another obvious reason is the growth of the public sector, e.g., the Central Government, local authorities and public enterprises such as nationalised industries accounted for 45% of gross fixed investment in the United Kingdom in 1963, compared with 33% in 1938. A technique which is explicitly concerned with the wide consequences of investment decisions is obviously of much more interest to-day than it was twenty-five years ago. Another reason for increasing interest by economists is the rapid development in recent years of such techniques as operations research, systems analysis, etc., both in the public and the private sectors of the economy. This is a point on which McKean [53] has laid particular emphasis.

It is always important, and perhaps especially so in economics, to avoid being swept off one's feet by the fashions of the moment. In the case of cost-benefit analysis, one must recognise that it is a method which can be used inappropriately as well as appropriately. There are two very clear general

---

[1] Alternatively, one can look at earlier works to see what their authors had to say about the principles of public investment expenditures. If one selects Dalton [16] for this purpose—and in doing this one can hardly be accused of selecting someone uninterested in the subject—one finds the following kind of statement:

" There is thus a large field for the intervention of public authorities to increase economic provision for the future and to create a better balance between its component elements. These two objects furnish the key to nearly all public expenditure designed to increase productive power " (op. cit., p. 157).

This is unexceptionable but hardly a complete guide to policy-makers.

limitations of principle (as distinct from the many more of practice) which must be recognised at the outset. First, cost-benefit analysis as generally understood is only a technique for taking decisions within a framework which has to be decided upon in advance and which involves a wide range of considerations, many of them of a political or social character. Secondly, cost-benefit techniques as so far developed are least relevant and serviceable for what one might call large-size investment decisions. If investment decisions are so large relatively to a given economy (*e.g.*, a major dam project in a small country), that they are likely to alter the constellation of relative outputs and prices over the whole economy, the standard technique is likely to fail us, for nothing less than some sort of general equilibrium approach would suffice in such cases. This means that the applicability of the technique to underdeveloped countries is likely to be less than is sometimes envisaged, as so many investment projects involve large structural changes in such areas. Of course, this does not rule out all applications of this technique in such countries, as a number of valuable studies (*e.g.*, Hawkins [34], Farmer [22]) bear witness. Nor should it do so, given the shortage of capital resources in such countries. The point is simply that one must remain more acutely aware of the limitations of the technique in these cases.

So much for the general limitations of cost-benefit analysis. It must be made clear at this point that this survey has particular limitations as well. First, cost-benefit analysis has many facets and many applications [1] which we cannot hope to cover fully. There are therefore gaps in both subject matter and references. Secondly, a good deal of the material in the field lies unpublished in the files of government departments or international agencies and is therefore inaccessible. Third, there is no discussion of such maximisation methods as linear and non-linear programming, simulation, game theory, etc. Finally, we shall confine ourselves to the applications of these techniques in economies which are not centrally planned and where there is a reasonable amount of recognition of the principle of consumer sovereignty. This should not be taken to mean that we think that cost-benefit analysis has no relevance at all in centrally planned economies, but simply that we are not attempting to deal with such cases.

II. General Principles

1. Preliminary Considerations

(a) *Statement of the Problem*

As we have seen, cost-benefit analysis is a way of setting out the factors which need to be taken into account in making certain economic choices. Most of the choices to which it has been applied involve investment projects

---

[1] The bibliography cited by McKean [53] contains references to works on, *e.g.*, government budgeting, capital budgeting, strategy, investment theory, welfare economics, highway pricing, operational research, staff and management control.

and decisions—whether or not a particular project is worthwhile, which is the best of several alternative projects, or when to undertake a particular project. We can, however, apply the term " project " more generally than this. Cost-benefit analysis can also be applied to proposed changes in laws or regulations, to new pricing schemes and the like. An example is furnished by proposals for regulating the traffic on urban roads. Such schemes involve making economic choices along the same lines as investment schemes. As choice involves maximisation, we have to discuss what it is that decision-makers want to maximise. The formulation which, as a description, best covers most cost-benefit analyses examined in the literature we are surveying is as follows: the aim is to maximise the present value of all benefits less that of all costs, subject to specified constraints.

This formulation is very general, but it does at least enable us to set out a series of questions, the answers to which constitute the general principles of cost-benefit analysis:

1. Which costs and which benefits are to be included?
2. How are they to be valued?
3. At what interest rate are they to be discounted?
4. What are the relevant constraints?

Needless to say, there is bound to be a certain degree of arbitrariness in classifying questions under these four headings, but that cannot be helped.

(b) *A General Issue*

Before we can take these questions seriatim it is convenient to discuss an issue which involves more than one of these questions. It arises because the conditions for a welfare maximum are not likely to be fulfilled throughout the economy. If they were, and so resource allocation were optimal, the marginal social rate of time preference and the (risk-adjusted) marginal social rate of return from investment would coincide. A single rate of interest would then serve both to compare benefits and costs of different dates and to measure the opportunity cost of that private investment which is displaced by the need to provide resources for the projects in question. As things are, however, no single rate of interest will fulfil both functions simultaneously; in a non-optimal world there are two things to be measured and not one.

The problem has been discussed by a number of authors, including Eckstein [20, 21], Steiner [80], Marglin [48] and Feldstein [23, 24, 25]. They suggest that the costs and benefits of a project are the time streams of consumption foregone and provided by that project. The nature of this approach emerges clearly from Feldstein's remarks on the social opportunity cost of funds transferred from the private sector to the public sector in [25]:

" Part of the money taken from the private sector decreases consumption immediately, while the rest decreases investment and therefore future consumption. A pound transferred from consumption in a particular year has, by definition, a social value in that year of £1. But a pound transferred from private investment is worth the discounted value of the future consumption that would have occurred if the investment had been made. The original investment generates an income stream to investors and workers. Some of this income is spent on consumption and the remainder is invested. Each of these subsequent investments generates a new income stream and thus consumption and further investment. The final result is an aggregate consumption timestream generated by the original investment. It is the current value of this aggregate that is the social opportunity cost of a one pound decrease in private investment.''

The application of this approach to both costs and benefits produces a complicated expression for the present worth of a project's benefits less its costs. Nobody has as yet succeeded in quantifying such expressions, however,[1] so at present the approach can only serve as a reference-standard for judging simpler but more practicable ways of tackling the problem. Meanwhile, we note that the problem arises to the extent: (i) that a project's benefits are reinvested or create new investment opportunities, or (ii) that some of the funds used for the project would otherwise have been invested or that the project renders impossible some other and mutually exclusive investment project. If neither of these conditions is fulfilled; if, in other words, benefits and costs both consist exclusively of consumption (directly provided and, respectively, precluded by the project), then these complications do not arise, and the problem is reduced to one of choosing an appropriate social time preference rate of discount.

2. The Main Questions

(a) Enumeration of Costs and Benefits

(i) *Definition of a Project.* In most cases the scope and nature of the projects which are to be submitted to cost-benefit analysis will be clear. For the sake of completeness, however, we must make the point that if one authority is responsible for producing A goods and B goods, then in judging between A goods investment projects of different sizes it must take into account the effect of producing more A goods on its output of B goods. There are all sorts of complications here: relationships between A and B goods may be on the supply or demand side, they may be direct (in the sense of A influencing B) or indirect (in the sense of A influencing C, which influences B) and so on. One illustration is the operations of an authority responsible for a long stretch of river; if it puts a dam at a point upstream this will affect the water level, and hence the operations of existing or potential dams downstream. Construction of a fast motorway, which in

---

[1] " Estimating many of the variables and parameters needed to calculate net social benefit may indeed be difficult " (Feldstein [23], p. 126).

itself speeds up traffic and reduces accidents, may lead to more congestion or more accidents on feeder roads if they are left unimproved. All that this amounts to saying is that where there are strong relationships on either the supply or the demand side, allowances must be made for these in cost-benefit calculations. We shall return to this point later (see p. 176 *infra*), when discussing investment criteria.

(ii) *Externalities*. We now come to the wide class of costs and benefits which accrue to bodies other than the one sponsoring a project, and the equally wide issue of how far the sponsoring body should take them into account. We shall discuss the general principles at stake and then apply them to particular cases.

McKean [53, Ch. 8] discusses the distinction between technological and pecuniary *spillovers* at length. The essential points are that progenitors of public investment projects *should* take into account the external effects of their actions in so far as they alter the physical production possibilities of other producers or the satisfactions that consumers can get from given resources; they *should not* take side-effects into account if the sole effect is via prices of products or factors. One example of the first type is when the construction of a reservoir by the upstream authority of a river basin necessitates more dredging by the downstream authority. An example of the second type is when the improvement of a road leads to greater profitability of the garages and restaurants on that road, employment of more labour by them, higher rent payments to the relevant landlords, etc. In general, this will *not* be an additional benefit to be credited to the road investment, even if the extra profitability, etc., of the garages on one road is not offset by lower profitability of garages on the other, which are now less used as a result of the traffic diversion. Any net difference in profitability and any net rise in rents and land values is simply a reflection of the benefits of more journeys being undertaken, etc., than before, and it would be double counting if these were included too. In other words, we have to eliminate the purely transfer or distributional items from a cost-benefit evaluation: we are concerned with the value of the increment of output arising from a given investment and not with the increment in value of existing assets. In still other words, we measure costs and benefits on the assumption of a given set of prices, and the incidental and consequential price changes of goods and factors should be ignored.[1]

No one can pretend that this distinction is a simple one to maintain in practice; there may well be results from investment which are partially technological and partially pecuniary. Nor is the task of unravelling made easier by the fact that some of the transfers occasioned by investment projects may affect the distribution of income significantly, and hence the pattern of demand. But as a general guiding principle the distinction is most valuable.

We now consider the application of this principle. First of all, an invest-

---

[1] Apart from allowances necessary to get a measure of the change of surplus (see p. 163 *infra*).

ing agency must try to take account of obvious technological spillovers, such as the effects of flood control measures or storage dams on the productivity of land at other points in the vicinity. In some cases no explicit action may be needed, *e.g.*, these effects may be internal to different branches of the same agency, or some system of compensation may be prescribed by law. But in others there should at least be an attempt to correct for the most obvious and important repercussions. Although in principle corrections are needed whatever the relationship between the interacting organisations, it must be expected that in practice the compulsion to take side-effects into account will be much greater if similar organisations are involved, *e.g.*, one local authority is more likely to take account of the costs it imposes on other bodies if those mainly affected are one or two other local authorities than if they are a large multitude of individuals.

(iii) *Secondary Benefits*. The notion that some pecuniary spillovers are properly included in benefits has appeared in a particular guise in arguments about secondary benefits. The American discussion of this matter has centred on the benefit estimation procedures used by the Bureau of Reclamation in respect of irrigation projects. In their analysis of the problem, McKean [53], Eckstein [20] and Margolis [52] all start by describing these procedures. The essential principle can be made clear by taking the case of irrigation which results in an increase in grain production, where the direct or primary benefits are measured as the value of the increase in grain output less the associated increase in farmers' costs.

The increased grain output will involve increased activity by grain merchants, transport concerns, millers, bakers and so on, and hence, it is asserted, will involve an increase in their profits. If the ratio of total profits in all these activities to the value of grain at the farm is 48% then secondary benefits of 48% of the value of the increase in grain output are credited to the irrigation project. These are called " stemming " secondary benefits. " Induced " secondary benefits, on the other hand, are the extra profits made from activities which sell to farmers. The profit rate here has been computed as averaging 18% of farmers' purchases.

All the three authors mentioned are highly critical of these notions, as they were set out by the Bureau of Reclamation in 1952. We shall not give a blow-by-blow account of the arguments of each author, but instead attempt to provide our own synthesis.

Where the output of a project has a market value this value plus any consumers' surplus can be taken as the measure of the gross benefit arising from the project. But where the output either is not sold or is sold at a price fixed solely with reference to cost-sharing considerations, it is necessary to impute a value to the output. Thus, in the case of irrigation water, a value is obtained by working out what the water is worth to farmers as the excess of the value of the increased output which it makes possible over the cost of the necessary increase in all the farmers' other inputs. The question now arises whether we should not impute a value to the increased farm output just as we have imputed one to the water instead of taking the market value of that output. Thus, supposing (to simplify the argument) that wheat is the only farm output, that all the wheat is used to make flour and that all the flour is used to make bread, why should we not value the water by taking the value of the increased output of bread and deducting the increase in farmers', millers' and bakers' costs? Consumption is, after all, the end of all economic activity, so is not what matters the value of the increase in consumption of bread made possible by the irrigation project less the sacrifice of alternative consumption involved—as measured by increased farming, milling and baking costs?

The answer must be that a properly functioning price mechanism performs the function of imputing values for us. It does so not only as regards the increase in farmers' costs (as the argument implicitly assumes) but also as regards the increase in their output (as it seems to deny). The market demand for wheat is a derived demand, and so reflects the value of extra bread and the marginal costs of milling, baking, etc. Imputation of values by the analyst is thus necessary only where there is no market for a product, *i.e.*, only for the water itself.

We conclude, therefore, that if the conditions for optimal resource allocation are fulfilled in the rest of the economy the estimate of benefits obtained by using the price of wheat and the price of farming inputs constitutes an adequate measure. Putting the matter the other way round, we need worry about secondary benefits (or, for that matter, costs) only to the extent that market prices fail to reflect marginal social costs and benefits. The real problem concerning secondary benefits (and costs) is thus a matter of second-best allocation problems.

(iv) *Project Life.* Estimation of length of life is clearly a highly subjective process depending on assessments of the physical length of life, technological changes, shifts in demand, emergence of competing products and so on. The effect of any error will depend on the rate of discount adopted; the higher this is, the less do errors of estimation matter. Some investigations seem to show that different assumptions about lengths of life do not affect the viability of schemes to an enormous extent (Foster and Beesley [28]). We have here, incidentally, one example of the scope for sensitivity analysis, where the calculations are repeated many times for different values of variables. This is an extremely important tool when estimates of costs and benefits are uncertain.

(b) *Valuation of Costs and Benefits*

(i) *The Relevant Prices.* When we are dealing with costs and benefits which can be expressed in terms of money it is generally agreed that adjustments need to be made to the expected prices of future inputs and outputs to allow for anticipated changes in relative prices of the items involved (including expected changes in interest rates over time), but not for expected changes in the *general* price level. The essential principle is that all prices must be reckoned on the same basis, and for convenience this will usually be the price-level prevailing in the initial year.[1] Future developments in output levels have also to be taken into account, *e.g.*, it is customary in cost-benefit studies of highway improvements to allow for the long-term trend of traffic growth.

(ii) *Non-marginal Changes.* With the exceptions discussed below, market prices are used to value the costs and benefits of a project. Difficulties arise when investment projects are large enough to affect these prices. In the case of final products, the benefits accruing from investment cannot be measured by multiplying the additional quantum of output either by the old or the new price. The former would give an over-estimate and the latter an underestimate. What is needed, as has long been recognised (Dupuit [19]), is a measure of the addition to the area under the demand curve, which, on the assumption that the marginal utility of money remains unchanged, is an appropriate measure of the money value of the benefits provided, in the sense of assessing what the recipients would pay rather than go without them. When the demand curve is linear an unweighted average of before and after prices will suffice; but more complicated techniques are necessary for other forms of demand function—when they are known. In the case of intermediate products, the demand curve is a derived one, and so it can only be a perfect reflector of social benefit if the optimum welfare conditions are met all along the line. If this condition is satisfied the gross benefit arising from a project concerned with intermediate products is measured by the market value of sales plus any increase in consumers' and producers' surplus in respect of any final products based on the intermediate ones.

On the costs side there is a double problem, clearly distinguished in Lerner's treatment of indivisibilities [45]. First, it is necessary to adjust prices of factors so as to eliminate any rental elements, which will be measured by excesses over transfer earnings in their next best alternative use. Second, one has an exactly analogous problem to the demand side, in that as more and more of a factor is absorbed in any one line of output the price of the alternative product which it might have been making rises further and further. Therefore we are faced with the choice between valuation of factors at the original price (*i.e.*, that ruling prior to the expansion of output of the commodity in question), the ultimate price, or some intermediate level. On the assumption of linearity, a price half-way between the original and ultimate levels will meet the bill, as on the demand side. Obviously, either or both of these two types of adjustments may be necessary at any

---

[1] Hirshleifer [37, p. 143] argues that, since the " true " interest rate lies below the " monetary " one when prices are expected to rise, a downward adjustment should be made to market rates to allow for this.

particular time, and so to this extent the adjustments for indivisibilities on the costs side are likely to be more complex than those on the benefit side.

(iii) *Market Imperfections.* Departures from Pareto-optimum situations arise when monopolistic elements or other imperfections in goods or factor markets are such as to twist relative outputs away from those which would prevail under competitive conditions. In cases of this kind investment decisions based on valuations of costs and benefits at market prices may not be appropriate; failure to correct for these distortions is likely to lead to misallocations of investment projects between different industries.

The relevance of this point for public decisions concerning investment is several-fold. First, if a public authority in a monopolistic position behaves like a private monopolist in its pricing and output policy its investment decisions will not comply with the principles of efficient allocation of resources unless the degree of monopoly is uniform throughout the economy. Secondly, complications may arise when there is monopolistic behaviour at a later stage in the production process. This can be illustrated by the example of an irrigation project which enables more sugar-beet to be grown, and hence more sugar to be refined. If the refiners enjoy a monopolistic position the sugar-beet farmers' demand for irrigation water will not be a sufficient indication of the merits of the irrigation project. If the refiners were producing at the (higher) competitive level they would absorb more beet, and this would in turn react back on the demand for irrigation water.

A third illustration is in respect of factor supplies. If the wages which have to be paid to the labour engaged on an investment project include some rental element and are greater than their marginal opportunity costs, then a deduction must be made to arrive at an appropriate figure: conversely, if wages are squeezed below marginal opportunity costs by monopsony practices.

Fourthly, there may be an excess of average over marginal costs. This raises the well-known difficulty that if prices are equated to short-run marginal costs, as they must be to ensure short-period efficiency, the enterprise will run at a loss. Various ways (see, *e.g.*, Hicks [36]) of getting over the problem have been suggested, but there are snags in all of them. Charges can be made, *e.g.*, by means of a two-part tariff, but this is likely to deter some consumers whose marginal valuation of the output exceeds its marginal cost. Various systems of discriminatory charges can be devised, but these may imply inquisitorial powers on the part of the authorities. Voluntary subscriptions can be asked for, but this runs into the Wicksell objection in respect of collective goods.[1] If none of these solutions are acceptable one must be prepared to countenance losses. So this is still another case where investment decisions have to be divorced from accounting computations of profits. Instead, they must be based on notions of what people would be willing to

---

[1] See *infra*, p. 168.

pay or what the project " ought to be " worth to customers, as Hicks [36] puts it. It must be emphasised that this is not a case where prices of goods or factors are imperfect measures of benefits and costs *per se*, but where the present value of net receipts no longer measures benefits.

These are all examples of what is fundamentally the same problem: the inapplicability of investment decision rules derived from a perfectly competitive state of affairs to a world where such a competitive situation no longer holds. It should be noted that there are two possible ways of making the necessary accounting adjustments: either a correction can be made to the actual level of costs (benefits), or the costs (benefits) arising from the market can be taken as they stand but a corresponding correction has to be made to the estimation of benefits (costs). Normally, the first of these two methods would be less complicated and less liable to cause confusion.

(iv) *Taxes and Controls.* Imperfect competition constitutes only one case of divergence between market price and social cost or benefit. Another is that of taxes on expenditure. Most economists prefer to measure taxed inputs at their factor cost rather than at their market value, though the latter would be appropriate when the total supply of the input in question has a zero elasticity of supply, *e.g.*, an imported item subject to a strict quota. A possible extension of this particular example relates to the cost of imported items in an economy with a fairly high level of tariff protection where it could be argued that price including duty is the best measure of social cost, because in the absence of protection the country's equilibrium exchange rate would be lower. Perhaps the most important example of a tax which it has been decided to exclude from costs occurs in the estimation of fuel savings resulting from road improvements [14].

Public decisions may properly differ from private ones in the investment field in respect of direct tax payments too. While private profit-making decisions should allow for income and profits tax payments, this is not apposite in the public sector. What one is primarily concerned with here is a measurement of cost which corresponds to the use of real resources [1] but excludes transfer payments. Hence profits or income taxes on the income derived by a public authority from its project are irrelevant.

As an example of government controls, we may take agricultural price supports and production controls. There seem to have been cases in the past in the United States (*e.g.*, the Missouri Basin project) where estimates of the benefits from sugar-beet production were made without taking any notice of existing sugar-beet quotas or considering whether sugar-beet production would actually be allowed to increase! Hard as it is to cope with refinements

---

[1] Additional government expenditures necessitated by a public authority project should be included as part of its costs. But whether these expenditures are, or are not, financed by taxes on that authority is irrelevant.

When public projects are being compared with private ones there must obviously be a common standard of comparison in respect of transfers to and by government, the simplest being to ignore them.

of this sort, obviously some attempt must be made to take cognisance of the more blatant discrepancies.

(v) *Unemployment.* A divergence of social cost from private cost which is sometimes of major importance arises when there is unemployment. When there is an excess supply at the current market price of any input that price overstates the social cost of using that input. Furthermore, when there is general unemployment, expenditure upon a project, by creating a multiplier effect, will create additional real incomes in the rest of the economy. Hence the use of market values to ascertain direct costs and benefits of a project overstates its social costs and underestimates its total benefits (by the amount of "induced benefits"). Under these conditions almost any project is better for the country than no project, so that, to achieve sub-optimisation, autonomous public agencies should bring these considerations into their benefit and cost calculations, while agencies subject to central government control over their expenditure should either choose the same or be told to do so. This simple picture only holds, however, when there is but one issue to decide: shall a particular project be initiated or not? But such a choice never exists in this solitary state. The Government can choose between public works and other methods of curing unemployment. The agencies responsible for the public works can choose between a number of possible projects, some of them mutually exclusive (*e.g.*, the choice between building a four- or six-lane motorway along a particular alignment). And it is not at all obvious that unemployment-adjusted estimates of costs and benefits constitute the right tool for making these choices.

The arguments against correcting costs for an excess of the market price of factors over the price which would clear the market for them and against including multiplier effects in benefits are largely [1] practical (cf. McKean [53]):

(*a*) It is easier to allow for the overpricing of labour which is to be used in constructing or operating a project than to allow for the overpricing of equipment, fuel, materials, etc., which are overpriced because they, too, include in their costs some overpriced labour. Yet if correction is made for project labour costs only, the relative social costs of project labour and of other inputs may be more poorly estimated than if no correction at all is made.

(*b*) Correcting future costs requires estimates of future unemployment. Government agencies are not usually equipped to make such forecasts, and governments may be reluctant to provide them on a realistic basis in view of the difficulty of keeping them out of public notice.

[1] But not entirely: it is possible to conceive of an unemployment situation in which shadow cost pricing would make a very large number of investment projects pass a cost-benefit test—in fact, a larger number than would be needed to reach full employment. The problem is to fix the shadow prices so that one can select the best projects but not so many of them that one has more than full employment.

(c) The effect of a project upon unemployment depends not only upon the expenditure which it involves but also upon the way it is financed, and this may not be known to the people doing the cost-benefit analysis (e.g., in the case of an agency financed by government grants).

These arguments suggest that in most cases it is best for unemployment policy to be left to the central government and for the agencies responsible for public works to confine their corrections of market prices on account of under-employment (i.e., overpricing) to divergences which are local or which relate to some specialised factor of production. National unemployment, to take an example, should be no concern of the National Coal Board, but the alleged lack of alternative employment opportunities for miners in certain coalfields should.

(vi) *Collective Goods.* Market prices clearly cannot be used to value benefits which are not capable of being marketed. Thus we meet the collective goods issue (Samuelson [72, 73, 74], Musgrave [60], Head [35]). The essential point is that some goods and services supplied by Government are of a collective nature in the sense that the quantity supplied to any one member of the relevant group cannot be independently varied. For example, all members of the population benefit from defence expenditure, all the inhabitants of any given district benefit from an anti-malaria programme, and all ships in the vicinity benefit from a lighthouse. The difference between separately marketable goods and such collective goods can be shown as in Figs. 1 (a) and 1 (b), following Bowen [8].

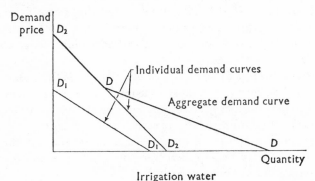

FIG. 1 (a).—Marketable Goods.

Whereas aggregation of individual demand curves is obtained by *horizontal* summation in the Fig. (1) (a) case, it is obtained by *vertical* summation in the Fig. 1 (b) case. This reflects the fact that though individuals may differ in their marginal valuation of a given quantity of a commodity, they all consume the same amount, in that each unit is consumed by all of them. For example, flood control afforded to different individuals is a joint product.

157

Ever since Wicksell, it has been recognised that any attempt to get consumers to reveal their preferences regarding collective goods founders on the rock that the rational thing for any individual consumer to do is understate his demand, in the expectation that he would thereby be relieved of part or all of his share of the cost without affecting the quantity obtained. Although a number of people (notably Lindahl) have attempted to find ways

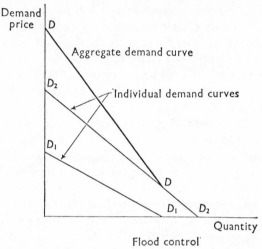

FIG. 1(b).—Collective Goods.

out of this impasse, it seems safe to say that no one has succeeded. In fact, the difficulties have multiplied rather than diminished, as Samuelson [72, 73, 74] and Musgrave [60] have demonstrated that even if the non-revelation of preferences problem is ignored, there is still another major snag, in that there is no single best solution but rather a multiplicity of alternative optimum solutions.

The relevance of this discussion for our purposes is that where commodities are supplied at zero prices or at non-market clearing prices which bear no relationship to consumer preferences, there is no basis for arriving at investment decisions by computing the present values of sales. Of course, the problem does not apply to collective goods alone; a whole range of other goods and services may be supplied free (or at nominal prices) by government for a whole variety of reasons.

(vii) *Intangibles.* Some costs and benefits (such as the scenic effect of building electricity transmission lines) cannot be quantified, and others, although they can be quantified, cannot be valued in any market sense (*e.g.*, a reduction in lives lost). Such costs and benefits have been called intangible costs and benefits. They are obviously important in many cases and, equally obviously, have to be presented to the decision-maker in the prose which accompanies the cost-benefit arithmetic, since they cannot be incorporated in the arithmetic itself. It may be possible to gain some idea of their importance on the basis of consumer questionnaires, but one has to be careful of the well-known difficulties inherent in such efforts (Yates [90]).

There is one possible exception in the case of quantifiable items. Consistency requires that the net marginal cost of, say, saving an average citizen's life be the same whether it be achieved by hiring more traffic police or by having more ambulances. If there were consistency and if the marginal cost were known, then it would measure how much decision-makers were ready to pay to save a life, and hence it could be used for valuing lives saved. So the importance attached to particular " intangibles " may sometimes be inferred from private or public behaviour. Thus, one might suggest that British public standards of visual amenity are higher than the private standards manifest in most back gardens!

(c) *Choice of Interest Rate*

(i) *The Social Time Preference Rate.* The literature on the choice of appropriate interest rates for public investment projects is voluminous, and we cannot hope to survey it in detail. But starting from the constellation of rates that one finds in the private sector, various questions have to be raised. Even if one can select a single or average risk-free long-term rate, it is not clear what significance can be attached to it. Straightaway we come up against all the old arguments about whether market rates of interest do bear any close relationship to the marginal productivity of investment and time preference or whether the relationship is so blurred as to be imperceptible. This is partly a matter of different interest theories (neo-Classical, Keynesian, Robertsonian, etc.) and partly a matter of how particular economies tick at particular times—do governments intervene in capital markets with any effectiveness, how well organised and unified is the capital market in a country, etc.? Both pure theory and imperfections in the capital market are thus involved.

Another issue is whether any market-determined interest rate would suffice for community decisions even if neo-classical theory is accepted and a perfectly functioning capital market assumed. Some writers believe that social time preference attaches more weight to the future than private time preference and that it is the former which is relevant for determining the allocation of society's current resources between investment and consumption. A number of arguments in favour of such a proposition have been produced over the years. Pigou [65], for instance, suggested that individuals were short-sighted about the future (" defective telescopic faculty ") and that government intervention might be needed to give adequate weight to the welfare of unborn generations (*op. cit.*, pp. 24–30). More recently, other arguments, which seek to avoid the objection that the Pigou position is a fundamentally authoritarian one, have been put forward (Eckstein [21], Marglin [49]). One point made really relates to a special kind of externality. It is that any one individual's preference for current consumption, relatively

159

to future consumption by himself or his successors, will be less if there is some sort of government-organised programme for imposing sacrifices on everybody—or at least on a large section of the population—than if the solution is left to the market. More generally, one might follow the lines indicated by Feldstein [24] and distinguish between: (1) market preferences; (2) preferences expressed through the ballot box; (3) what the Government in its wisdom thinks is good for this generation; and (4) what the Government thinks is good for this generation and future generations taken together.

Whatever the ultimate pros and cons of these arguments, there are two difficulties, if one tries to give effect to them. The first is actually to determine the social rate of discount. Marglin accepts that this does pose serious difficulties, but goes on to suggest that one can set about it by choosing the growth rate for an economy and thence (on the basis of the marginal capital/output ratio) determine the rate of investment; the social rate of discount must then be equated with the marginal productivity of investment. The practicability of such a procedure does not commend itself to us; but we must leave this to others to judge.

Another difficulty of operating with a social rate of discount is that we have the very awkward problem that different rates of interest would be used in the public and private sectors. There is then likely to be considerable inefficiency in the allocation of funds inside the investment sector—in the sense that if the Government is, say, responsible for electricity and the private sector for oil, inferior projects of the former kind will supplant superior projects of the latter kind.[1] This particular difficulty leads us right back to the point discussed at the beginning of Section II, *i.e.*, that one rate of interest cannot perform two functions in a non-optimal situation. One way out of this is to recommend making the situation an optimal one. For instance, Hirshleifer [37] has suggested that the Government should take action to push down market rates of interest to the social rate, so that all investment decisions, whether in the public or private sectors, should be taken on the same basis. While applauding this idea in principle, other writers quite reasonably feel that in practice economists will still have to deal with sub-optimisation problems.

(ii) *The Social Opportunity Cost Rate.* The government borrowing rate is a popular and easily applicable measure of costs, both because it is a financial cost in the case of government financed investment and, more academically, because it can be regarded as " the " risk-free rate of interest.[2] Yet despite the recent empirically founded recrudescence of belief in the interest elasticity of private investment, no one has demonstrated that the latter's marginal efficiency does actually equal the interest rate. A direct attempt to measure marginal rates of return on private investment is therefore required. Even if such a measure were made, however, it would be

---

[1] Defining " inferior " and " superior " in terms of present values of net benefits.

[2] Abstracting from uncertainty about the price level.

relevant only in so far as the costs being evaluated consisted exclusively of displaced private investment.

Recognising this problem, Krutilla and Eckstein [43] assumed that the alternative to public investment would be a tax cut, considered the ways in which a likely tax cut would affect income groups, and then asked how the notional recipients would utilise their hypothetical receipts, thus finally arriving at a weighted average rate of return. An alternative postulate was that the additional public investment would be offset by tighter monetary policy; it was then asked which individuals would suffer and what sort of weighted interest rate could thence be derived. The general result from both assumptions was that Federal capital in the United States in the late 'fifties had an opportunity cost of 5–6%. Quite apart from the logical and statistical problems associated with the techniques of assigning tax cuts to the different income groups, etc., as Eckstein himself has noted [21], this approach deals with only two out of many relevant alternatives (*e.g.*, more public investment might be met instead by less public consumption). It has also been severely criticised by Hirshleifer [37] on the grounds that the composite interest rate finally derived has an unknown allowance for a risk premium in it. Feldstein has also commented on this approach [25].

(iii) *Adjustment for Uncertainty*. The various ways in which uncertainty impinges upon cost-benefit analysis are discussed by Dorfman [48, Ch. 3], McKean [53, Ch. 4], Eckstein [21, Section 5], Hirshleifer [37, pp. 139–41] in their admirable surveys, and we need only add two remarks here. The first point is that there is no reason to argue that public investment projects are free of uncertainty (see, especially, Hirshleifer [37]). The second is that allowances for uncertainty can be made: (1) in the assessments of annual levels of benefits and costs; (2) in the assumptions about length of life; and (3) in the discount rate. The first is most appropriate if the risk of dispersion of outcomes (or inputs) is irregularly, rather than regularly, distributed with time. If the main risk is that there may be a sudden day of reckoning when benefits disappear or costs soar, the second type of adjustment is needed. The third correction, a premium on the discount rate, is appropriate where uncertainty is a strictly compounding function of time.

(iv) *The Need for an Interest Rate*. When the problem of choice involves no opportunity cost of capital—as happens when all of a fixed budget is to be spent—there is obviously no need for an opportunity-cost rate of interest. It has been argued by some authors, *e.g.*, McKean [53], that in this case there is no need for a social discount rate of interest either. This can be generally true, however, only if the maximand is not the present worth of benefits less costs, for if it is, some rate of discount is obviously required. We shall not elaborate this point here, since one of us has already published a purely expository note on the subject in this JOURNAL [83].

(v) *Principles* vs. *Practice*. Discussions about social rates of time prefer-ence, social opportunity cost, etc., do not cut very much ice in most empirical work, and we have not been able to discover any cases where there was any convincingly complete application of such notions.[1] Nor do ideas about allowing for future changes in interest rates seem to receive much attention. In practice, the most usual kind of procedure is to select an interest rate or rates, on the basis of observed rates ruling at the time, for calculating present values, etc. For example, Weisbrod [86] takes a rate of 10% to represent the opportunity cost of capital in the private sector (on the basis that the observed yield of 5% for corporate stocks should be grossed up to approximately double that figure to allow for the corporate profits tax) [2] and one of 4% to represent the cost of Federal Government borrowing. He then makes his present value calculations on both bases. It can obviously be said that this may give ambiguous results, *e.g.*, that project A is preferable to project B on one basis, but project B is preferable on the other. This is indisputable; but there are also examples to show that the choice of varying discount rates does not, within the 4–8% band, make much difference to assessments of a project (Foster and Beesley [28]), though the same conclusions do not necessarily hold for a rather wider band. The truth of the matter is that, whatever one does, one is trying to unscramble an omelette, and no one has yet invented a uniquely superior way of doing this.

(d) *Relevant Constraints*

(i) *Introduction.* Eckstein [21] has provided a most helpful classification of constraints. First, there are physical constraints. The most general of these is the production function which relates the physical inputs and outputs of a project, but this enters directly into the calculation of costs and benefits. Where choice is involved between different projects or regarding the size or timing of a particular project, external physical constraints may also be relevant. Thus, one particular input may be in totally inelastic supply, or two projects may be mutually exclusive on purely technological grounds.

Next there are legal constraints. What is done must be within the framework of the law, which may affect matters in a multiplicity of ways, *e.g.*, rights of access, time needed for public inquiries, regulated pricing, limits to the activities of public agencies and so on. Third, there may be administrative constraints, related to limits to what can be handled administratively. Fourth, uncertainty can be introduced by constraints, for example, by the introduction of some minimum regret requirement. Finally, there are distributional and budgetary constraints; these need more extended discussion.

(ii) *Distributional Constraints.* The notion that the choice between projects can be made solely on the grounds of " economic efficiency," because

---

[1] Eckstein [21] concluded after several pages of discussion " thus the choice of interest rates must remain a value judgment " (*op. cit.*, p. 460).

[2] It might be argued that a further correction should also be made to bridge any gap between earnings yield and dividend yield. This would make for a wider spread of the rate band.

any unfavourable effects on income distribution can be overcome by making some of the gainers compensate some of the losers, is rarely applicable in practice.

It is perfectly possible to compensate property-owners not only for property which is expropriated but also for property which is reduced in value. Similarly, it is possible to levy a charge in respect of property which has been enhanced in value. These payments of compensation and charges, being lump sums, are not likely to have any direct effects upon resource allocation. Another way in which extra money can be raised from the beneficiaries of a project without affecting resource allocation arises where some of the project outputs are sold and intra-marginal units of these outputs can be priced at more than marginal units. (Thus electricity consumers may be charged on a two-part tariff.)

In general, however, attempts to get beneficiaries to pay more than the marginal social cost of the project outputs they consume will affect the allocation of resources. Such attempts may be made either because of a desire not to raise the real income of the beneficiaries to an extent regarded as unfair or because of a desire to raise funds to compensate a group who are made worse off by the project or simply because of a general belief that projects ought to break even. Whatever the reason, the pricing policy adopted will affect project outputs, and hence project costs. Tolls on a motorway, for instance, will affect the volume of traffic, and this may affect the appropriate width at which it should be constructed. Thus, benefits and costs are not independent of pricing policy.

This can affect cost-benefit analysis in either of two ways. The first is relevant when pricing rules have been laid down in advance in the light of political or social notions about income distribution. Here the task is to maximise the present value of benefits less costs subject to certain specified financial requirements, i.e., subject to one or more constraints. The second way in which income distribution requirements may affect cost-benefit analysis occurs when the authorities have not laid down any specific financial rules but do clearly care about income distribution. In this case it is up to the analyst to invent and present as alternatives a number of variants of a project which differ both as regards the particular people who pay (or are paid) and the prices charged and, in consequence, as regards outputs and inputs. For each alternative, the analyst will have to set out not only total costs and benefits but also the costs and benefits for those particular groups whose economic welfare is of interest to the decision-maker.

In cases like this the choice can be formalised—if the decision-taker allows it—by expressing it in terms of maximising the excess of total benefits over total costs subject to constraints on the benefits less costs of particular groups. Alternatively, it can be expressed in terms of maximising the net gain (or minimising the net loss) to a particular group subject to a constraint relating to total benefits and costs. Whether or not this is helpful in practice s not known, but at least it may explain why income distribution considerations have been brought into this survey under the heading of constraints.

It should be noted that these considerations may relate to many different kinds of groups. In one context notions of " fairness " to workers may predominate, while in another it may be notions of " equity " between different geographical areas which are important. If one is taking a regional, rather than a national, viewpoint the assessment and measurement of costs and benefits may be quite markedly different. For instance, it has been argued that one of the benefits of the Morecambe Bay barrage scheme would be the attraction of more industry to the Barrow area. This would no doubt benefit Barrow; but it is perfectly conceivable that there would be equivalent or even greater losses to South Lancashire, or for that matter other regions of the United Kingdom. Therefore one gets an entirely different picture of benefits and costs, if one looks at them from the viewpoint of the Barrow area, from that prevailing for the whole of the North-west or the whole of the United Kingdom.

(iii) *Budgetary Constraints.* Discussions of this topic combine (and sometimes confuse) three issues: first, ought such constraints to exist; second, what form do they take; and third, how can they be incorporated into investment criteria? We shall deal with the third issue shortly when we reach the general subject of investment criteria. We do not propose to discuss the first point, but might note that Hirshleifer [37] has argued that if the budgeting authorities are worth their salt the amount allocated to the sub-budgets will take account of the productivity of the projects available to them and the costs of obtaining the necessary funds. If this is not done, it is argued, the answer is to recast the system of budget allocation rather than to go into python-like contortions at the sub-budget level. This argument, however, is rather unrealistic. For the present, at any rate, many decisions are in fact taken within the framework of a budget restraint, and the economist might as well help people to sub-optimise within this framework, even if, as a long-run proposition, he thinks in his private capacity that it should be changed.

On the second issue there is not much to be said in general terms. There may be a constraint upon total capital expenditure over one or more years, as, for instance, when the projects undertaken by a public agency have to fit within a budget framework determined in advance. The sums involved may be either maxima which do not have to be reached or amounts which are to be spent entirely.[1] In the first case, but not the second, the expenditure in question has an opportunity cost, since once the decision is made to use funds, they are effectively a bygone. There can be other kinds of constraint applying to capital expenditure, such as a prescribed percentage of self-financing, and constraints can also apply to current expenditure and/or to revenue, for example, a financial target for gross or net accounting profits.

[1] " Maximum " or " specific " rationing to use the convenient terminology of Hirshleifer [37].

3. Final Considerations

(a) Investment Criteria

We believe that the most common maximand where projects involve only costs and benefits expressed in terms of money is the present value of benefits less costs. Other maximands are possible, however, such as capital stock at a final date. We shall not attempt to argue the relative merits of different maximands, but, continuing to accept present value, now introduce the subject of investment criteria or, as they are sometimes called, decision algorithms.

Where no projects are interdependent or mutually exclusive, where starting dates are given and where no constraints are operative, the choice of projects which maximises the present value of total benefits less total costs can be expressed in any of the following four equivalent ways: [1]

(1) select all projects where the present value of benefits exceeds the present value of costs;

(2) select all projects where the ratio of the present value of benefits to the present value of costs exceeds unity;

(3) select all projects where the constant annuity with the same present value as benefits exceeds the constant annuity (of the same duration) with the same present value as costs;

(4) select all projects where the internal rate of return exceeds the chosen rate of discount.

Once the various complications just assumed away are introduced, more complicated rules are required. We shall explain the impact of these

[1] Symbolically, these criteria can be summarised as follows.

Let $c_1, c_2, \ldots c_n$ = series of prospective costs in years $1, 2, \ldots n$;

$\quad c$ = constant annuity with same present value as $c_1, c_2, \ldots c$;

$b_1, b_2, \ldots b_n$ = series of prospective benefits in years $1, 2, \ldots n$;

$\quad b$ = constant annuity with same present value as $b_1, b_2, \ldots b_n$;

$\quad s$ = scrap value;

$\quad i$ = appropriate rate of discount for annual compounding;

$\quad r$ = internal rate of return.

Then we may write the rules as follows: select projects where

$$(1) \quad \frac{b_1}{(1+i)} + \frac{b_2}{(1+i)^2} + \cdots + \frac{b_n+s}{(1+i)^n} > \frac{c_1}{(1+i)} + \frac{c_2}{(1+i)^2} + \cdots + \frac{c_n}{(1+i)^n}$$

$$(2) \quad \frac{\dfrac{b_1}{(1+i)} + \dfrac{b_2}{(1+i)^2} + \cdots + \dfrac{b_n+s}{(1+i)_n}}{\dfrac{c_1}{(1+i)} + \dfrac{c_2}{(1+i)^2} + \cdots + \dfrac{c_n}{(1+i)^n}} > 1$$

$$(3) \quad b > c$$

Finally, select projects where $r > i$, where r is given by

$$(4) \quad \frac{b_1 - c_1}{(1+r)} + \frac{b_2 - c_2}{(1+r)^2} + \cdots + \frac{b_n - c_n}{(1+r)^n} = 0$$

complications in terms of the present-value approach without claiming that it is always the most convenient one. Which approach is most convenient will vary with the facts of the case. Where a rule which is not algebraically equivalent to the present value approach is used, the issue is not one of convenience, but involves either error [1] or a different maximand.

Where the costs and/or benefits of two schemes A and B are interdependent in the sense that the execution of one affects the costs or benefits of the other (see pp. 159–60 *supra*), they must be treated as constituting three mutually exclusive schemes, namely A and B together, A alone and B alone. Thus, if one wants to improve communications between two towns one has the choice between a road improvement, a rail improvement and a combination of road and rail improvements.

Mutual exclusivity can also arise for technological reasons. Thus, a road intersection can be built as a cross-roads, a roundabout or a flyover. Similarly, a large or a small dam, but not both, may be put in one place. Whatever the reason for mutual exclusivity, its presence must be allowed for in formulating investment rules.

Where there is a choice of starting date it must be chosen so as to maximise the present value of benefits less costs at the reference date.

Constraints cause the biggest complications, particularly when there is more than one of them and when mutual exclusivity and optimal timing are also involved. Indivisibilities also complicate matters when constraints are involved.

We shall not venture into the algebraic jungle of constructing decision algorithms. Anyone who seeks examples can turn to Marglin's discussion of income distribution and budgetary constraints in his exemplary synthesis of much of cost-benefit analysis [48] or to his monograph on dynamic investment planning [51]. A most useful discussion is also to be found in an article on capital budgeting by Dryden [18].

(b) *Second-best Matters*

Since cost-benefit analysis is essentially a practical tool for decision-making, it is not worth our while pursuing the second-best problem into the higher reaches of welfare economics. The non-fulfilment of the conditions for a welfare maximum elsewhere in the economy is relevant to cost-benefit analysis only in so far as it makes the market values of outputs and inputs obviously biased measures of benefits and costs. Small and remote divergences from the optimum will cause biases in these measures which fall within their margin of error, while large divergences of an unknown sort create unknowable biases which are necessarily irrelevant to action. Only those divergences which are immediate, palpable and considerable thus deserve

---

[1] A naïve error in early writings was the use of benefit–cost ratios to choose between two mutually exclusive projects. One project may have the lower benefit–cost ratio, yet will be preferable if the *extra* benefits exceed the *extra* costs. This is clearly brought out by McKean [53, pp. 108 ff.].

our attention. We have discussed some of these already, and will bring in further examples in our survey of particular applications of cost-benefit analysis.

Ideally, all such divergences should be taken into account, for otherwise a sub-optimum will not be achieved. Yet it does not follow that public agencies ought always to take account of them; the ideal involves administrative costs. It has to be recognised that public agencies have defined spheres of competence and that the responsibility for wide issues lying outside these spheres rests not with them but with the Government which created them and their tasks. It is not the business of, say, the Scottish Development Department to decide whether or not the currency is overvalued, for instance, and it is not within its competence to put a shadow price upon the foreign-exchange content of proposed expenditure. Either it must value imports at their import price or it must be told to adopt a shadow rate for planning purposes by the central government, whose function it is to consider such matters. The division of labour in administration which is necessary if the public sector is to avoid monolithic sluggishness requires each part of the machine to act as if the rest were doing its job properly. After all, to continue with this example, it may be better if all government agencies value foreign exchange at a uniform but incorrect exchange rate than if they each have their own different shadow rates.

BIBLIOGRAPHY

Note: This is mainly the list of articles, books, etc., to which we have referred in the text and in no sense is a complete bibliography of the subject.

1. G. S. Becker, *Human Capital* (New York: Columbia University Press, 1964).
2. M. E. Beesley, " The Value of Time Spent in Travelling: Some New Evidence," *Economica*, Vol. XXXII, May 1965.
3. M. E. Beesley and C. D. Foster, " The Victoria Line: Social Benefits and Finances," *Journal of the Royal Statistical Society*, Vol. 128, Part 1, 1965.
4. M. E. Beesley and J. F. Kain, " Urban Form, Car Ownership and Public Policy: An Appraisal of Traffic in Towns," *Urban Studies*, Vol. 1, No. 2, November 1964.
5. M. Blaug, " The Rate of Return on Investment in Education in Great Britain," *The Manchester School*, Vol. XXXIII, No. 3, September 1965.
6. M. E. Borus, " A Benefit Cost Analysis of the Economic Effectiveness of Retraining the Unemployed," *Yale Economic Essays*, Vol. 4, No. 2, Fall 1964.
7. H. C. Bos and L. M. Koyck, " The Appraisal of Road Construction Projects," *Review of Economics and Statistics*, Vol. XLIII, February 1961.
8. H. R. Bowen, *Toward Social Economy* (New York: Rinehart, 1948).
9. Mary J. Bowman, " Social Returns to Education," *International Social Science Journal*, Vol. XIV, No. 4, 1962.

10. British Railways Board, *The Reshaping of British Railways* (The Beeching Report) (H.M.S.O., 1963).
11. J. M. Buchanan and W. C. Stubblebine, " Externality," *Economica*, Vol. XXIX, November 1962.
12. Marion Clawson, " Methods of Measuring the Demand for and Value of Outdoor Recreation," *Resources for the Future, Inc.* (Washington, D.C., 1959).
13. R. H. Coase, " The Problem of Social Cost," *Journal of Law and Economics*, Vol. III, October 1960.
14. T. M. Coburn, M. E. Beesley and D. J. Reynolds, *The London–Birmingham Motorway: Traffic and Economics*, Road Research Laboratory Technical Paper No. 46. D.S.I.R., H.M.S.O., 1960.
15. J. A. Crutchfield, " Valuation of Fishery Resources," *Land Economics*, Vol. XXXVIII, May 1962.
16. H. Dalton, *Principles of Public Finance* (4th edn. revised), (London: Routledge & Kegan Paul, 1954).
17. Otto Davis and Andrew Whinston, " Externalities, Welfare, and the Theory of Games," *Journal of Political Economy*, Vol. LXX, June 1962.
18. M. M. Dryden, " Capital Budgeting: Treatment of Uncertainty and Investment Criteria," *Scottish Journal of Political Economy*, Vol. XI, November 1964.
19. J. Dupuit, " On the Measurement of Utility of Public Works," *International Economic Papers*, Vol. 2 (translated from the French).
20. Otto Eckstein, *Water Resource Development* (Cambridge, Mass.: Harvard University Press, 1958).
21. Otto Eckstein, " A Survey of the Theory of Public Expenditure Criteria," in James M. Buchanan (ed.), *Public Finances: Needs, Sources and Utilization* (Princeton: Princeton University Press, 1961).
22. B. H. Farmer, *Ceylon. A Divided Nation* (London: Oxford University Press, 1963).
23. M. S. Feldstein, " Net Social Benefit Calculation and the Public Investment Decision," *Oxford Economic Papers*, Vol. 16, March 1964.
24. M. S. Feldstein, " The Social Time Preference Discount Rate in Cost Benefit Analysis," ECONOMIC JOURNAL, Vol. LXXIV, June 1964.
25. M. S. Feldstein, " Opportunity Cost Calculations in Cost Benefit Analysis," *Public Finance*, Vol. XIX, No. 2, 1964.
26. I. Fisher, " Report on National Vitality: Its Wastes and Conservation," *Bulletin of One Hundred on National Health*, No. 30 (Washington, 1909).
27. C. D. Foster, *The Transport Problem* (London: Blackie, 1963).
28. C. D. Foster and M. E. Beesley, " Estimating the Social Benefit of Constructing an Underground Railway in London," *Journal of the Royal Statistical Society*, Vol. 126, Part 1, 1963.
29. I. K. Fox and O. C. Herfindahl, " Attainment of Efficiency in Satisfying Demands for Water Resources," *American Economic Review*, Vol. LIV, May 1964.
30. G. Fromm, " Civil Aviation Expenditures," R. Dorfman (ed.) *Measuring Benefits of Government Investments* (Washington, D.C.: Brookings Institution, 1965).
31. Zvi Griliches, " Research Costs and Social Returns: Hybrid Corn and Related Innovations," *Journal of Political Economy*, Vol. LXVI, October 1958.
32. R. J. Hammond, *Benefit–Cost Analysis and Water Pollution Control* (Stanford, California: University Press, 1958).
33. W. L. Hansen, " Total and Private Rates of Return to Investment in Schooling," *Journal of Political Economy*, Vol. LXXI, April 1963.
34. E. K. Hawkins, *Roads and Road Transport in an Underdeveloped Country. A Case Study of Uganda*, Colonial Office, Colonial Research Studies No. 32 (London: H.M.S.O., 1962).

35. J. G. Head, " Public Goods and Public Policy," *Public Finance*, Vol. XVII, 1962.
36. J. R. Hicks, " Economic Theory and the Evaluation of Consumers' Wants," *Journal of Business*, Chicago, Vol. 35, July 1962.
37. J. Hirshleifer, J. C. de Haven and J. W. Milliman, *Water Supply, Economics, Technology and Policy* (Chicago: University of Chicago Press, 1960).
38. C. J. Hitch and R. N. McKean, *The Economics of Defense in the Nuclear Age* (London: Oxford University Press, 1960).
39. S. J. Hunt, " Income Determinants for College Graduates and the Return to Educational Investment," *Yale Economic Essays*, Fall 1963.
40. Inter-Agency River Basin Committee (Sub-Committee on Costs and Budgets), *Proposed Practices for Economic Analysis of River Basin Projects* (" The Green Book ") (Washington, D.C., 1950).
41. International Institute for Land Reclamation and Improvement, *An Assessment of Investments in Land Reclamation* (Wageningen, Holland, 1960).
42. H. E. Klarman, " Syphilis Control Problems," R. Dorfman (ed.) *Measuring Benefits of Government Investments* (Washington D.C.: Brookings Institution, 1965).
43. J. V. Krutilla and Otto Eckstein, *Multiple Purpose River Development* (Baltimore: Johns Hopkins Press, 1958).
44. T. E. Kuhn, *Public Enterprise Economics and Transport Problems* (Berkeley and Los Angeles: University of California Press, 1962).
45. A. P. Lerner, *The Economics of Control* (New York: Macmillan, 1944).
46. J. Lesourne, *Le Calcul Economique* (Paris: Dunod, 1964).
47. N. Lichfield, *Cost Benefit Analysis in Urban Redevelopment*, Research Report, Real Estate Research Program, Institute of Business and Economic Research (Berkeley: University of California, 1962).
48. A. Maass, M. M. Hufschmidt, R. Dorfman, H. A. Thomas, S. A. Marglin and G. M. Fair, *Design of Water Resource Systems: New Techniques for Relating Economic Objectives, Engineering Analysis, and Governmental Planning* (London: Macmillan, 1962).
49. S. A. Marglin, " The Social Rate of Discount and Optimal Rate of Investment," *Quarterly Journal of Economics*, Vol. LXXVII, February 1963.
50. S. A. Marglin, " The Opportunity Costs of Public Investment," *Quarterly Journal of Economics*, Vol. LXXVII, May 1963.
51. S. A. Marglin, *Approaches to Dynamic Investment Planning* (Amsterdam: North Holland, 1963).
52. Julius Margolis, " Secondary Benefits, External Economies, and the Justification of Public Investment," *Review of Economics and Statistics*, Vol. XXXIX, August 1957.
53. R. N. McKean, *Efficiency in Government through Systems Analysis* (New York: John Wiley & Sons, 1958).
54. R. N. McKean, " Cost-benefit Analysis and British Defense Expenditure," in A. T. Peacock and D. J. Robertson (eds.), *Public Expenditure, Appraisal and Control* (Edinburgh: Oliver and Boyd, 1963).
55. Ministry of Transport, *Panel on Road Pricing* (Smeed Report) (H.M.S.O., 1964).
56. Ministry of Transport, *Traffic in Towns: A Study of the Long Term Problems of Traffic in Urban Areas* (Buchanan Report) (H.M.S.O., 1963).
57. H. Mohring, " Land Values and the Measurement of Highway Benefits," *Journal of Political Economy*, Vol. LXIX, June 1961.
58. H. Mohring and N. Harwitz, *Highway Benefits: an Analytical Framework* (Northwestern University Press, 1962).
59. L. N. Moses and H. F. Williamson, " Value of Time, Choice of Mode, and the Subsidy Issue in Urban Transportation," *Journal of Political Economy*, Vol. LXXI, June 1963.

60. R. A. Musgrave, *The Theory of Public Finance. A Study in Public Economy* (New York: McGraw-Hill, 1959).
61. R. A. Musgrave and A. T. Peacock, *Classics in the Theory of Public Finance* (London: Macmillan, 1958).
62. Selma J. Mushkin, " Health as an Investment," *Journal of Political Economy,* Vol. LXX (Supplement), October 1962.
63. National Council of Applied Economic Research (New Delhi), *Criteria for Fixation of Water Rates and Selection of Irrigation Projects* (London: Asia Publishing House, 1959).
64. R. R. Nelson, " The Simple Economics of Basic Scientific Research," *Journal of Political Economy,* Vol. LXVII, June 1959.
65. A. C. Pigou, *The Economics of Welfare* (4th edn.) (London: Macmillan, 1932).
66. A. R. Prest and I. G. Stewart, *The National Income of Nigeria 1950–51,* Colonial Office Research Series (H.M.S.O., 1953).
67. G. F. Ray and R. E. Crum, " Transport: Notes and Comments," *National Institute Economic Review,* No. 24, May 1963.
68. E. F. Renshaw, *Towards Responsible Government* (Chicago: Idyia Press, 1957).
69. E. F. Renshaw, " A Note on the Measurement of the Benefits from Public Investment in Navigation Projects," *American Economic Review,* Vol. XLVII, September 1957.
70. D. J. Reynolds, " The Cost of Road Accidents," *Journal of the Royal Statistical Society,* Vol. 119, Part 4, 1956.
71. J. Rothenberg, " Urban Renewal Programs," R. Dorfman (ed.) *Measuring Benefits of Government Investments* (Washington, D.C.: Brookings Institution, 1965).
72. P. A. Samuelson, " The Pure Theory of Public Expenditure," *Review of Economics and Statistics,* Vol. XXXVI, November 1954.
73. P. A. Samuelson, " Diagrammatic Exposition of a Theory of Public Expenditure," *Review of Economics and Statistics,* Vol. XXXVII, November 1955.
74. P. A. Samuelson, " Aspects of Public Expenditure Theories," *Review of Economics and Statistics,* Vol. XL, November 1958.
75. F. M. Scherer, " Government Research and Development Programs," R. Dorfman (ed.) *Measuring Benefits of Government Investments* (Washington, D.C.: Brookings Institution, 1965).
76. J. R. Schlesinger, " Quantitative Analysis and National Security," *World Politics,* January 1963.
77. W. R. D. Sewell, J. Davis, A. D. Scott and D. W. Ross, *Guide to Benefit-Cost Analysis* (Resources for Tomorrow) (Ottawa: Queen's Printer, 1962).
78. Arthur Smithies, *The Budgetary Process in the United States* (Committee for Economic Development Research Study) (New York: McGraw-Hill, 1955).
79. N. V. Sovani and N. Rath, *Economics of a Multiple-purpose River Dam: Report of an Inquiry into the Economic Benefits of the Hirakud Dam,* Gokhale Institute of Politics and Economics Publication No. 38 (Poona, 1960).
80. P. O. Steiner, " Choosing Among Alternative Public Investments in the Water Resource Field," *American Economic Review,* Vol. XLIX, December 1959.
81. J. Thédié and C. Abraham, " Economic Aspect of Road Accidents," *Traffic Engineering and Control,* Vol. II, No. 10, February 1961.
82. A. H. Trice and S. E. Wood, " Measurement of Recreation Benefits," *Land Economics,* Vol. XXXIV, August 1958.
83. Ralph Turvey, " Present Value versus Internal Rate of Return—An Essay in the Theory of the Third Best," Economic Journal, Vol. LXXIII, March 1963.
84. Ralph Turvey, " On Investment Choices in Electricity Generation," *Oxford Economic Papers,* Vol. 15, November 1963.

85. Ralph Turvey, " On Divergences between Social Cost and Private Cost,"
    Economica, New Series, Vol. XXX, August 1963.
86. B. A. Weisbrod, *Economics of Public Health: Measuring the Economic Impact of
    Diseases* (Philadelphia: University of Pennsylvania Press, 1960).
87. B. A. Weisbrod, " Education and Investment in Human Capital," *Journal of
    Political Economy*, Vol. LXX (Supplement), October 1962.
88. B. R. Williams, " Economics in Unwonted Places," ECONOMIC JOURNAL,
    March 1965.
89. D. M. Winch, *The Economics of Highway Planning* (Toronto: Toronto Univer-
    sity Press, 1963).
90. F. Yates, *Sampling Methods for Censuses and Surveys* (London: Griffin, 1960).

ON THE SOCIAL RATE OF DISCOUNT

By William J. Baumol

Few topics in our discipline rival the social rate of discount as a subject exhibiting simultaneously a very considerable degree of knowledge and a very substantial level of ignorance. Economists understand thoroughly just what this variable should measure: The opportunity cost of postponement of receipt of any benefit yielded by a public investment. They agree also on the components that should be considered in making up this figure: Primarily the welfare foregone by not having these benefits available for immediate consumption or reinvestment and (perhaps) a premium corresponding to the risk incurred in undertaking government projects. Above all, economists are quite generally in accord on the view that a very serious misallocation of resources can result from the use of an incorrect estimate of the value of this variable in a cost-benefit calculation. Yet, while they agree that externalities can play a significant role in the matter, there is some considerable question even about the direction of these effects. There is substantial obscurity and divergence of views in discussions of the implications of differences (if indeed there are any) in the degree of risk that is incurred when a given project is undertaken by a private firm on the one side and by government on the other. And as a result of these and other sources of shaky understanding of some basic principles, we are treated to what may with little exaggeration be described as a sorry spectacle—outstanding members of our profession providing in print estimates of the social discount rate ranging from four and one half to eight or nine percent. Some calculations by governmental agencies and others have even employed discount rates as low as three per cent (see March [10]) or have even discounted at a zero rate! (see Klarman [6]). Since the choice of investment projects can be so sensitive to the magnitude of this variable, little help is provided to the decision maker who is confronted by such an enormous range of estimates.

I do not presume in this paper to settle the major issues outstanding. But by going at the matter slowly and in terms of its elementary components I hope to introduce some illumination on these matters. It will be maintained however that there has been some misunderstanding of the relative magnitude of the components of the social discount rate.

THE AMERICAN ECONOMIC REVIEW, September, 1968, Vol. 58, No. 4, pp. 788-802.

172

I will conclude that both risk and corporate taxes play a more important role than is sometimes ascribed to them, though, curiously, risk derives its significance from the comparative risklessness of investments from the point of view of society, the very fact that has played a central part in the argument of those who oppose the inclusion of a risk premium in the discount rate for government projects.

Perhaps more important, I will show that, given our institutional arrangements, there is an unavoidable indeterminacy in the choice of that rate. The figure which is optimal from the point of view of the allocation of resources between the private and public sectors is necessarily higher than that which accords with the public's subjective time preference. As a result, neither the higher nor the lower figure that has been proposed can, by itself, satisfy the requirements for an optimal allocation of resources, and we find ourselves forced to hunt for a solution in the dark jungles of the second best.

Finally, I shall suggest that the intertemporal externalities that have been discussed in the literature are significant for the overall levels of the optimal private and public discount rates rather than for the *differential* between the two rates. That is, if, e.g., externalities were in fact to imply that society invests too little for the future, then this means that the private and social rates should both be lowered, not that public projects should be evaluated in terms of a rate that is low relative to the cost of capital to private industry. I shall, then, reexamine the externalities issue and review the nature of the misallocations which are likely to result if inappropriate policy decisions are made in response to them.

In covering our subject it will prove convenient to proceed by stages, first dealing with a world in which taxes are present but in which there is no uncertainty and the role of time preference and externalities are ignored. In subsequent sections these other influences will be reintroduced one at a time and so we will be able to see more clearly the consequences of each.

I. *The Basic Model: The Role of Taxes*

The basic premise on which the analysis will proceed is that the appropriate rate of discount for public projects is one which measures correctly the social opportunity cost. The decision to devote resources to investment in a public project means, given the overall level of employment in the economy, that these resources will become unavailable for use by the private sector. And this transfer should be undertaken whenever a potential project available to the government offers social benefits greater than the loss sustained by removing these resources from the private sector. The social rate of discount, then, must be chosen in such a way that it leads to a positive number for the evaluated net benefits of a public project if and only if its gross benefits exceed its opportunity costs in the private sector. I repeat this banality because it seems to me to be the criterion which is relevant for investigations of the discount rate, and because it forms the basis for all of the discussion that follows.

Let us begin with a very simple model that brings out some of the critical elements in the analysis. For these purposes I utilize the following assumptions in the discussion of the present section, many of which will be dropped later in the paper: (1) The overall level of employment of all resources by the economy is fixed so that any increase in the use of resources by the public sector unavoidably produces a concomitant decrease in their utilization by private enterprise; (2) There is no risk or uncertainty—the future returns of any investment project can be foreseen perfectly. (We will return to the subject of risk in the next section); (3) All goods and services in the economy other than those provided by the government are supplied by corporations, an assumption which permits us to abstract from the difference in tax treatment of corporations and other types of firm; (4) Corporations in this riskless world are financed entirely by equity; (5) Corporate income is subject to a uniform tax rate of 50 per cent; (6) There is a unique rate of interest, r, at which the government borrows money.

Suppose now that the government considers undertaking a project whose construction requires the use of a set of input resources, R, for some given period of time. How does one calculate the opportunity cost of this use of resources? Since R is composed of inputs and since the corporations are the only alternative users of such items it follows that, in the first instance, R must all be obtained by taking it out of the hands of the corporations. The opportunity cost can then be calculated simply by determining the returns which could have been obtained if R had been left for corporate use during the period in question.

Our premises enable us to determine the equilibrium value of this magnitude, given the rate of interest on government securities. For in this riskless world investors will expect exactly the same rate of return on money invested either in the private or the public sectors. This means that the corporations must return r per cent to their stockholders. But with a 50 per cent tax on corporate earnings it follows that corporate resources must provide a gross yield of $2r$. In other words, the resources, R, if left in the private sector would have produced a real rate of return evaluated by the market at $2r$. For this purpose it makes no difference whether or not product prices are affected by monopolistic elements or other influences causing them to depart from competitive levels.[1] The

---

[1] However, externalities do make a difference. If a private firm obtains a private return on its

174

fact is simply that the transfer of our resources R has led to a reduction in outputs for which consumers would have been willing to pay enough to provide a rate of return $2r$ on corporate capital. Specifically, even if a monopoly charges prices above marginal cost, its sales will be cut sufficiently so that its outputs' prices still represent the money measure of the goods' marginal utilities to their consumers.[2] Hence, with the usual reservations about interpersonal comparisons and income distribution these amounts do still represent the opportunity costs of the outputs foregone.

The form of this argument can easily lead to one sort of misunderstanding. It would seem to suggest that all government projects must draw their resources from private investment and that none of them can be taken from private consumption. But nothing of this sort is implied or intended. It is obviously possible that the steel used in some governmental undertaking is all taken from consumers and so results in no reduction in the output of producers' goods. The consequent decrease in manufacture of automobiles, refrigerators and bird cages then represents the real cost of the government project. But this in no way conflicts with my way of regarding the matter which states only that

investment but imposes external costs equivalent to 3 per cent, the net social yield will obviously be only 12 per cent. For precisely the same sort of reason, as will be observed later, we may well consider it desirable to subsidize further the production of public goods in order to increase their output beyond its current level.

Note, incidentally, that the preceding argument does *not* necessarily imply that the individual firm can shift any or all of the burden of the corporate income tax. As with an increase in fixed costs under competitive equilibrium, the rise in taxes may raise the gross rate of return simply by driving some firms out of business even though no company can do anything about it.

[2] Professor Abba Lerner, in a letter to me, has commented on this point, suggesting that the presence of monopoly in the private sector does make a difference. "It is true that a dollar spent on the monopolized article yields the same marginal utility as one spent on an item produced under perfect competition, but the marginal return on the monopolized investment derives from the *marginal revenue* received by the monopolist and this is less than the *price*, so that there is here an additional reason for not taking resources away from the monopolist whose marginal social product is greater than his marginal private product because of his monopolistic restriction."

To put the argument another way, let p, mc, mr and I respectively represent price, marginal cost, marginal revenue and incremental investment, where the marginal cost includes no normal return, i.e., no "cost of capital." Then the monopolist will select an output at which his marginal rate of return on I is $2r$, i.e., at which $(mr\text{-}mc)/I = 2r$ so that

$$I = (mr - mc)/2r.$$

But, using price as the measure of marginal consumer benefits, the social rate of return will then be

$$(p - mc)/I = 2r(p - mc)/(mr - mc).$$

Since price is normally larger than the monopolist's marginal revenue, this social opportunity cost figure will then be greater than $2r$ and it may in fact be considerably greater. If, e.g., $p = \$2$, $mc = \$1.40$ and $mr = \$1.50$ the marginal social rate of return will then be $12r$ while if $mc = \$1.45$ this opportunity cost rate will rise to $22r$!

175

this transfer of resources must take place *through the agency of the corporation*. The automobile factory will have fewer tons of steel to process, as will the producer of refrigerators and other steel product consumer's goods. And I am arguing only that the outlays of these firms on the steel which they would otherwise have used would have brought them a rate of return of *2r as a result of the consumers' marginal valuation of these commodities.*

In these simple circumstances that is all there is to the matter. But it is important to bring out clearly how this discussion differs from much of the standard literature. This it does in two respects; in method of approach and in its implications for policy. In method, the approach of this model avoids the technique associated with Krutilla and Eckstein [7, ch. 4], (see also Otto Eckstein [3, pp. 81–104]) the attempt to trace out the sources of the money funds "used to finance" the project. Their method is to ask whether the adoption of the project will lead to further taxes or will be financed by further borrowing and seeks to measure opportunity cost by estimating the real consequences for the taxpayers or lenders involved. Such a calculation can easily be questioned from the viewpoint of the literature of functional finance which tells us that, in the last analysis, the purpose of such fiscal measures is not to "pay for" governmental activity, but to offset inflationary pressures. Real resources can be transferred to the government without either increased taxation or added borrowing from the public, inflation being left the task of providing the necessary forced saving. And, looked at from this point of view it is by no means obvious that the tax equivalent of a D dollar government expenditure is exactly D dollars in taxes. The balanced budget multiplier literature suggests strongly that it takes more than D dollars in taxes and borrowing from the private sector to offset the impact of a D dollar public outlay. But whether or not one is prepared to go along with this functional finance criticism of the sources of funds approach to the estimation of opportunity cost one can surely argue that the method is unnecessarily complex. If it is true that, in real terms, what the government takes from the private sector is input resources, then to determine the relevant rate of discount one need not inquire beyond the rate of return currently being earned by users of such inputs. One can ignore in this calculation the subjective time preferences of consumers, the difference between the disutility of paying taxes and of lending and a host of other issues which clutter unnecessarily some of the public project discount rate calculations. That the government's use of resources does deprive consumers of some goods is true but beside the point because consumers implicitly but very definitely indicate how they feel about this foregone consumption through the rate of return they are currently providing to business firms. And the costs of taxation versus borrowing are considerations relevant to the choice of strategy of stabilization policy. They should not determine whether or not a specific project is undertaken.[3]

In addition, the proposed calculation has significant consequences for public policy, via its implication that, with a 5 per cent rate of interest on government bonds for the relevant time period, the correct rate of discount on government projects is not anything near 5 per cent but is on the order of 10 per cent per annum. This conclusion means that a number of longer-term government projects which are currently passing muster should be rejected. If this conclusion were accepted it might lead to very considerable changes in public investment programs— changes whose nature will be discussed later in this paper.[4]

II. *Some Modifications: The Role of Risk*

So far the argument has deliberately abstracted from risk, a matter with which much of the discount rate discussion has concerned itself. A minor issue that arises from the presence of risk is that it leads corporations to finance themselves in part by means of debt rather than equity in the hope of attracting funds from investors who wish to limit their risk. Since in fact corporate income taxes apply neither to the interest payments on debt, nor to the earnings of firms which have avoided the corporate form of organization, one may conclude that our estimate of the opportunity cost of resources should be reduced somewhat below the figure of $2r$ arrived at in the preceding section. One should decrease the figure for the corporate sector perhaps proportionately to its use of debt financing and then the overall discount figure should presumably be reduced in proportion to the resources that would come from noncorporate enterprises.[5]

[3] There is, however, a reasonable ground for objection to this last statement. If the decision to undertake a government project contributes to inflationary pressures the real cost or the cost of the counterinflationary measures should be deducted from the anticipated benefits of the project, and the reverse should hold in a period of unemployment where the calculation proposed in the text is incorrect in any event, since an increased use of resources by the government need require no corresponding reduction in their utilization by private industry.

[4] Readers will recognize that this conclusion has much in common with the views of Hirshleifer, DeHaven and Milliman [4, pp. 139–50]. However, we come to this result not entirely for the same reasons, as will be noted presently. On the other hand my position on this particular point *is* similar to one taken by Machlup [9] and by Vickrey in some brief remarks [16].

[5] That is, if e per cent of corporate financing is obtained from equity, and if c per cent of the government's input resources are derived from corporations, the social discount rate becomes

$$(1 - c)r + c[(1 - e)r + e(2r)] = r + cer.$$

Thus if, say, 80 per cent of the nation's goods and services were produced by the corporate sector ($c = 0.8$) and 80 per cent of corporate finances were accounted for by equity, one might estimate the discount rate for public projects at $(1.64)r$.

Even this smaller ratio may overstate the proper differential between this allocative discount rate and the bond rate of interest. It is easy to show that if a company's earnings are growing

177

But this is not the main issue in the risk discussion, which has centered about the role of risk in private borrowing, where, in addition to tax payments, investments must produce a rate of return sufficiently high to compensate the investor for the risks he undertakes in providing the finances to the company. Thus, suppose a private corporation earns 16 per cent on investment, half of which goes into taxes and, that of the remaining 8 per cent we have reason to suppose 3 per cent is a risk premium. Should the social rate of discount be 10 per cent (the 5 per cent riskless rate of return plus the tax payment on that amount) or should it be 16 per cent?

The argument for exclusion of a risk premium from the discount rate on public investment has been provided by economists as eminent as Samuelson [12] and Arrow[1]. It proceeds somewhat as follows. The government undertakes a very large number of highly variegated projects. Thus, under the law of large numbers, the overall outcome becomes virtually certain. On insurance principles, each one should be evaluated in terms of its expected value with no distinction made between projects whose outcomes have different dispersions. In such a context a project offering two possible payoffs, $90 and $110 with equal probability, is neither better nor worse than another offering $50 or $150 since each has an expected value of $100.

It has been objected that one should take into account not only the total risk and the total expected yield of all government projects but also their *marginal* risk contribution and their *marginal* expected yield. It may appear at first glance that as a proportion of the government's total investment program both of these are apt to be insignificant for a single project, but that the ratio of the marginal risk to the marginal expected value contribution is not negligible. However, this view ignores some relevant considerations. If the outcomes of the various projects are independent, so that their covariance is zero (an assumption which is not obviously as valid a representation of the facts as is sometimes suggested—cf. Hirschleifer [5, pp. 268–75, esp. n. 6]) the distribution of the entire set of outcomes for all projects combined will tend to approach the normal distribution. Hence if the expected yield of a single representative project is y and its standard deviation is σ, for n projects the total expected yield will be yn while its standard deviation will be $\sqrt{n}\sigma$. A project's marginal contribution to expected yield will therefore be $dyn/dn = y$, while its contribution to standard deviation will be $\sigma/2\sqrt{\eta}$ which approaches zero with growing n. Thus if, for example, we

---

at a rate g per annum then a 50 per cent tax rate will reduce the company's rate of return from P to P' where these are related by $P = 2P' - g$. Hence if $g = 0$ the company will indeed have to earn $2r$ to provide an investor a net reurn of r neglecting the considerations of the preceding paragraph. But if, say, $g = .03$ and P', the desired after tax rate, is $.05$, then P, the before tax rate, will be only $2P' - g = .07$ per cent. I am indebted to E. P. Howrey for this observation.

consider as a rough measure of "safety level" (minimum anticipated earnings) a number k standard deviations below the mean, this figure for all government projects together will be $yn - \sqrt{n}k\sigma$ and a project's marginal contribution to safety level will be $y - k\sigma/2\sqrt{n}$ which for large values of n will be approximately equal to y, the project's expected yield.

But this still does not tell us about the opportunity cost. From the point of view of society (with the exception of one element that will be mentioned presently) a private project is equally riskless with a public one. Society benefits from the entire set of investment projects currently undertaken, whether they are public or private. The mere transfer of an investment's sponsorship from private hands to government does not per se affect its flow of benefits to society[6] nor does it mean that its risks are any more or less offsetable against the risks of other projects. That is to say, in line with the argument of the preceding paragraphs *all* investments should be evaluated at their expected earnings. Transfer into government hands may reduce the risk of an investment slightly in only one way. A private firm faces some danger of insolvency, in which case a project that has been undertaken may never be completed. Even here the distinction is not clear-cut; a change in administration with a new election can also cut off a public project before its invested resources can begin to bear fruit. But in any event, with increasing numbers of projects the marginal value of this sort of risk, too, will be negligible. Thus, from the social point of view the "law of large numbers" argument cuts both ways—it says that risk in either public or private projects is irrelevant for the returns society can expect.

But does this mean that the risk discount component in private cost of capital figures should be ignored in the social rate of discount calculation, as is often suggested in the literature? On the contrary, paradoxically, *the very absence of real risk means that the private risk discount should also enter the social discount rate.* Here private risk plays precisely the same role as the corporation tax. It induces firms to invest in such a way that the marginal investment yield is higher than it would other-

---

[6] In a letter William Whipple Jr. of Rutgers University has pointed out to me that this conclusion is not quite correct as it stands. When the resources are in private hands, the risk involved in their use constitutes a disutility to the investor, a psychic cost which has no counterpart in public investment. Hence, the removal of resources from the private sector where they yield a rate of return S involves an opportunity cost lower than S by the amount of this psychic cost to investors. It may perhaps even be argued that this investor risk disutility is exactly equal to the risk premium on private investment so that for this reason the rate of discount on government projects should include no risk premium, contrary to what is argued in this section on the basis of the evaluation of the yield of the resources *by consumers*. In any event, it is clear that the opportunity cost of the transfer must be larger than one would have thought if one had believed the returns to the private project to be uncertain from the point of view of society and there must therefore be some distortion in a discount rate on government projects that does not take into account the low social risk of private projects.

wise be. And the transfer of resources from the private sector therefore imposes a correspondingly high opportunity cost. Take the example of our corporation earning a 16 per cent rate of return, which in the absence of a risk premium would be reduced to 10 per cent. The expected return on its investment is then in fact 16 per cent which, as we have seen, *is virtually certain from the viewpoint of society.* Then, clearly, the social opportunity cost of a transfer of resources from the corporate to the public sector is 16 and not 10 per cent, and that is all there is to be said on the subject. It is irrelevant to argue that this high return is produced by artificial distortions—taxes, risks which for society do not exist, etc. The fact that the source of this rate of return is "artificial" makes the resulting yield figure no less substantive. Society cannot come out ahead by taking resources that have been bringing in annual benefits amounting to 16 per cent of the resource values and transferring them to uses where they will yield only 5 per cent.

III. *Reassessment: Total Investment and its Allocation Between the Public and Private Sectors*

There are certain to be readers who find the preceding arguments to be offensive, and who will be led to this feeling by instincts that are perfectly reasonable. Surely, one may say, a 16 per cent discount rate means that far too little will be invested in the future. And in all this we have taken no account of the public's true preference and the relevant externalities. To some of these specific issues I will turn presently. But we should note first that this objection may well arise because we tend to overlook a distinction which has not often come across clearly in the literature. Involved in the choice of discount rate are several distinct issues:

(1) How much should be invested altogether? (2) How should this investment activity be divided up between the private and public sectors? (3) Given the level of investment of the public sector how much should be allocated to long-term projects—how much to short-term projects?

It must be emphasized that up to this point this paper has addressed itself exclusively to the second of these questions. It is perfectly consistent with what has been said for us to conclude in accord with the Pigovian point of view that our telescopic faculty is indeed defective. If so, the rate of interest on government securities should be lowered drastically. The value of r should perhaps be reduced by a cheap money policy to $2\frac{1}{2}$ per cent. *But this should serve to encourage longer term investment by both the private and public sectors,* and, for example, in our riskless-world-with-corporate-tax model it does not in any way affect the conclusion that the rate of discount on public projects should be $2r$, a figure which would in these circumstances fall to 5 per cent.

Thus, nothing said so far argues for or against low rates of discount. It states merely that society will not benefit if it increases long-term investment in a wasteful and inefficient manner, by forcing the transfer of resources from employments with a high marginal yield to uses with a low marginal yield. For that is exactly what can be expected to result from the usual sort of figure of, say, 5 per cent for discount rates on public projects when the corporate rate of return is perhaps three times that high.

IV. *The Role of Consumers' Subjective Time Preference*

But so far our leading actor has only been lurking in the wings. Where in all this is the subjective time preference? Is this, too, equal to some multiple of the rate of interest on government bonds? A moment's thought indicates that it is not. Suppose all consumers were willing to purchase government bonds at r per cent and were not doing so merely in response to appeals to their patriotism. This means, surely, that they consider the proposition to be good business, i.e., their time discount rate must then be no higher than r per cent. In practice the motive in buying government bonds may often be somewhat mixed, and not all persons hold some of these instruments. But it seems safe to conclude that at least for some members of the public r per cent is the riskless rate of time preference.[7]

We are thus left with the following unpleasant pair of conclusions: as we saw in the preceding section, efficiency in resource allocation between the private and public sectors requires a social rate of discount equal to kr where k is some number considerably greater than unity, because otherwise one would end up drawing resources from uses providing a return of kr and putting them into uses providing a far lower yield. Yet the public's time preference calls for a discount rate of r per cent for otherwise one allocates to the future resources much smaller than the amount desired by society. This observation immediately

[7] Or, more accurately, r per cent *exceeds* their time preference rate by the expected rate of rise in the price level plus some risk premium corresponding to the lenders' risk of being repaid in depreciated money.

In any event, the r per cent rate to be used in this calculation is surely the market yield to maturity of some government bond with a suitably long period of time to maturity. This observation offers no support to the rather curious discount rate calculation procedure currently utilized (under presidential directive) by the corps of engineers in the evaluation of water resource projects. Their figure is obtained by averaging the coupon rates (!) on all government securities *"which upon original issue,* had terms to maturity of 15 years or more." Thus the June 30, 1965 discount rate of 3 1/8 per cent apparently included in its average bonds which had less than two years left to run and whose (nominal) coupon rate was 2 1/2 per cent.

suggests one explanation for the diversity of economists' views on our subject, a hypothesis which a study of the literature seems to confirm. Different writers seem to have focussed on different optimality conditions—some on the requirement for efficiency in the allocation between public and private investments, and others on the requirements of the private subjective time preference rate, and each has concluded that the discount rate that satisfied the one corresponding optimality requirement was in fact optimal.

However, we see now that no optimal rate exists. The rate that satisfies the one requirement cannot possibly meet the conditions of the other. In part the difficulty is caused by the corporate income tax which, our discussion suggests, may well be a very serious cause of resource misallocation in our economy.[8]

But even if the corporation tax were eliminated it would not solve the problem because of the risk premium on private investments. Repeal of the corporate income tax might, in line with our numerical example, reduce the rate of return to corporate resources from perhaps 16 down to 8 per cent. But it would never get it down to the illustrative 5 per cent on government bonds because of the risk incurred by the individual who lends his money to a private firm, a risk which for society is negligible. Since the discount rate cannot simultaneously be 5 and 8 per cent, one of the optimality requirements must still be violated unless a negative tax (a subsidy) on corporate investment were substituted for the corporation income tax.[9]

In the absence of such a subsidy there remains an inescapable indeterminacy in the choice of discount rate on government projects. There is perhaps something to be said for a figure higher than that currently employed on the grounds discussed in the preceding section. But if the discount rate is raised it should surely be done by all government agencies simultaneously. For otherwise the change will only produce wastes in the interagency allocation of resources beyond those that

[8] Or as Professor Lerner, in a letter to me, prefers to put it, "for avoidance of bias between public and private investment the public investment should pay the same taxes." Some writers, e.g., Whipple, have argued that tax-induced differences in opportunity cost rate such as that between the corporate and noncorporate sectors are a matter of deliberate policy, suggesting, in effect, that corporate activity generates undesirable externalities which Congress, in its wisdom, has implicitly decided to discourage. My opinion is that this is an excessively charitable view of the logic of the legislation which is a compound of expediency and failure to consider its consequences with sufficient care. Surely it requires a heroic reinterpretation of history to take the selection of a source of tax funds that is likely to cause little damage to the career of a politician and elevate it into a decision of high social principle.

[9] Hirshleifer [5, p. 270] recognizes the appropriateness of the risk compensating subsidy in these circumstances, and makes the very cogent remark that a larger subsidy would have to be paid to the small firm that incurs a substantial private risk than is given, say, to General Motors whose substantial number of investments offset one another's private risk to a considerable extent.

already characterize the apportionment of inputs between the government and private enterprise.

V. *Investment as a Public Good: The Externalities Argument*

Since the time when Pigou wrote on the subject there has been an increase in the sophistication of the argument against a market-determined discount rate as the proper criterion for the quantity and durability of investment. But much of the literature seems to accept the view that a free market will make inadequate provision for the future and that therefore the social rate of discount should be lower than that which would produce market equilibrium.

Apparently the most widely accepted justification for this conclusion is one for which I must admit some degree of responsibility.[10] It maintains that the social yield of investment is characteristically higher than its private return so that on the usual logic of the externalities argument the market will not provide enough investment. Specifically, there are three reasons why this is apt to be the case:

1. A project undertaken by an individual incurs a risk to him much greater than that which it imposes on society. Part of the source of this divergence has already been discussed—the insurance to society provided by the many projects simultaneously engaged in by the economy.

2. But there is another and perhaps equally significant reason for the distinction. A project undertaken by a private individual may for financial or other reasons be taken from him before he receives all of its benefits; he may lose it by going bankrupt, or he may die without heirs. Yet in either of these cases the benefits accrue unimpaired to society. Inheritance taxes clearly cause a substantial divergence between private and public returns from long-term investment.

3. Investment in the future is of the character of a public good. National pride leads many of us to want a promising future for our country. Or looked at the other way, many of us have an uneasy conscience at leaving to future generations a world despoiled and deprived of its productive capacity. But as with national defense, it is impossible to provide a brilliant future for the nation to one of today's citizens without simultaneously making it available to all.

---

[10] See Baumol [2], pp. 131–32. On the subsequent literature see Marglin [11] and Sen [13] [14]. The more recent of Sen's papers makes a very useful distinction between two related arguments on these matters: the "isolation paradox" whereby it pays no individual to save an optimal amount, whether or not everyone else does so, and the "assurance problem" in which the individual will save enough only if he is assured that others will also do so. Sen is right in pointing out that my argument seems to fall into the latter category. But that is a matter of careless phrasing on my part. On this I need not merely rely on distant memory which reminds me that I was well aware of the relevance of the prisoner's dilemma analogy when I wrote the passage in question. The discussion in Section 3 of my Chapter 11 makes the distinction between the two cases in some detail even if in a somewhat obscure manner.

These are all classic grounds for encouragement of additional supply and the direction of their force is clear. Yet when they were recently recapitulated, cogently argued and their implications explored by Marglin, his conclusions were strongly disputed in two replies.[11] One of these dealt primarily with what, for present purposes, may be considered technicalities and so it need not concern us here, though it is certainly worth reading. However, the other note, that by Tullock, makes an important point which in my view goes far to offset the conclusions implied by the externalities argument.

Tullock points out that an increase in investment, aside from its allocative consequences, constitutes a redistribution of income from present to future generations. That being so, he reminds us, it is incumbent on us to ask ourselves whether we really want to undertake such a redistribution of income—as in any such redivision of the pie the answer depends heavily on who the recipients are to be, and on their economic circumstances. In particular, in our economy if past trends and current developments are any guide, a redistribution to provide more for the future may be described as a Robin Hood activity stood on its head—it takes from the poor to give to the rich. Average real per capita income a century hence is likely to be a sizeable multiple of its present value. Why should I give up part of my income to help support someone else with an income several times my own?[12]

Tullock puts the matter in a more attractive light by posing the alternative in a different way. Suppose we feel we can afford to give up some fixed amount for the benefit of others. We must then ask ourselves whether there are so few diseased, illiterate, underprivileged today, so few persons who excite our sympathy that we must look to the prospectively wealthy future for a source of worthy recipients of our bounty.

Let us then pull together the pieces of the argument and see where they lead. We have seen that there is a basic contradiction in the optimality requirements for the social rate of discount. The condition for efficiency in the allocation of resources between the private and public sectors requires a discount rate significantly higher than that called for by the public's time preferences. Only by the elimination of the corporate income tax and the substitution of a subsidy to private investment

[11] See Lind [8] and Tullock [15].

[12] Of course, if the capital market were perfect the discount rate would fully take into account the prospective rate of increase in real incomes. This is why I find Sen's argument [14] convincing for the pure competitive model but not for decision making in practice. Under pure competition the differences in present and future wealth will be reflected fully in the market's discount rate so that the reluctance to invest described by the Marglin-Sen-Baumol argument will certainly make for a misallocation of resources. In practice, where capital markets are riddled with imperfections and subject to the tergiversations of government policy it is my judgment that the probable wealth of future generations is given inadequate weight in interest rate policy so that the Marlin-Sen-Baumol externalities may well prove benign in their effects.

to offset the difference between public and private risks can the two requirements be reconciled. Since neither of these changes seems, to say the least, very likely to be instituted in the foreseeable future, some arbitrary choice will have to be made. It is my inclination at the moment to look with some favor at a figure toward the higher end of the range—at a discount rate closer to what may be considered the cost of capital to private firms. My grounds for this preference are hardly convincing even to me—they rest largely on the feeling that there is a very tangible loss in the transfer of resources from a high rate of return use to an employment in which their yield is very low. On the other hand I can attribute much less significance to a time preference rate which is constantly shifted about and made to adjust to the dictates of monetary policy.

My other major conclusion (which, unavoidably, is also largely a matter of opinion) would appear to be that in our economy, by and large, the future can be left to take care of itself. There is no need to lower artificially the social rate of discount in order to increase further the prospective wealth of future generations. The rate of interest should presumably then be set by the market and the needs of public policy— the requirements of stabilization, equilibrium in international trade, etc., and no attempt should be made to subsidize the future by artificial reductions in discount rates designed only for that purpose.

However, this does not mean that the future should in every respect be left to the mercy of the free market. There are important externalities and investments of the public goods variety which cry for special attention. Irreversibilities constitute a prime example. If we poison our soil so that never again will it be the same, if we destroy the Grand Canyon and turn it into a hydroelectric plant, we give up assets which like Goldsmith's bold peasantry, ". . . their country's pride, when once destroy'd can never be supplied." All the wealth and resources of future generations will not suffice to restore them. Investment in the preservation of such items then seems perfectly proper, but for this purpose the appropriate instrument would appear to be a set of selective subsidies rather than a low general discount rate that encourages indiscriminately all sorts of investment programs whether or not they are relevant.

Moreover, one can envision circumstances in which a more general program of encouragement to investment commends itself to us. In a country which is stagnating and where only a major restriction of current consumption can put life into its development program, one may well wish to make the sacrifice for tomorrow, for in such a case, without it the future generation will be as impoverished as the present.

There is a final consequence of the Tullock suggestion which should not be overlooked. The idea that we may want to redistribute income in favor of the poor of today's generation rather than the future poor is *not* an argument against government activity. On the contrary, it is perfectly consistent with the rather persuasive Galbraithian view that the supply of public goods is far too small. We may want far more governmental activity than is currently being undertaken to remove today's slums, to combat today's air pollution, to help put down today's crime. But wanting *more* government projects is not tantamount to a desire for more *long-term* government projects. What our society's interests may well require is more but less durable government investments, and a low rate of discount on public projects is precisely the wrong way to go about their achievement.

REFERENCES

1. K. J. ARROW, "Discounting and Public Investment Criteria," in A. V. Kneese and S. C. Smith, eds., *Water Research*, Baltimore 1966.
2. W. J. BAUMOL, *Welfare Economics and the Theory of the State*, 2nd ed. Cambridge Mass. 1965.
3. OTTO ECKSTEIN, *Water-Resource Development: The Economics of Project Evaluation.* Cambridge, Mass. 1961.
4. JACK HIRSHLEIFER, J. C. DeHAVEN AND J. J. MILLIMAN, *Water Supply; Economics, Technology and Policy.* Chicago 1960.
5. JACK HIRSHLEIFER, "Investment Decision Under Uncertainty: Applications of the State-Preference Approach," *Quart. Jour. Econ.,* May 1966, *80,* 252–77.
6. H. E. KLARMAN, "Syphilis Control Programs," in Robert Dorfman, ed., *Measuring Benefits of Government Investments*, Washington 1965.
7. J. V. KRUTILLA AND OTTO ECKSTEIN, *Multiple Purpose River Development.* Baltimore 1958.
8. R. C. LIND, "Further Comment," *Quart. Jour. Econ.,* May 1964, *78,* 336–44.
9. FRITZ MACHLUP, Discussion of a paper by Weisbrod, in Dorfman, editor [6].
10. M. S. MARCH, Discussion of a paper by Weisbrod, in Dorfman, editor [6].
11. S. A. MARGLIN, "The Social Rate of Discount and the Optimal Rate of Investment," *Quart. Jour. Econ.,* Feb. 1963, 77, 95–112.
12. P. A. SAMUELSON, "Principles of Efficiency: Discussion," *Am. Econ. Rev.,* Proc., May 1964, *54,* 93–96.
13. A. K. SEN, "On Optimizing the Rate of Saving," *Econ. Jour.,* Sept. 1961, *71,* 479–96.
14. ———, "Isolation, Assurance and the Social Rate of Discount," *Quart. Jour. Econ.,* Feb. 1967, *81,* 112–24.
15. GORDON TULLOCK, "The Social Rate of Discount and the Optimal Rate of Investment: Comment," *Quart. Jour. Econ.,* May 1964, *78,* 331–36.
16. WILLIAM VICKERY, "Principles of Efficiency: Discussion," *Am. Econ. Rev.,* Proc., May 1964, *54,* 88–92.

THE BENEFIT-COST RATIO

IN RESOURCE DEVELOPMENT PLANNING

George A. Pavelis

The stimulus for this article was an observation that resource development in the United States is of a lumpy or whole project-by-project character. We seem to have looked at resource development proposals in isolation from other worthwhile activities and to have been preoccupied with the magnitude of "benefit-cost ratios" in evaluating and comparing individual resource development activities, projects, or programs. Unless properly interpreted, however, such ratios can mislead planners and legislators to invest capital and other inputs in a way that leads to a less than fully efficient pattern of resource development, even where the objective is only to maximize quantifiable monetary benefits. Accordingly, this analysis examines the "benefit-cost ratio" in the context of an income-producing efficiency objective and elementary production theory. Such other currently emphasized objectives as environmental quality improvement are treated implicitly, though not within a multiobjective framework. For a more complete treatment of these see Miller and Holloway [9] who have illustrated an application of multiobjective resource planning principles recently issued by the Water Resources Council [15]. Other particular papers and reports dealing with multiobjective resource development planning are [3, 4, 5, 7, 9, 13 and 14].

To begin with, the mathematical ratio of total development benefits over total costs is first interpreted in economic terms. Legitimate uses of the ratio as a choice criterion are then reviewed for cases where the ratio does not vary with the scale of an individual development project or activity, where it varies with project scale, and where a series of de-

SOUTHERN JOURNAL OF AGRICULTURAL ECONOMICS, 1971, Vol. 3, No. 1, pp. 161-166.

velopment alternatives are under consideration. Relations between planning on the basis of benefit-cost ratios versus examining comparative rates of return on investment capital as such are discussed briefly. Some concluding remarks deal with the question of supporting or not supporting additional research aimed at improving techniques of economic analysis as applied to resource development.

UNDERLYING DEFINITIONS AND CONCEPTS

The benefit-cost ratio, as commonly used in resource development planning, can be defined as dollars of total capitalized benefits divided by dollars of total capitalized cost, where capitalized costs and benefits can be expressed either as discounted (present value) or recurring (annual) amounts. Program, project, and activity costs include expenditures required to obtain the use of productive factors employed in realizing benefits. Such expenditures can be considered as the values foregone by not incurring them for other economic activities. Land, labor, capital, and management are principal classes of productive factors usually involved. In general, all construction, operation, and maintenance expenses can be associated with one or another of these classes of factors. Outlays may take the form of purchase prices or rent for land, wages for labor, and interest on capital investment.

Monetary benefits represent market or imputed values of goods or services rendered by a development through employment of the productive factors mentioned above. Benefits are computed by multiplying physical quantities of goods or services, such as kilowatt-hours of electric power or acre-feet of storage capacity in reservoirs, by their estimated unit values. The unit value of power is usually taken as its selling price or marketable value per kilowatt-hour. The unit value of storage capacity, however, depends on the particular purposes for which the capacity is utilized; that is, whether it is used for recreation, power generation, flood control or irrigation.

The benefit-cost ratio can be calculated at any level of aggregation. It can refer to programs or projects in total, project activities, individual beneficiaries or participants, or project subareas. The main requirement in this regard is that costs and benefits be accurately associated. Net benefits are total benefits less total costs. Consequently, the ratio of net benefits over total costs (or dollars of "profit" for each dollar invested) is computed by subtracting 1.00 from the corresponding gross ratio of benefits over costs, and a value greater than zero is taken to justify the expenditure. However, the gross ratio is almost always the one presented and discussed in evaluation reports, and a value for it of unity is commonly regarded as the threshold value of justification. A recognition that development activities, projects or programs can each have a varying scale is essential in interpreting the subsequent discussion.

RESTRICTIONS ON INTERPRETATION OF THE RATIO

By definition, the popularly used benefit-cost ratio is an average. Average relations are properly utilized in allocating scarce resources (including money) if they are synonymous with marginal relations. Therefore, the benefit-cost ratio as popularly computed in resource evaluations is an appropriate criterion for deciding how to allocate resources to a project provided it satisfies the following condition, called Condition X: *The ratio does not change with the amount of money represented by the total costs assigned to a particular program, project, or activity.*

Condition X Satisfied

In Figure 1 there is a straight-line relation between total costs and total benefits. Slopes of the three benefit lines A, B, and C do not change with costs, so they denote ratios of marginal changes in benefits to marginal changes in cost as well as ratios of total benefits divided by total costs.

Condition X Not Satisfied

In Figure 2 there is not a straight-line relation between total costs and total benefits. Line II, as the marginal benefit-cost ratio and the plotted slope of line I, changes as costs change and so is not the same as average benefit or the conventionally figured benefit-cost ratio. The latter is shown as line III. Marginal and average relations (lines II and III) coincide at one point in Figure 2—where costs total q dollars. At this point, the benefit-cost ratio is a maximum but net benefits are definitely not maximum. The case shown in Figure 2 can be expected much more frequently than the case illustrated by Figure 1.

Where benefit-cost relationships are not of a straight-line nature, programs, projects, or activities can be compared validly by the benefit-cost ratio criterion alone only if the scale is fixed at the same cost level among all programs, projects, or activities.

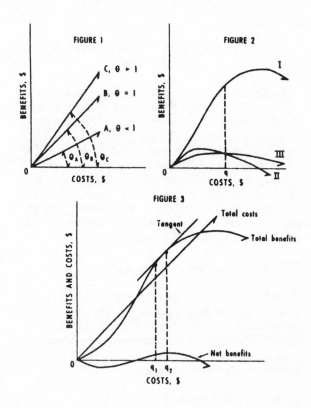

FIGURES 1, 2, and 3. SCHEMATIC BENEFIT-COST RELATIONS

Example:

Project	Gross Benefits	Total Costs	Net Benefits	B/C Ratio
1	$3,000	$2,000	$1,000	1.50
2	7,500	6,000	1,500	1.25
3	6,600	6,000	600	1.10

Costs of projects 1 and 2 are not equal in this example. Net benefits are greater in project 2, although its benefit-cost ratio is less than that of project 1. Moreover, there is no *a priori* justification for inferring that the ratios for either projects 1 or 2 would remain the same if costs were not as shown. Because costs for projects 2 and 3 are equal, their B/C ratios can be compared. Project 2 is clearly preferable to project 3 for the expenditure of $6,000, as it is 2.5 times as efficient as project 3 in yielding net benefits.

USEFULNESS OF THE BENEFIT-COST RATIO

The examples illustrated by Figures 1 and 2 show how the benefit-cost ratio can be used as an efficiency standard if Condition X is met or is not met. The general guide is to determine what the same cost will do in different programs, projects, or activities, without assuming, however, that such comparisons will remain valid if costs are either increased or decreased in any of the programs, projects, or activities. The essential point is that proper use of the benefit-cost ratio in incurring costs or appraising projects, while still based on the relation between costs and benefits, allows for any changes in the relation as costs are changed. Some different uses are explained next. The discussion hinges on whether the gross benefit-cost functions are linear or are not linear.

Linear Functions

Three possible subcases are described, based on constant magnitudes of the function slope.

A. If the benefit-cost ratio is less than unity, money will be lost, whatever benefits are received, and losses will increase proportionately with costs.

Refer to line A in Figure 1, where tan $\theta < 1$. A broad decision rule here would be that, unless more-than-compensating net intangible values can be realized, no expenditure is justified.

B. If the benefit-cost ratio is equal to unity, net benefits will be zero regardless of the total benefits received. Refer to line B in Figure 1, where tan $\theta = 1$. The decision rule here is that the expenditure is a matter of indifference unless the existence of associated net intangible values or net intangible losses was established, and the decision was modified accordingly.

C. If the benefit-cost ratio exceeds unity, net benefits will increase proportionately with cost. Refer to line C in Figure 1, where tan $\theta > 1$. The broad decision rule in this case is that expenditure is essentially limited only by more lucrative alternatives and the cost that could be incurred. However, associated intangible benefits and costs should be considered here too, as the existence of associated net intangible losses considered significant by the decision-makers could limit or at least qualify their judgment of the desirability of the activity.

Nonlinear Functions

Determining justified cost if the benefit-cost function is not linear, or if the benefit-cost ratio is not constant and so is in contradiction to Condition X, is discussed with reference to whether the scale of only one alternative (Case D) or the scales of more than one alternative (Case E) are being considered. The discussion assumes that associated intangible values or losses may be involved in either case and could modify the decisions implied.

Case D. If the appropriate scale of only one project or activity is under consideration, the economic rule is to incur costs to the point where added total cost is equal to added total benefit obtained. Expected net benefits are a maximum by so doing. Referring to Figure 3, the optimum cost to incur is shown as q_2 dollars. The amount q_2 is identified by drawing to the gross benefits function a tangent that parallels the total cost function, and then dropping a perpendicular to the horizontal or cost axis from the tangency point. The total cost function will be at 45 degrees from the horizontal, as in Figure 3, if scales of the horizontal and vertical axes are drawn the same.

The hypothetical data given in Table 1 elaborate these points and approximate the relations drawn in Figure 3. Column 2 in the table shows gross benefits, denoted by the upper curve in the figure. The benefit-cost ratios of Column 3 are not plotted in Figure 3 but would have the general form of line III in Figure 2. Column 4 in the table represents the net benefit curve of Figure 3. Columns 5 and 6, respectively, indicate successive incremental or marginal changes in gross benefits and total costs.

Net benefits of $9.60 in Table 1 approximate the highest point of the net benefit curve in Figure 3. The precise maximum is slightly more than this, as a comparison of marginal benefits and costs (columns 5 and 6) will indicate. Net benefits will begin to decline after costs and benefits are found to be increasing at the same rate (at just under q_2), not at q_1 where the ratio of benefits to costs is greatest. Incurring costs of more than $12 or q_1 where the benefit-cost ratio is greatest is clearly justified, because marginal or incremental benefits of $4.40 at q_1 are more than twice the $2 of marginal or incremental cost.

Case E. If the appropriate scales of a series of projects are under consideration, the general rule is that net benefits will be maximized if costs are incurred among the projects so that marginal net benefits are the same in all projects undertaken, and would not be greater if the equivalent cost were to be devoted to any omitted project. The rule fits those situations where resources may be sufficient to undertake each project at scale q_2, thus getting maximum net benefits in each one by pushing its marginal net benefits to zero. But the rule also recognizes that, owing to capital, engineering, or perhaps political or institutional constraints, it may not be possible to incur the cost that would push to zero the rate of increase in net benefits for an entire series of projects.

193

TABLE 1. HYPOTHETICAL SCHEDULE OF BENEFITS AND COSTS

(1) Total cost	(2) Total benefits	(3) Ratio (2)/(1)	(4) Net benefits (2) − (1)	(5) ΔBenefits	(6) ΔCosts
$ 0	$ 0		$ 0	$ 0	$ 0
2	1.00	0.50	−1.00	1.00	2
4	3.00	0.75	−1.00	2.00	2
6	6.60	1.10	0.60	3.60	2
8	11.60	1.45	3.60	5.00	2
10	16.00	1.60	6.00	4.40	2
12, q_1	20.40	1.70	8.40	4.40	2
14	23.10	1.65	9.10	2.70	2
16	25.60	1.60	9.60	2.40	2
17, q_2	26.60	1.56	9.60	1.00	1
18	27.00	1.50	9.00	0.40	1
20	25.00	1.25	5.00	−2.00	2

194

Moreover, some projects may be omitted entirely if budgets are tight, because marginal net benefits for such projects, even though they may be quite substantial at low-cost levels, may be exceeded by those for other projects at equivalent cost levels.

The general rule for Case E can be validated with principles from basic economic theory. Carlson's text [1] is excellent for this purpose. The procedure is also covered by many other authors, often under the theory of price descrimination. Figure 4, as taken from reference [11], illustrates a practical planning problem of discriminately deciding the optimum total and separable capacities of a dual-purpose reservoir designed to serve irrigation (i) and municipal-industrial water demands (m). The curves B_i and B_m in Figure 4 denote gross benefits obtained by storing water for each purpose in relation to respective separable allocations of any total capacity that might be planned. Incremental benefits for each purpose are the derivatives of their respective gross benefits and are denoted by B_i' and B_m' in the lower section of the diagram. Total incremental benefits B_t' stemming from either or both purposes are synonymous with B_m' at capacities under S_x. Thereafter, B_t' is composited from B_i' and B_m' by horizontal adding. The total benefit curve B_t in the upper section is not the sum of B_i and B_m. It is the compound integral of B_t'. Total cost as related to total capacity is given by C_t and marginal cost is C_t'. Corresponding aggregate net benefits as total benefits less costs are N_t.

Aggregate net benefits N_t in Figure 4 would be maximized if S_t units of total storage were planned, with S_i units allocated to irrigation and S_m units to municipal-industrial purposes. At these optimal capacities, incremental costs of storage are shown (in the lower section) to be equal to incremental total benefits as well as to incremental benefits for each purpose. Optimal positions on total benefit and cost functions are indicated by the small circles in the upper section of the figure. These denote points at which slopes of tangents to the functions would be equal, according to the condition $C_t' = B_t' = B_i' = B_m'$.

CAPITAL RESTRICTIONS AND RATES OF RETURN

Nearly all of the preceding discussion has focused on evaluating and combining resource development

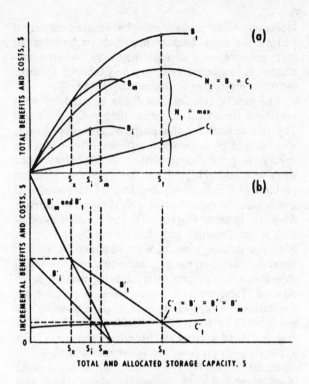

FIGURE 4. MAXIMIZING BENEFITS FROM WATER STORAGE

projects with reference to relations between total capitalized costs, total capitalized benefits, net benefits, the B/C ratio as average benefit per unit cost, and the incremental or marginal benefit-cost rates as representing primary choice indicators. No particular emphasis was placed on returns to investment capital as such which, in a planning environment of capital scarcity, may be of overriding concern in evaluating project feasibility and establishing development priorities. Investment returns were not stressed because of a belief that project planning in the United States is still by-and-large characterized by a preoccupation with the magnitude of B/C ratios and because of the article's related objective of clarifying their legitimate use for economic evaluation.

Giving more stress to the optimum use of investment capital as such would revolve around optimization principles conceptually similar to those already

196

presented. In idealized and simplified terms, for example, capitalized costs C are separable into capital investment I, and recurring operation and maintenance charges V. The latter can be deducted from recurring total benefits B to give B' as a measure of returns to capital investment. Then B' / I is a measure of the average return per unit of investment. The ratios $\Delta B' / \Delta I$ or dB' / dI, respectively, give arc or point measures of marginal rates of return. The variable B' as returns to capital is the item to maximize and so has a role similar to that of B - C or net benefits as previously discussed. Increased investment would be justified provided dB / dI as the "demand" for project investment funds exceeded a specified schedule of marginal interest rates as the investment "supply" function. The optimum or maximum justified investment would be the investment at which dB' / dI equaled the marginal interest rate. In allocating investment funds among competing projects, principles similar to those given for Case E above would be followed. That is, marginal returns to capital would be equated for all projects undertaken and should not exceed this rate in any project not undertaken.

AN ISSUE FOR FURTHER STUDY

The stimulus for this article was an observation that resource development in the United States is of a lumpy or whole project-by-project character. A related hypothesis is that this situation is due less to a preference for politically achieving an optimum "pork-barrel distribution" of projects than to the lack of information that would allow a distribution of development resources based on the internal economics of each project proposal. The points covered briefly herein, and more extensively in the various additional references listed, would be useful in examining the validity of this hypothesis.

Attracting the research resources necessary to examine this kind of issue is not easy, but a dynamic reordering of our research and other priorities may be necessary, if we are to justify the continued use of resources to improve the planning process through developing refinements in economic evaluation.

Validation of the hypothesis would imply that "process economic research" (research to improve techniques and standards for economic evaluation) should continue and possibly be increased. A nullified hypothesis would imply that such research should be curtailed. If the hypothesis is considered tenable and important but is not examined, the utilitarian values of "process" economic research will remain unknown. If the hypothesis is considered tenable but not important enough to test out, the utilitarian value of continued process research would be regarded as an unimportant unknown in resource development.

REFERENCES

1. Carlson, S., "Joint Production and Joint Costs," *A Study of the Pure Theory of Production*, pp. 10-28, Kelley and Milliman, Inc., New York, 1956.

2. Eckstein, Otto, *Water Resource Development: the Economics of Project Evaluation*, Harvard University Press, Cambridge, Mass., 1958.

3. Kalter, Robert J., W. B. Lord, D. J. Allee, E. N. Castle, M. M. Kelso, D. W. Bromley, S. C. Smith, S. V. Ciriacy-Wantrup and B. A. Weisbrod, "Criteria for Federal Evaluation of Resource Investments," Water Resources and Marine Sciences Center, Cornell University, Aug. 1969.

4. Knetsch, Jack L., J. L. Knetsch, R. H. Haveman, C. W. Howe, J. V. Krutilla, and M. F. Brewer, "Federal Natural Resources Development: Basic Issues in Benefit and Cost Measurement," Natural Resources Policy Center, The George Washington University, May 1969.

5. Krutilla, J. V., *Welfare Aspects of Benefit-Cost Analysis*, Resources for the Future, Inc., Reprint No. 29, 1961.

6. Lutz, F. and Vera Lutz, "Criteria of Profit Maximization," *The Theory of Investment of the Firm*, pp. 16-48, Princeton Univ. Press, 1951.

7. Maass, Arthur, "Benefit-Cost Analysis: Its Relevance to Public Investment Decisions," *Quarterly J. Econ.*, Vol. LXXX, pp. 209-226, May 1966.

8. McKean, R. N., *Efficiency in Government Through Systems Analysis: with Emphasis on Water Resource Development*, Wiley and Sons, Inc., New York, 1958.

9. Miller, Stanley F. and Milton L. Holloway, "Project Evaluation: A Case Study–Scoggins Creek, Oregon," *Proceedings of Western Agricultural Economics Association*, Tucson, Ariz., July 19-22, 1970.

10. Smith, Stephen C. and Emery N. Castle, *Economics and Public Policy in Water Resources Development*, pp. 9, 34 and 171, Iowa State University Press, Ames, 1964.

11. Steele, Harry A. and George A. Pavelis, "Economics of Irrigation Policy and Planning," *Irrigation of Agricultural Lands (Ch. 11)*, Am. Soc. Agron. Monograph No. 11, Am. Soc. Agron., Madison, Wisc., 1967.

12. Timmons, John F., "Economic Framework for Watershed Development," *J. Farm Econ.* 36 (5):1170-1183, 1954.

13. U. S. Department of Agriculture, Economic Research Service, Natural Resource Economics Division, *Proceedings of Symposium on Secondary Impacts of Public Resource Development*, Washington, D. C., Sept. 1968.

14. U. S. Senate, *Policies, Standards, and Procedures in the Formulation, Evaluation, and Review of Plans for Use and Development of Water and Related Land Resources*, Doc. No. 97, 87th Cong., 2nd Session, May 29, 1962.

15. U. S. Water Resources Council, *Principles for Planning Water and Land Resources: Report to the Council by the Special Task Force*, Washington, D. C., July 1970.